IMAGES
of America

DOWAGIAC

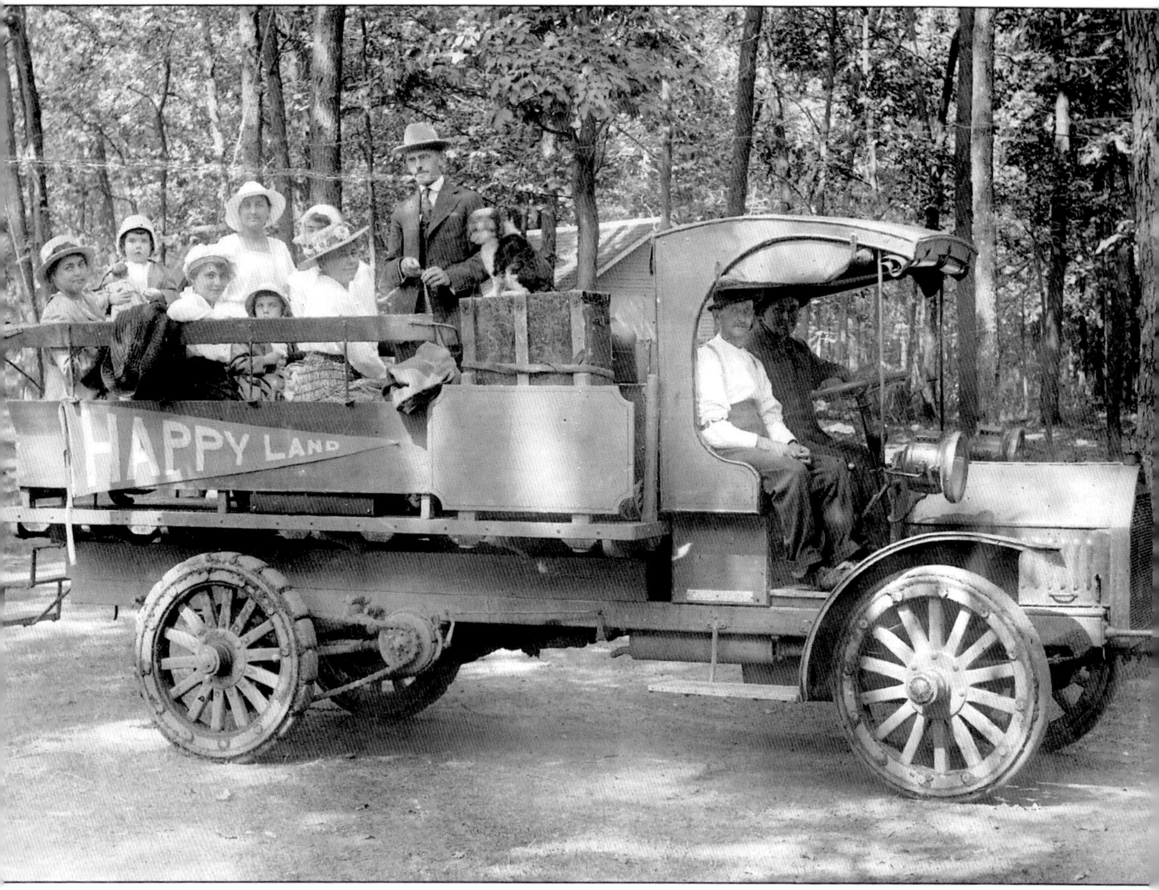

This *c.* 1910s photograph shows a group of happy people on their way to Happyland, a summer resort on Magician Lake in Dowagiac. Happyland was owned by Frederic Howe, a theatrical promoter with a unique business concept. His traveling troupe of actors assisted fraternal lodges throughout the country to present productions as fundraisers. Providing costumes, scenery, and "electrical effects," the Happyland players worked for a percentage of the event's income. During the summer months, Howe's troupe congregated at Happyland, writing new plays and rehearsing for the traveling season.

IMAGES
of America

DOWAGIAC

Steven Arseneau and Ann Thompson

ARCADIA
PUBLISHING

ISBN 978-0-7385-3422-0

Published by Arcadia Publishing
Charleston, South Carolina

Printed in the United States of America

Library of Congress Catalog Card Number: 2005926581

For all general information contact Arcadia Publishing at:
Telephone 843-853-2070
Fax 843-853-0044
E-mail sales@arcadiapublishing.com
For customer service and orders:
Toll-Free 1-888-313-2665

Visit us on the Internet at www.arcadiapublishing.com

Contents

ACKNOWLEDGMENTS

The authors would like to thank the many individuals who have donated their photographs to the Museum at Southwestern Michigan College. Due to their understanding that photographs provide invaluable information about the past, and that museums are safe repositories for those photographs, this book became possible. A special appreciation to those individuals who donated photographs with good identification!

We would like to acknowledge the many hours that our college-student worker, Maxwell Abrokwah Nkrumah, spent scanning photographs from our collection. Without the ability to assess the over-4,000-piece collection through this digitization, our jobs would have been immensely more difficult. Museum Educator Judy van der Linden proofread the final copy of our manuscript and we are grateful for her keen attention to detail.

In identifying the photographs we often used the research compiled by Genny Kroepel, former museum volunteer and employee, who traced the history of many Dowagiac businesses and locations throughout the years. Two books were especially helpful in providing historical facts: *The Round Oak Stove People and Other Dowagiac, Michigan Personalities* by Barbara and Grafton Cook, and *Round Oak: A Good Thing from Doe-Wah-Jack* by Leland Haines.

Finally, we would like to acknowledge the members of the Board of Trustees of Southwestern Michigan College, who over the years recognized the value of a community museum and its role in preserving and interpreting local history. Their support has allowed us to share the story of our region with thousands of museum visitors, and, in particular, the history of the city of Dowagiac and its people through the publication of this book.

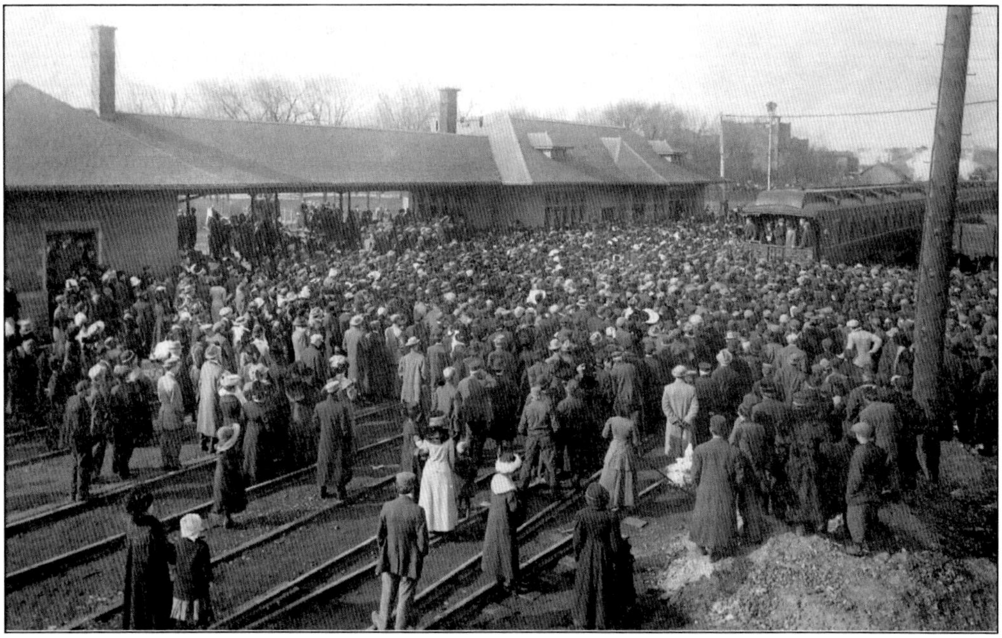

Theodore Roosevelt spoke in Dowagiac from the back of his special campaign train on March 30, 1912. Mr. Roosevelt arrived from Chicago and delivered a five-minute speech which opened, "Ladies and gentlemen and babies. . . ." This photograph shows many of the onlookers, some whom arrived from Benton Harbor, St. Joseph, and Eau Claire via the interurban railway. After his speech, Roosevelt was on his way to Detroit with a stop in Kalamazoo.

INTRODUCTION

Dowagiac is a small city located in southwestern Michigan, 25 miles north of South Bend, Indiana, and 90 miles east of Chicago. It lies in an area resplendent with lakes, rivers, and rich glacial till. The Potawatomi Indians began to inhabit the Dowagiac area and surrounding lands in the 17th century. The numbers of Potawatomi in southwestern Michigan were few when the first white settlers began to arrive in the area in the early 1800s. Most, except the Pokagon Band, were forced to leave the area and move west in 1838. Today the Pokagon Band numbers 2,700, with headquarters located in Dowagiac.

Hardwood forests, tall grass prairies, wildflowers, and game were abundant when the first settlers arrived. The earliest ones found life difficult—partially due to the fact that, though lush, the area was swampy or covered with hard prairie sod and timber. The first crops to be planted were corn, wheat, and other subsistence crops. An early settler, William Renesten, built a carding mill on the Dowagiac Creek in 1830, and built a grist mill a few years later. Over time, the grist mill became the property of H.F. Colby, and there has been an operating mill in Dowagiac ever since. The grist mill made the cash farming of wheat and other grains more lucrative for area farmers. The Colby Mill was purported to be the most photographed mill in America due to its picturesque setting on the mill pond.

Once the tough sod was broken, the labor of planting was underway. Locally invented and manufactured, the roller grain drill streamlined the planting process by planting and covering grain in one operation. The grain drill could be used in planting wheat, oats, barley, buckwheat, peas, beans, clover, and timothy. Over the years the Dowagiac area has proven to be superior for the cultivation of fruit trees, blueberries, peppermint, assorted vegetables, and the production of livestock. Continuing with the legacy provided by the Potawatomi, maple syrup continues to be produced today.

Dowagiac was platted in 1848 when the Michigan Central Railroad route was established from Detroit to Niles, Michigan. Incorporated as a village in 1858, Dowagiac grew to become a city in 1877. Slowly, buildings began to appear along Front Street, facing the railroad tracks. The railroad depot and freight depot were prominent in importance to the community. Taverns, cigar shops, hotels, clothing shops, and churches added to the city's bustle.

Like all new cities of this time, Dowagiac had its struggles. In 1858, scarlet fever hit the town and 30 children died. This epidemic returned in 1870 to kill another 30 children. Fires broke out in both 1863 and 1864, destroying many frame buildings in the commercial district. Brick buildings soon replaced them. Lumber mills, banks, restaurants, and a cemetery soon became part of the city's landscape. The population grew and by 1900, the city numbered over 4,000 people.

In addition to the manufacture of the roller grain drill, Dowagiac is known for other enterprising endeavors. One Dowagiac resident, James Heddon, was able to capitalize on the proximity of area lakes by manufacturing fishing lures. The nationally-known lures were produced in Dowagiac from 1902 to 1984. The story behind the business' beginnings reveals that Heddon became inspired after casting his first whittled piece of wood into the local mill pond. Heddon's "Wounded Minnow" and "Lucky 13" are just a few of the many lures produced. Another local product was the Lindsley automobile. This 10-horsepower runabout with a four-gallon gasoline tank under the seat could be purchased for $475 in 1908.

Dowagiac is rather typical of Midwestern cities in that it owes its existence to the arrival of the railroad, but in another way, Dowagiac's history is quite unique. The presence of the railroad was critical to the development of Dowagiac, but it was the enterprise of one man, Philo D. Beckwith, that is considered to be the reason the city grew during the latter 19th and early 20th centuries. His company, the Round Oak Stove Company, had a symbiotic relationship with the railroad. The Michigan Central Railroad contracted with Beckwith for heating stoves to be placed in depots all along its route, and the Round Oak Stove Company began to flourish.

It would be difficult to isolate the importance of the railroad and Beckwith's stove company from the development of Dowagiac, but the latter clearly sustained the new town. The company manufactured heating and cooking stoves and furnaces from 1868 to 1947. The patented Round Oak stove became known nationwide; local legend states that the Round Oak Stove Company made more heating stoves than any other company in America.

The success of the Round Oak Stove Company certainly impacted the city through employment opportunities, but also in less direct ways. P.D. Beckwith himself influenced Dowagiac's development. Beckwith was a pillar of the community who enjoyed the arts and culture. The Beckwith name is linked to a number of civic endeavors including a church, a library, a kindergarten, a community theater, a community band, and a baseball team. The houses built by the Beckwith family remain as proud reminders of its legacy and are the most elaborate and imposing structures the city has today.

Another unique feature of Dowagiac is its designation as the first stop of the "orphan train" in 1854. This social experiment is often cited as the precursor to foster care. Orphaned and destitute children from the slums of New York City were placed on trains for destinations in western states where it was hoped families would care for them. Over the course of many years, more than 120,000 children were placed in 45 states across the nation, but the first 45 children of the program were sent to Dowagiac.

This book covers the years from the 1860s to the 1940s. All of the images used in the book are owned by the Museum at Southwestern Michigan College, a local history and science museum in Dowagiac, whose major collection of Round Oak stoves and memorabilia is the best in the nation. The 200 images were chosen from a collection of over 4,000 for their historical interest and physical clarity, and also for the role they play in a comprehensive study of the history of Dowagiac. Regrettably, some aspects of Dowagiac's history are not represented in the museum's collections, so this book is not a definitive study. It is, however, an important glimpse into the past of a typical, but unique, Midwestern city: Dowagiac, Michigan.

One

A New Community

Dowagiac owes its settlement to two factors—the Dowagiac Creek and the Michigan Central Railroad. When William Renesten moved to what is now the eastern outskirts of Dowagiac and set up a carding mill on the Dowagiac Creek in 1830, he was simply using a power source. He probably had no idea that his move would lead to a booming village by the end of the century. In 1833 he dammed the creek and built a grist mill that would operate for over 100 years—the presence of the two mills led other settlers to the area and roads were built so they could access the mills.

Renesten did not stay long, but others grew interested in the land. Patrick and George Hamilton and James McOmber bought land and farmed the area for the next decade. Orlando Craine platted the village of Venice in 1836 in nearby Wayne Township—Venice never materialized but the plat did consist of part of present-day Dowagiac.

It took the arrival of the railroad in 1848, however, to plant the seeds of the city of Dowagiac. It was decided that the Michigan Central Railroad line between Chicago and Detroit would take a route through Dowagiac and Niles rather than through St. Joseph. In 1847, the railroad sent Nicholas Chesbro to southwest Michigan to purchase right-of-way land for the railroad. Mitchel Robinson of Pokagon Township accompanied him on his buying trip through Cass County.

Once the right-of-way was secured, Chesbro, Robinson, and Niles businessman Jacob Beeson began purchasing additional land from settlers like Patrick Hamilton. They quickly platted the land into 183 lots in a grid running parallel to the railroad tracks, which ran at a northeasterly angle between Niles and Kalamazoo. This plat became the original downtown Dowagiac, but later additions ran along a directional grid (north/south and east/west), which makes for an interesting town layout. By March of 1848, the first store in Dowagiac, Ezekiel Smith's general store, was open for business at the corner of Main Street and Front Street. Later that year, the Dowagiac House Tavern/Hotel opened across the street.

From these early happenings, Dowagiac began to take shape. Businessmen bought lots and erected a wide assortment of shops along Front Street—shoes, clothing, hardware, gunsmiths, blacksmiths, drug stores, livery stables, foundries—all were present in Dowagiac by 1860. Mark Judd's sawmill opened in 1859 and probably provided a great deal of the lumber that built the growing city—Judd's Lumber Company is still family-owned today and is the oldest lumber company in the state of Michigan.

Dowagiac was incorporated as a village in 1858; it quickly outgrew the village title and became a city in 1877. After fires in the 1860s, brick structures replaced wood ones in downtown Dowagiac. By 1890, many of the downtown buildings were already constructed—most still house businesses today.

Dowagiac residents of the 1850s and 1860s surely did not know what the future held for the village and it would take a manufacturing base for the town to develop and grow further. The manufacturer to take Dowagiac to the next level arrived in 1854, but his business venture would take another 25 years to mature.

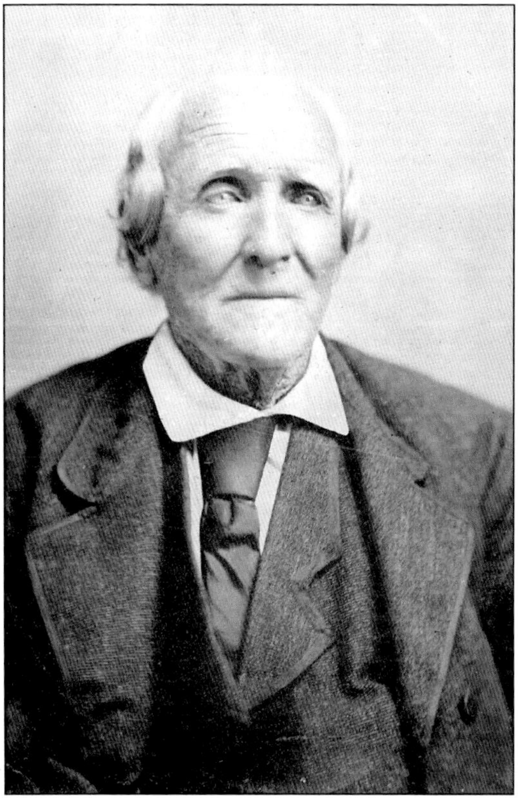

William Renesten became the first white settler in the Dowagiac area in 1830. In 1833, he dammed the Dowagiac Creek, creating the Mill Pond, and built a grist mill. He quickly lost interest in the mill business and sold the property to Erastus Spaulding in 1834 and moved to Berrien County. Spaulding expanded the mill and sold it to Horace Colby; the Colby Mills became landmarks in Dowagiac.

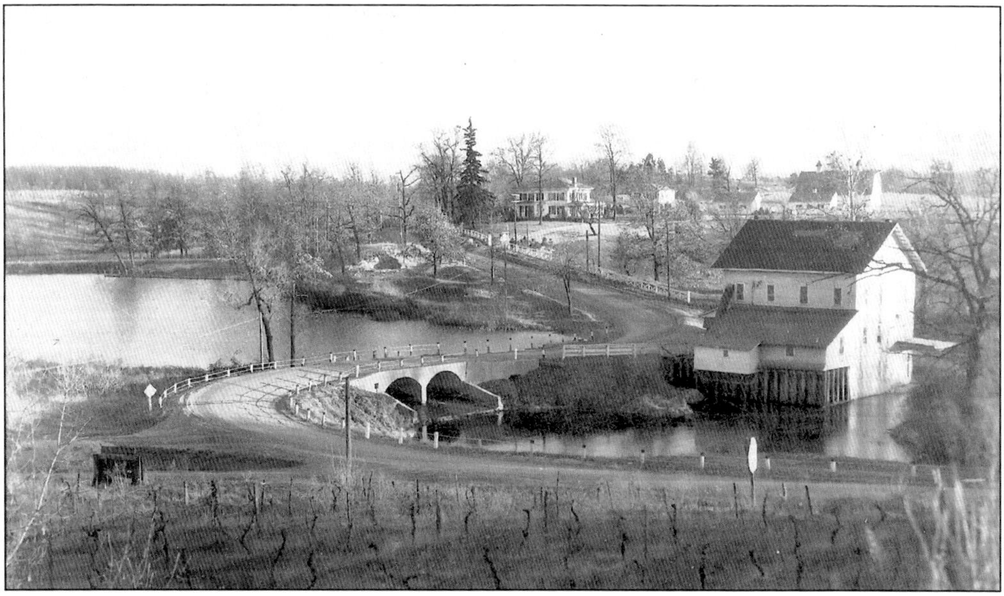

This photo shows the Upper Colby Mill and the Mill Pond in the early 1900s. Horace Colby, already the operator of what became known as the Lower Colby Mill, bought this mill, the expanded Renesten mill, from Erastus Spaulding in 1868. The Colby Mills made Colby one of the most successful millers in Michigan and this mill became known as one of the most photographed mills in the world.

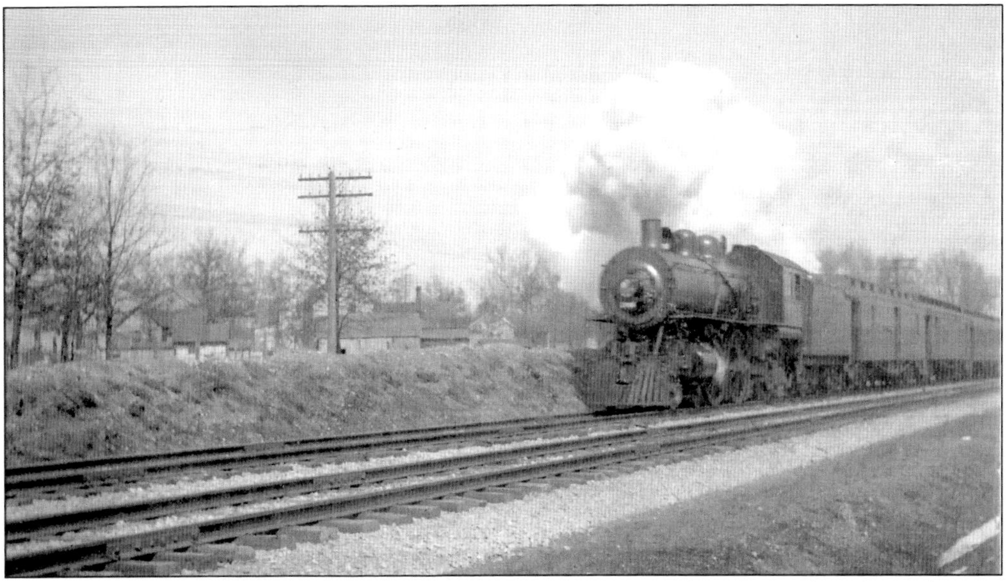

The railroad's arrival in Dowagiac in 1848 led to an influx of settlers. This photo shows a train rolling through Dowagiac in the early 1900s. Nicholas Chesbro, a representative of the Michigan Central Railroad, came to Dowagiac in 1847 to purchase right-of-way land for the company. Patrick Hamilton owned much of the land that constitutes present-day downtown Dowagiac and sold some to the railroad. Chesbro and Jacob Beeson of Niles platted the land in the final layout.

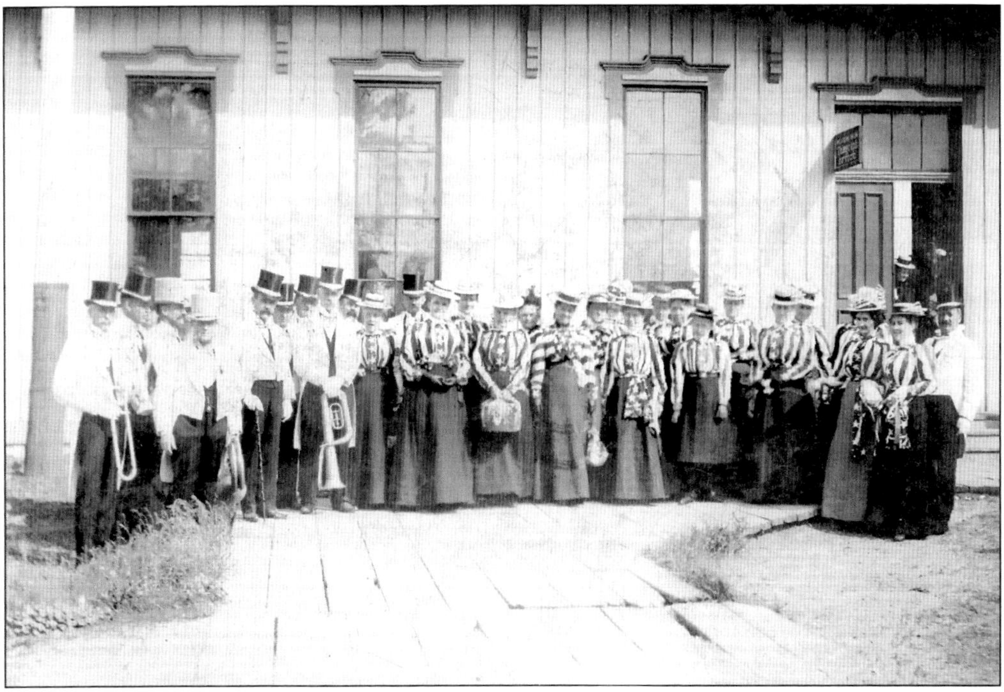

The occasion of this celebration is unknown, but this photograph shows a band and women's group in front of the old depot in Dowagiac. This depot was built in the 1870s and was replaced by the new depot in 1901.

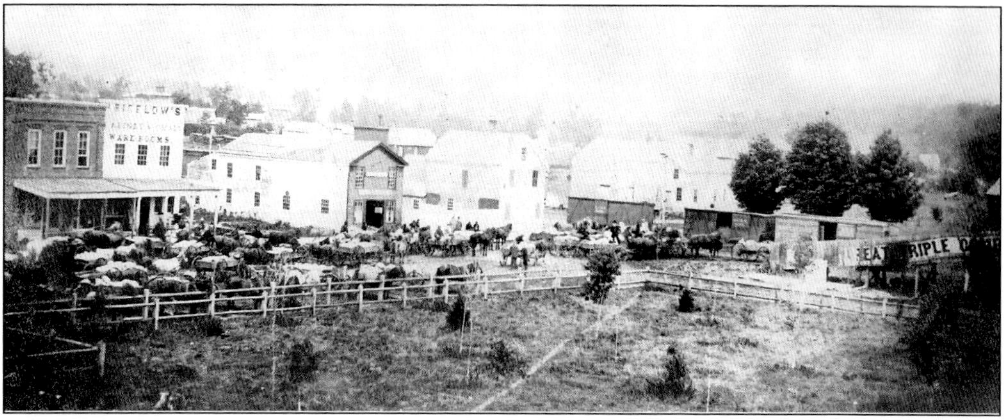

This is the oldest known photograph of Dowagiac, known as "Wheat Day 1860." It shows how two influential industries—agriculture and the railroad—affected Dowagiac. Farmers came from a 50-mile radius to load their wheat onto trains for shipment to mills. In the fall, 300 wagons of wheat could be loaded per day and the streets were lined with wagons, as this photo shows.

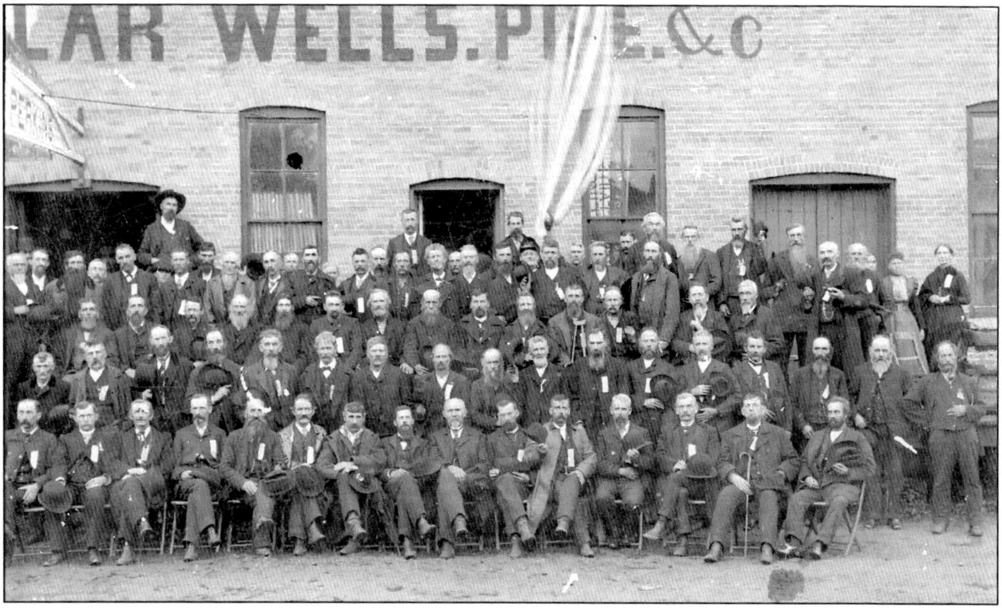

The 19th Michigan Infantry Regiment met and trained in Dowagiac in the summer of 1862 before heading south to fight in the Civil War. The regiment participated in many key battles and was a part of Sherman's March to the Sea at the end of the war. Like most Civil War units, the 19th held regular reunions, including this one in Dowagiac in the 1880s. This photo was taken in front of the L.J. Pray Building.

This photograph was taken from the roof of O.B. Dunning's photography studio on Front Street in 1865. Dunning was facing southwest and the image shows the corner of Commercial and Pennsylvania Streets and the growing village of Dowagiac.

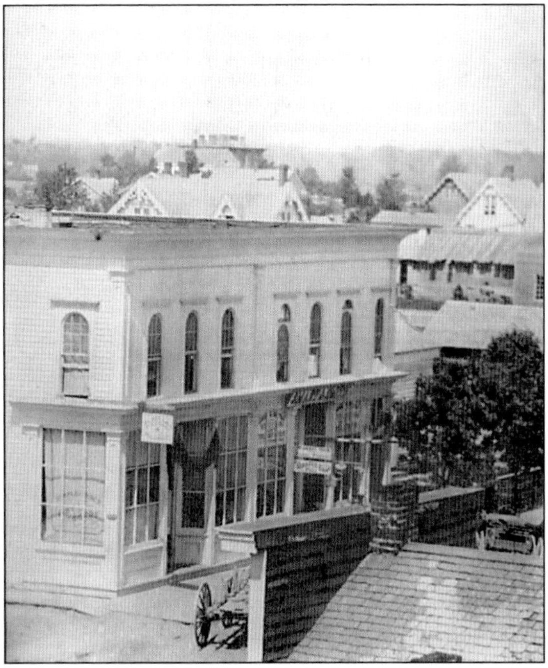

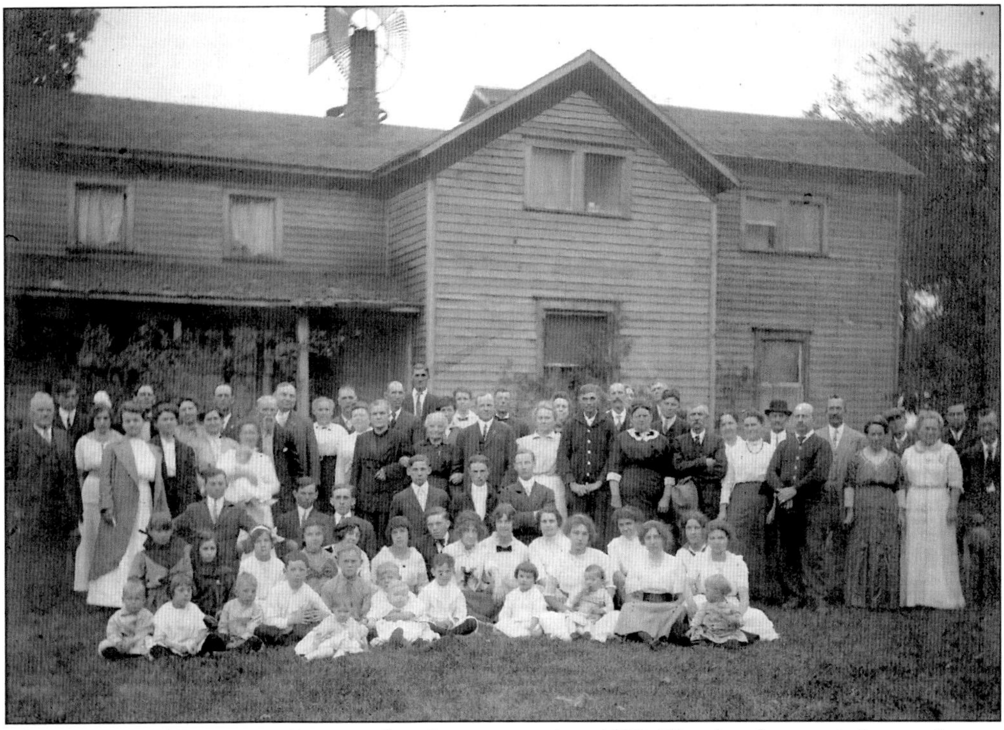

This reunion of Dowagiac German families occurred in 1912. The families settled east of town in the 1840s and 1850s in what was known as the Dutch Settlement (a road goes by that name today). The reunion was held at the home of Mr. and Mrs. Jacob Myers, who are standing in the center of the group under the window. Other families in the photo are the Gebhards, Shanafelts, Cooks, Bieks, and Gards.

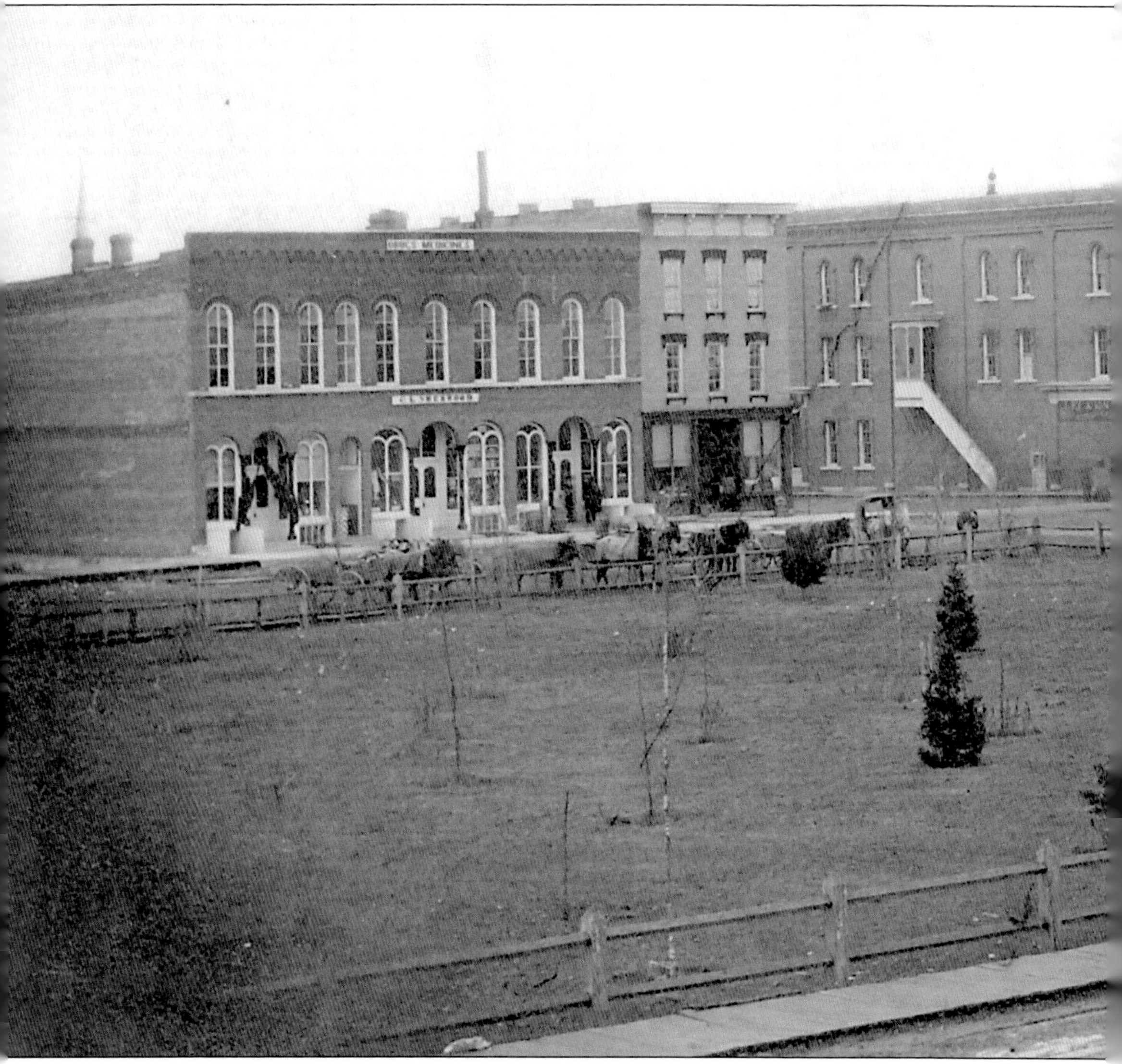

In 1874, the business district of Dowagiac consisted only of the west side of Front Street. All the buildings were constructed of brick, after several devastating fires in the 1860s. A sketch of Front Street in the *1882 History of Cass County* shows that the east side of the

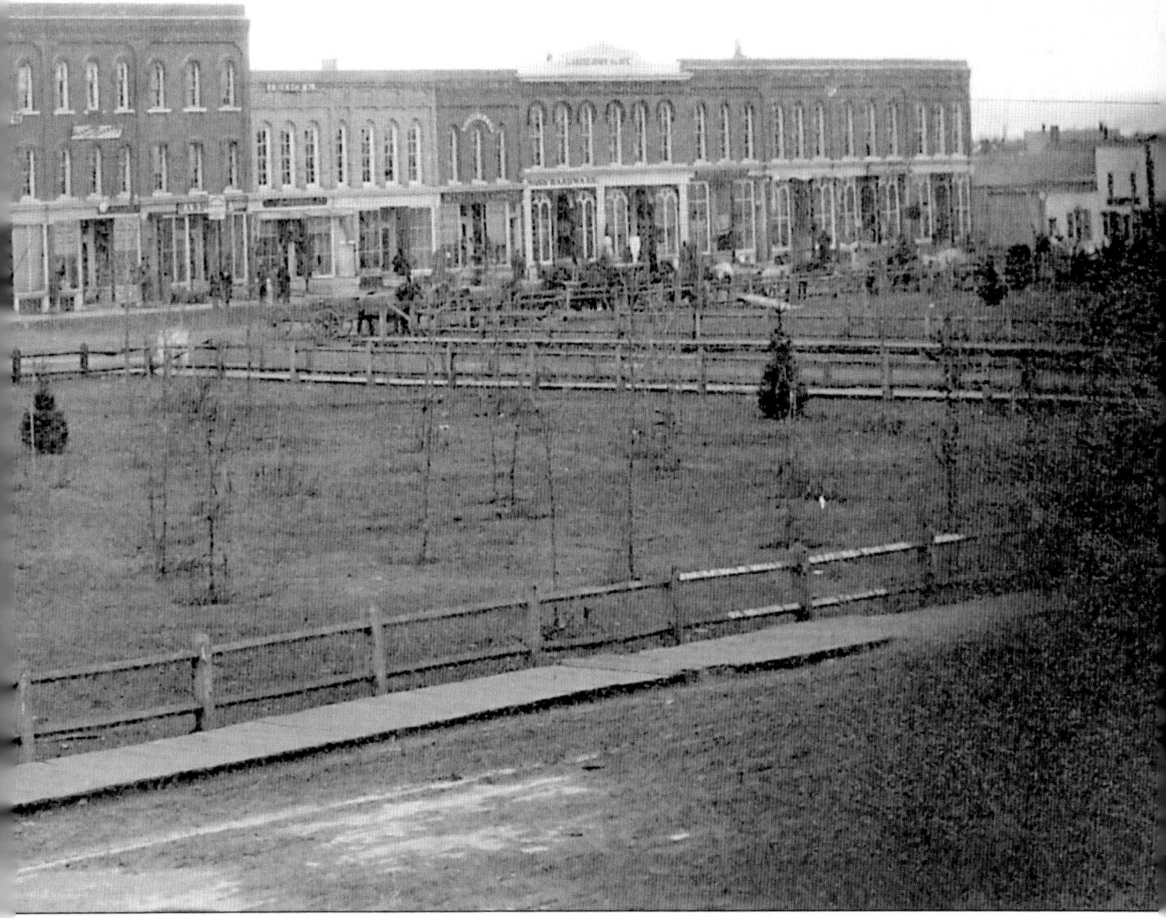

street was still undeveloped—that would change shortly. The park in the foreground of this photograph later became Michigan Central Railroad Park and would remain undeveloped well into the 20th century.

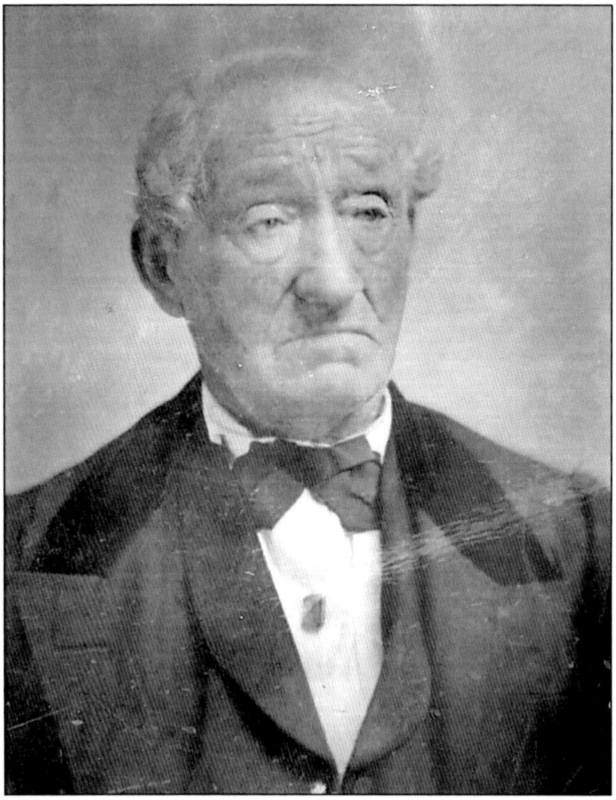

Nicholas Bock *(left)* claimed to have been a water boy in Napoleon Bonaparte's army at Waterloo. He opened an early hotel, the American House *(below)*, in Dowagiac in 1849. The American House was located on the northwest corner of Division and Front Streets and was a hub of activity in Dowagiac's early days. Dowagiac's first village election was held there in 1858, and the hotel featured a tavern for a time. Bock built two nearly identical Italianate homes at 104 Oak Street—the second was constructed of brick in 1877 after the first was destroyed by fire. Even after selling his interest in hotels, Bock continued to rent rooms to travelers at his residence. The photo below is of the American House in 1867—Bock is in a top hat, second from left.

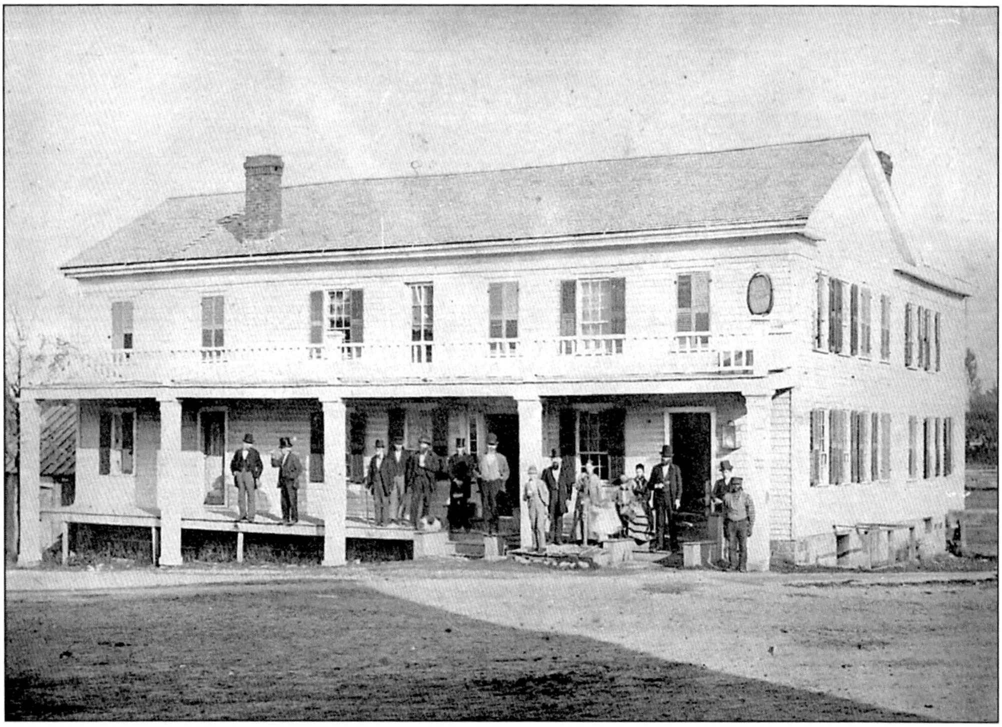

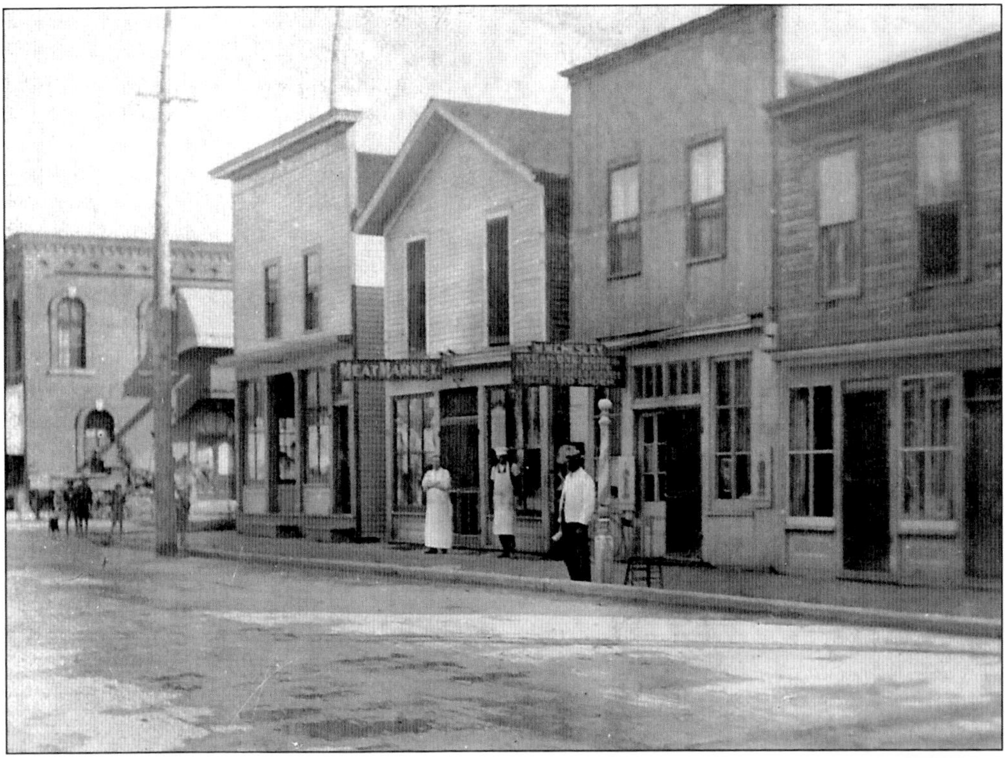

(above) Thomas Jefferson Martin stands in front of his barber shop on Commercial Street, probably in the 1880s. Martin was a noted orator and served as Grand Master of Michigan's Free and Accepted Ancient York Masons, Prince Hall Lodge. This photo shows the northeast corner of Commercial Street at Pennsylvania Street. This is the only photo of this section of town in the Museum's collection.

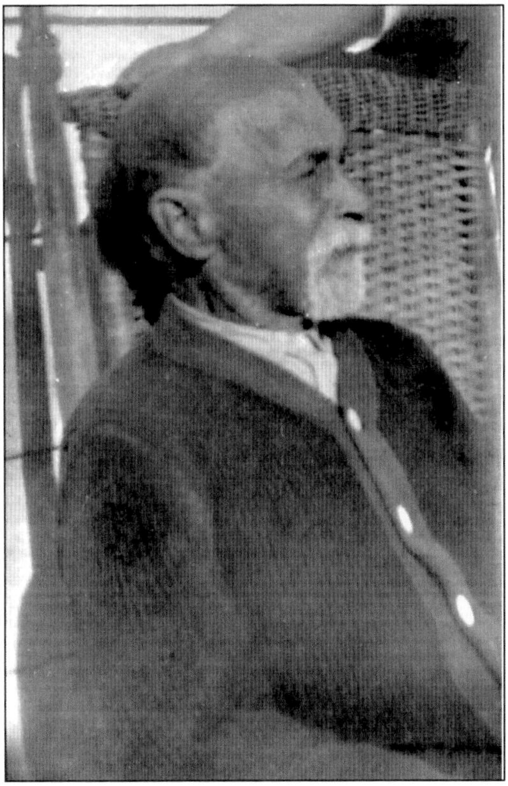

(right) Thomas Jefferson Martin (1820–1912) was one of the most enterprising African Americans in Dowagiac in the 1800s. Born in Tennessee, and a barber by the age of 12, Martin claimed to have shaved many noted Americans, including Abraham Lincoln, James Polk, and Jefferson Davis. He moved to Dowagiac in 1855 and maintained his barber shop, with help from his son, at various downtown locations into the 1900s.

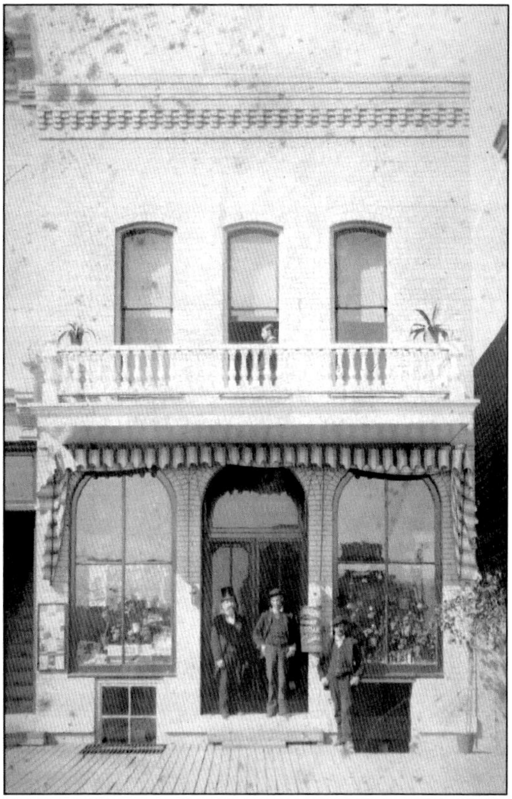

This drug store stood at 118 S. Front Street and was operated by Theophilus Rudolphi, c. 1880s. Rudolphi is in the doorway with his son, Arthur. Arthur worked in the pharmacy industry for a short time before embarking on a successful career with Round Oak Stove Company. He later founded the Rudy Furnace Company.

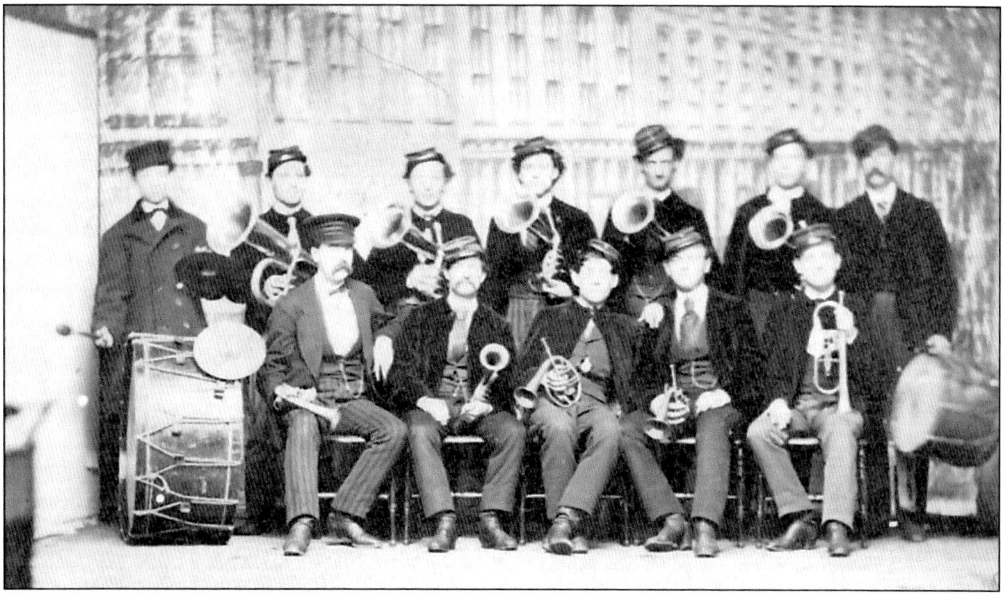

The Silver Cornet Band of Dowagiac, also known as the Beardless Band, was well known in the area in the 1860s and 1870s. The band played at the laying of the cornerstone for the Chicago Post Office in 1874, the occasion for this photograph. They also played for a similar ceremony for the Michigan State Capitol building in Lansing.

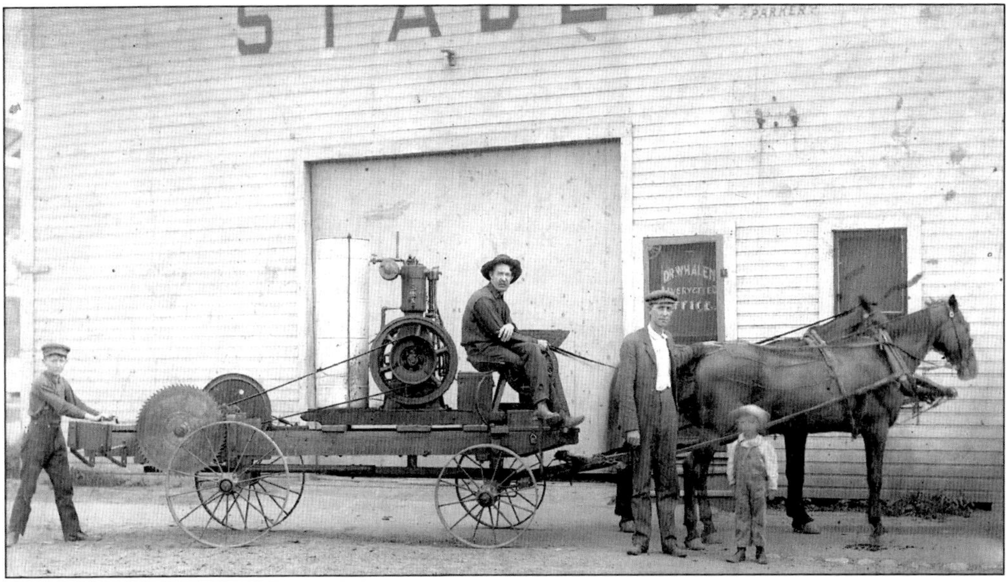

The livery and veterinary barn of Dr. Michael Whalen, located at 102 Park Place in Dowagiac is pictured here c. late 1890s. Whalen, possibly the man standing next to the horses, opened his stable and veterinary service in late 1895 and sold his business in 1914. Whalen's stable was conveniently located next door to the Elkerton Hotel. The origin of the mobile sawmill on the wagon is unknown.

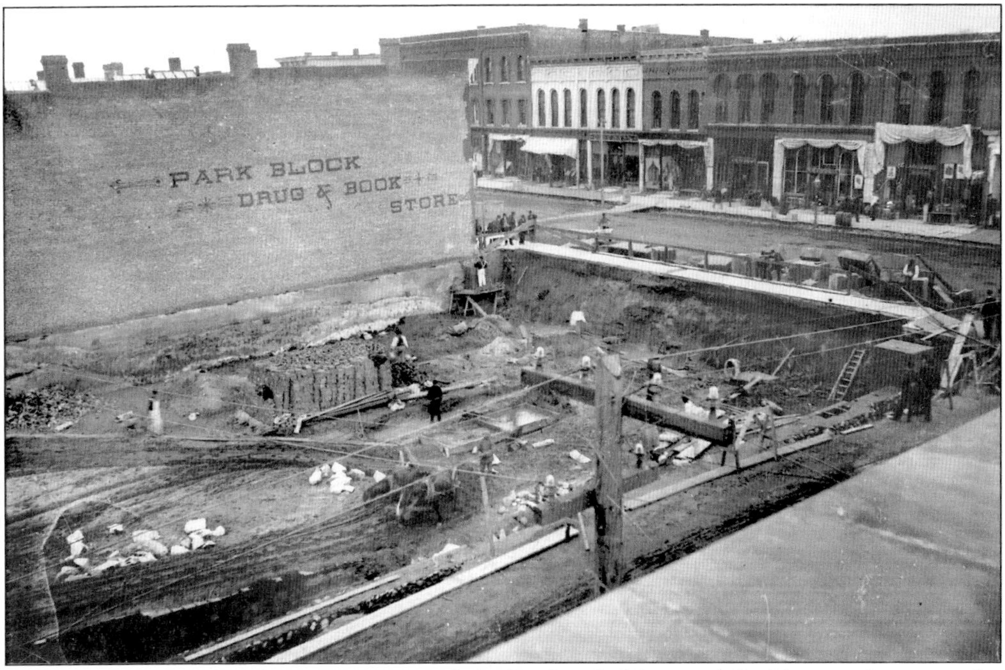

The excavation and early construction of the Beckwith Memorial Building is shown in the early 1890s. The photo was taken from a building on Beeson Street and shows the west side of Front Street in addition to the construction. At the far side of the site, a mason is visible with spectators overseeing his work. The building, which opened in January of 1893, significantly changed the business district.

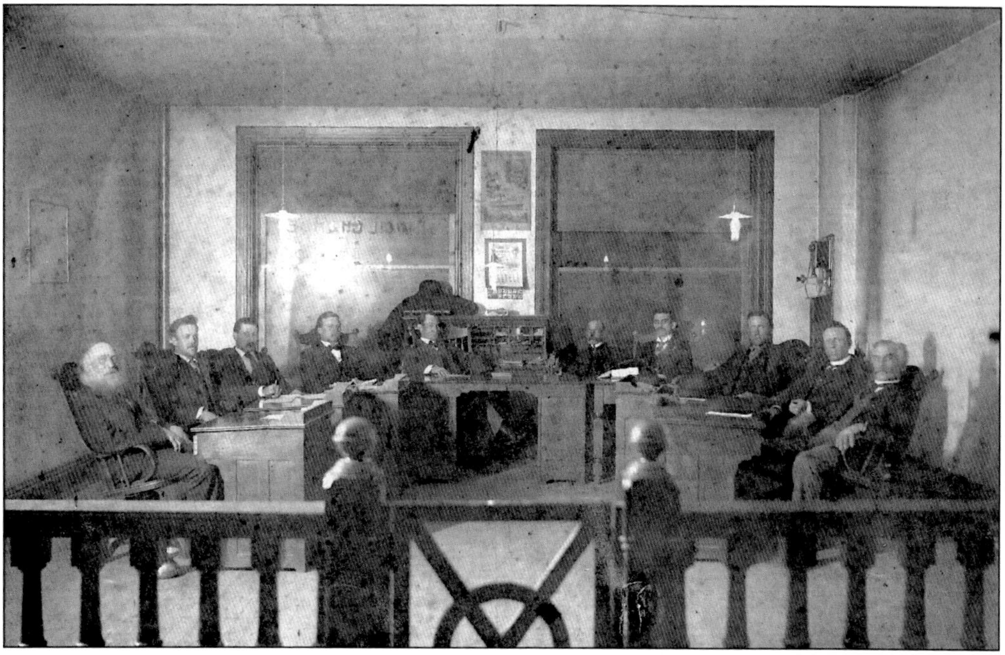

The Dowagiac City Council members are seated in the Council Chambers inside the Beckwith Building, c. 1899–1900. Pictured are, from left to right: H.A. Mason, Charles Lamareaux, Martin Herold, Coy Hendryx, Mayor Frank Richey, J.J. Ritter, Burt Thomas, S.W. Emmons, Charles Hubbard, and L. Gray. Richey was Dowagiac's mayor from 1899–1900.

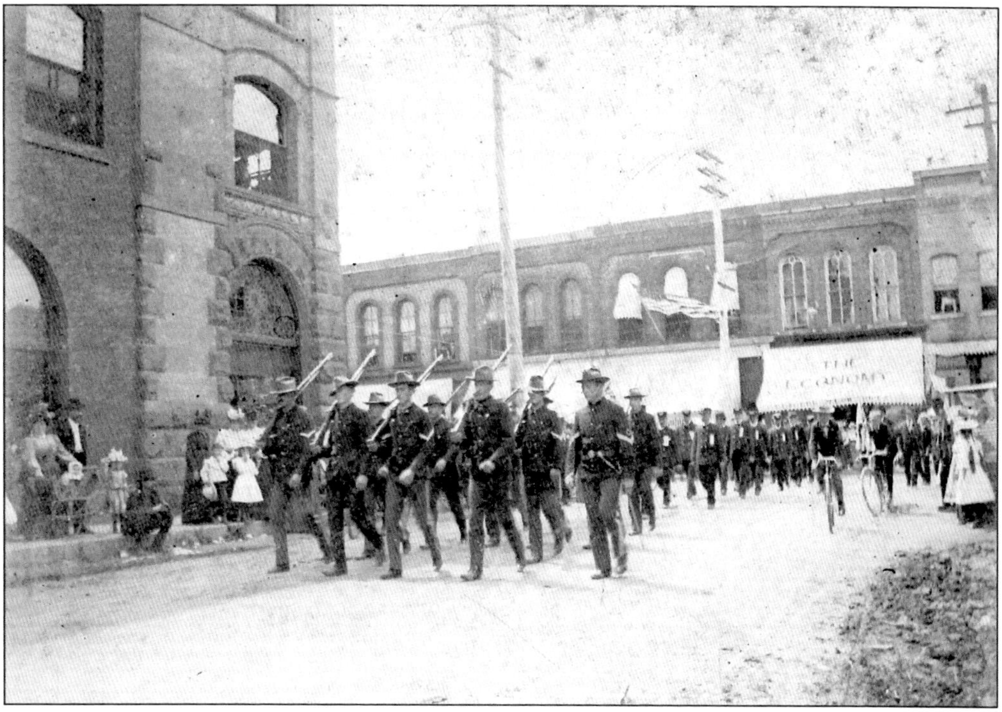

American soldiers march down Beeson Street during a parade in the Spanish–American War era, June 3, 1899. The Beckwith Memorial Building is at the left.

Two

Agricultural Roots

Whether through the direct tilling of soil, or through the manufacture of machines that make farming possible, Dowagiac has benefited from agriculture. Its glacier-enriched soil, indigenous forests, and abundant water have allowed people throughout time to eke out their livelihoods. Even the name, Dowagiac, has been translated as "foraging ground" from the Potawatomi language. Early residents tapped maple trees for sugar and early settlers planted corn and wheat.

Agricultural pursuits have been varied, with crops such as peppermint, ginseng, celery, cabbage, flax, potatoes, rye, and oats. Apiaries, maple sugar farms, fruit orchards, and blueberry patches dot the landscape. This variety of agricultural products allowed Dowagiac-area farmers to survive, and in many cases, to prosper. In one week alone in 1869, the local newspaper reported that 114,722 pounds of wheat were shipped out of Dowagiac by train, along with flour, corn meal, butter, hides, and tallow.

Farm machinery industries have also thrived in Dowagiac. One major industry was grain drills. A grain drill is a piece of equipment which, when pulled behind a horse or tractor, will plant corn or wheat seed in a furrow and cover it up as well. The manufacture of windmills, pumps, and engines also contributed to the city's prosperity and to its legacy as an agricultural center, which still survive today.

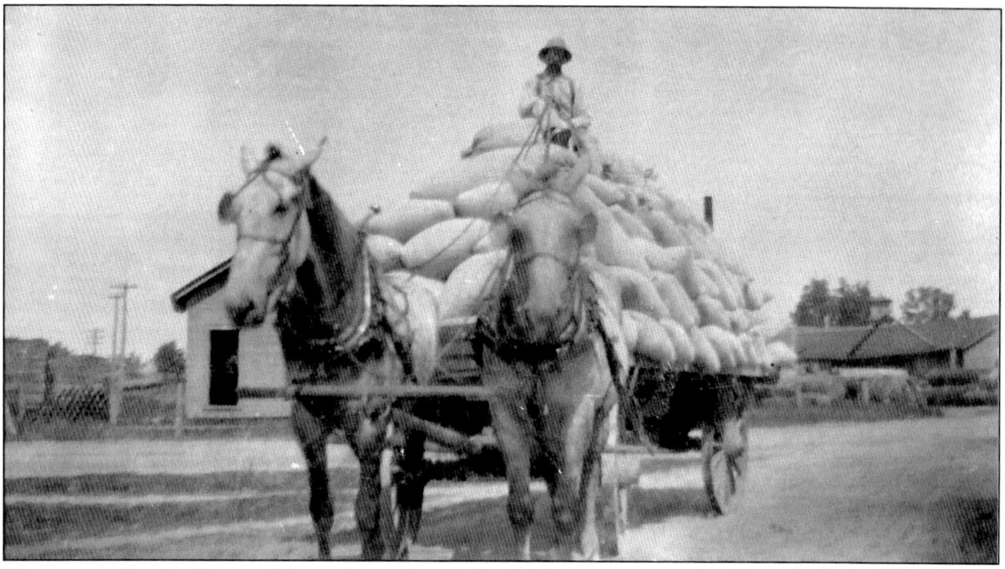

This wagonload of bagged flour from the Colby Mill was a typical sight in Dowagiac for many years. Horace Colby operated two grist mills for over 50 years, acquiring a mill that was built in 1833 by William Renesten. At the time of Colby's death, the local paper estimated that 10 million bushels of wheat were ground at the mills during his lifetime. A grist mill continues to operate in Dowagiac today.

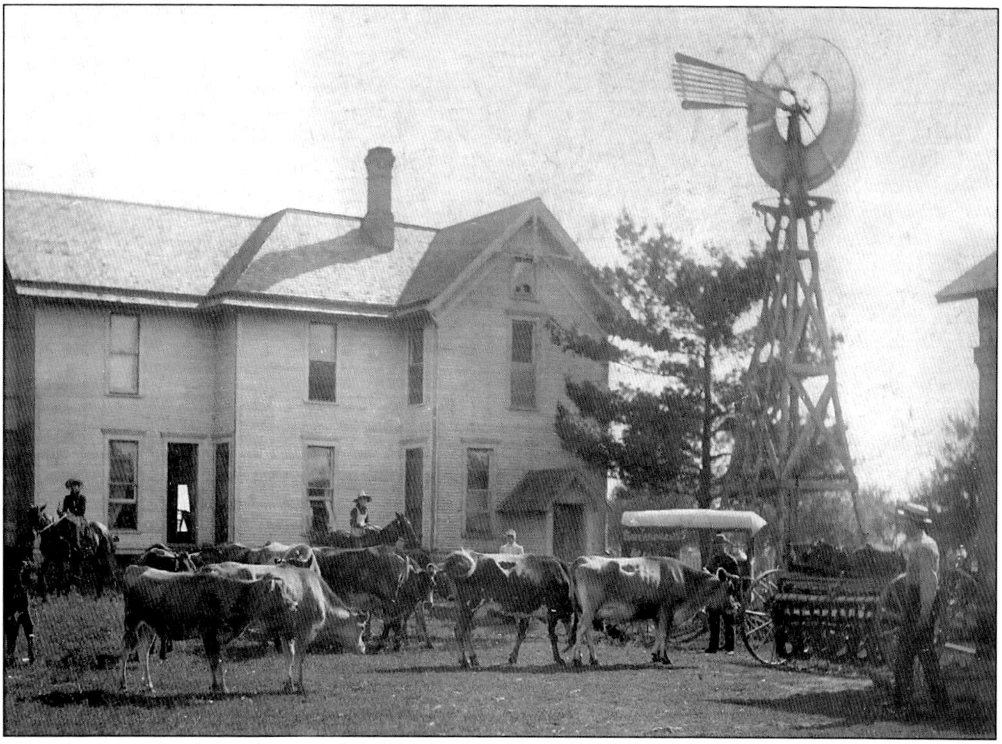

The photograph of this farm on Middle Crossing Road dates from c. 1900. This scene captures what life was often like in rural America at the time: a windmill for power, cows in the front yard, and no screens on the windows!

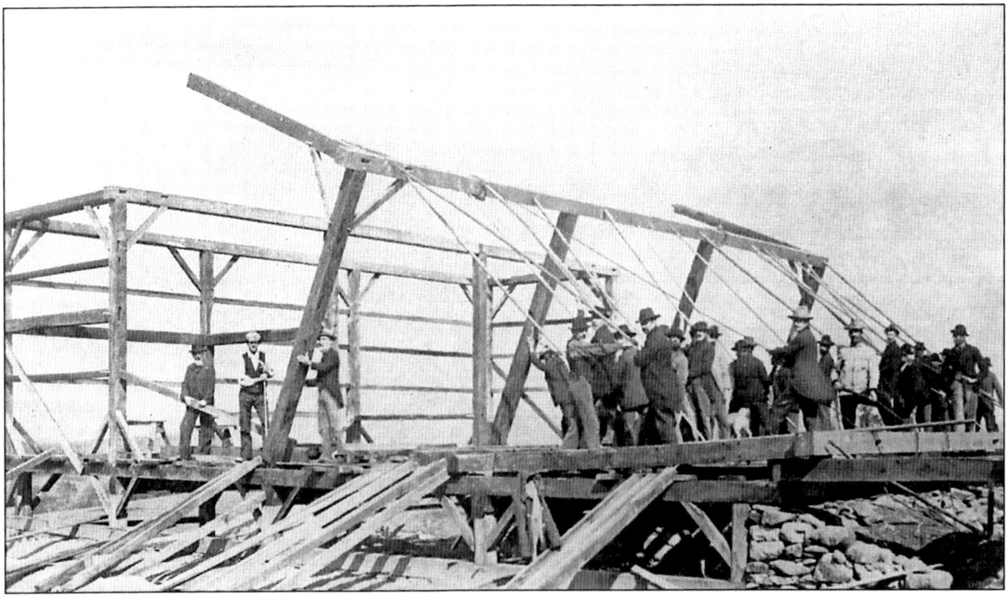

This unusual photograph shows the process of raising the wall of a barn in the early 1900s.

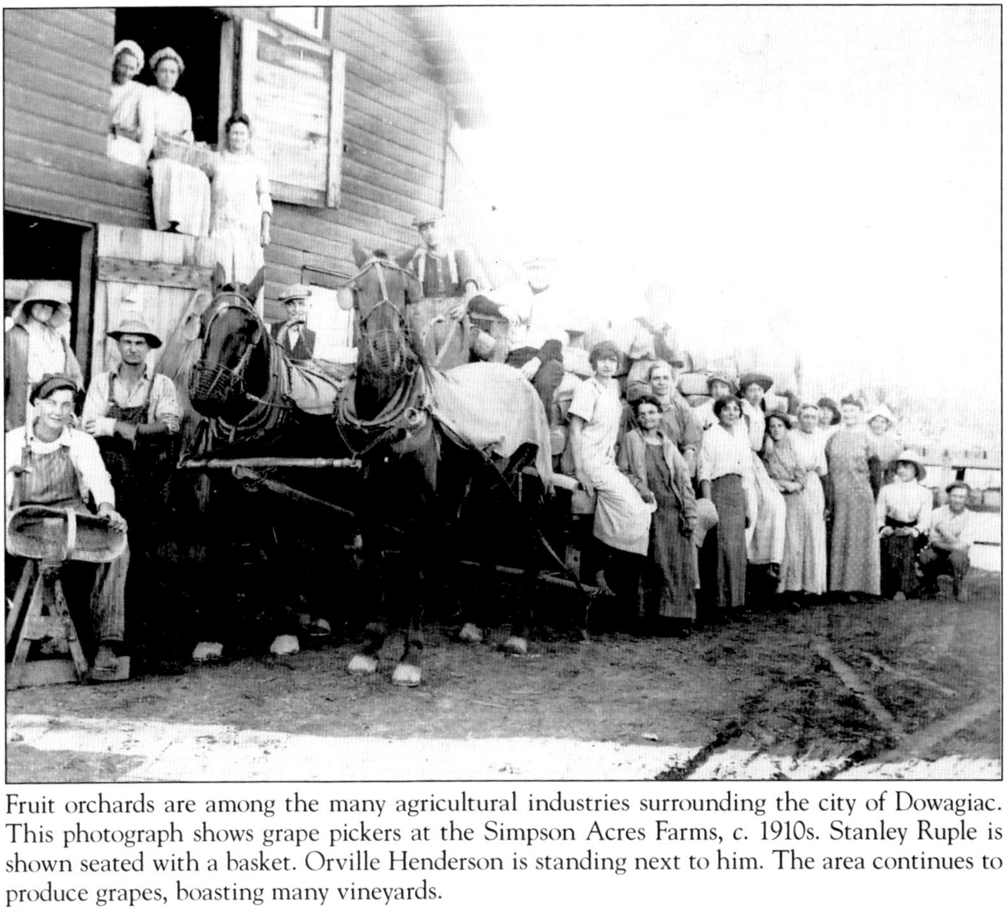

Fruit orchards are among the many agricultural industries surrounding the city of Dowagiac. This photograph shows grape pickers at the Simpson Acres Farms, c. 1910s. Stanley Ruple is shown seated with a basket. Orville Henderson is standing next to him. The area continues to produce grapes, boasting many vineyards.

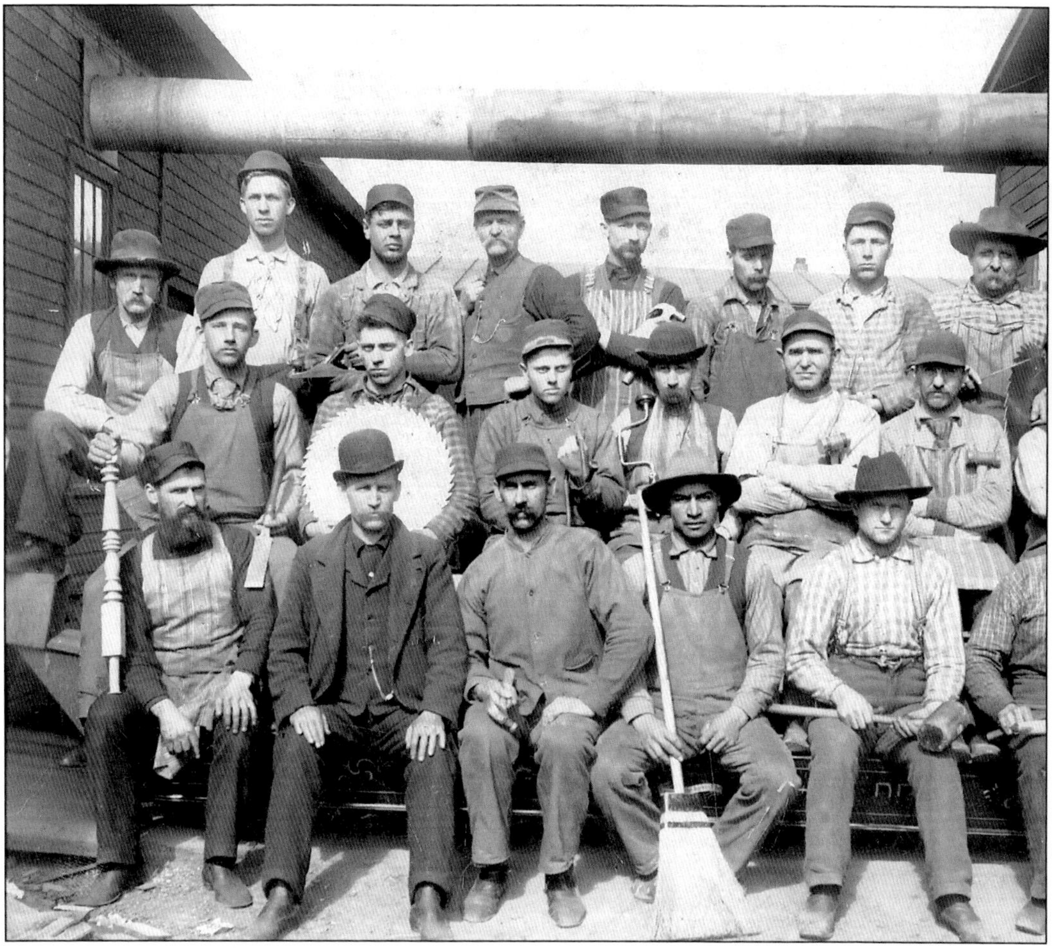

The Dowagiac Manufacturing Company produced grain drills and operated under a number of different names, among them the Dowagiac Drill Works, Warner and Tuttle Company, Chappel and Company, and the Dowagiac Shoe Drill Company. The workers in this 1880s photograph are sitting on the hopper of one of the grain drills and are holding the various tools needed to make them. The man seated second from left in the first row is probably J.P. Warner, one-time owner and longtime superintendent of the company.

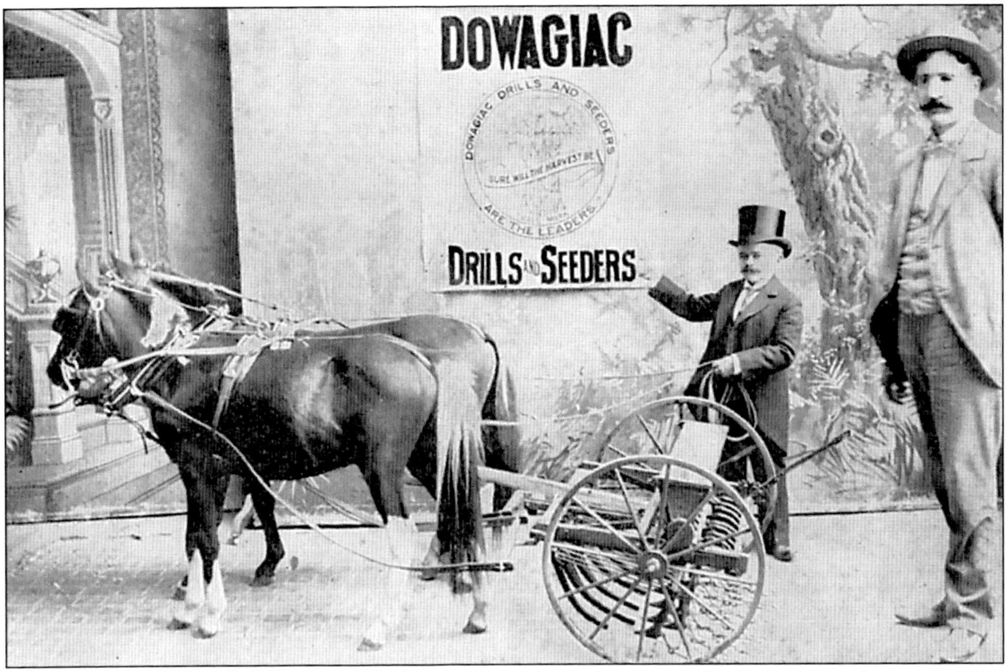

The Dowagiac Manufacturing Company used many marketing tools throughout the years. This c. 1890s trade card features Colonel C.W. Sparling, a little person, with a miniature grain drill and ponies. Colonel Sparling traveled to fairs throughout the country advertising the drill.

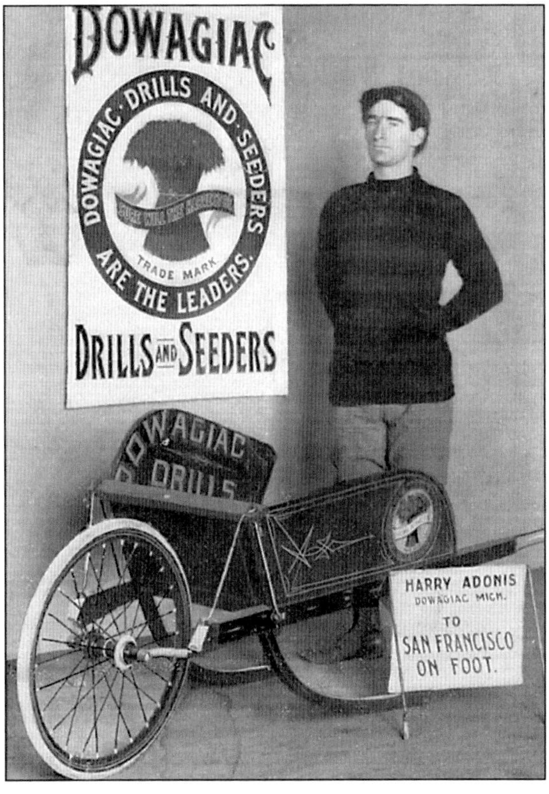

In this photo, c. 1912, a hired promoter, Harry Adonis, posed beside a wheelbarrow that advertised the company's famous grain drills. As a publicity stunt, Mr. Adonis pushed the wheelbarrow to San Francisco, California, from Michigan.

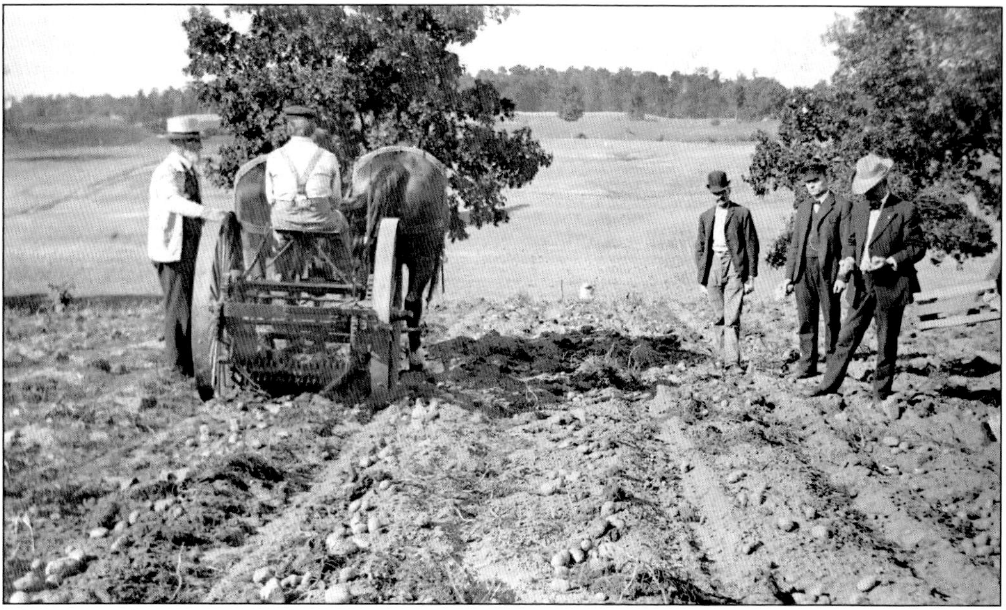

This scene shows a potato digger at work c. 1900. The potato digger was invented by Shepherd H. Wheeler, who is believed to be the man standing at the far left in this image. Mr. Wheeler was born in New York and was an early pioneer in the Dowagiac area. In 1867, he and William Tuttle Jr., a farmer in neighboring Van Buren County, patented a grain drill.

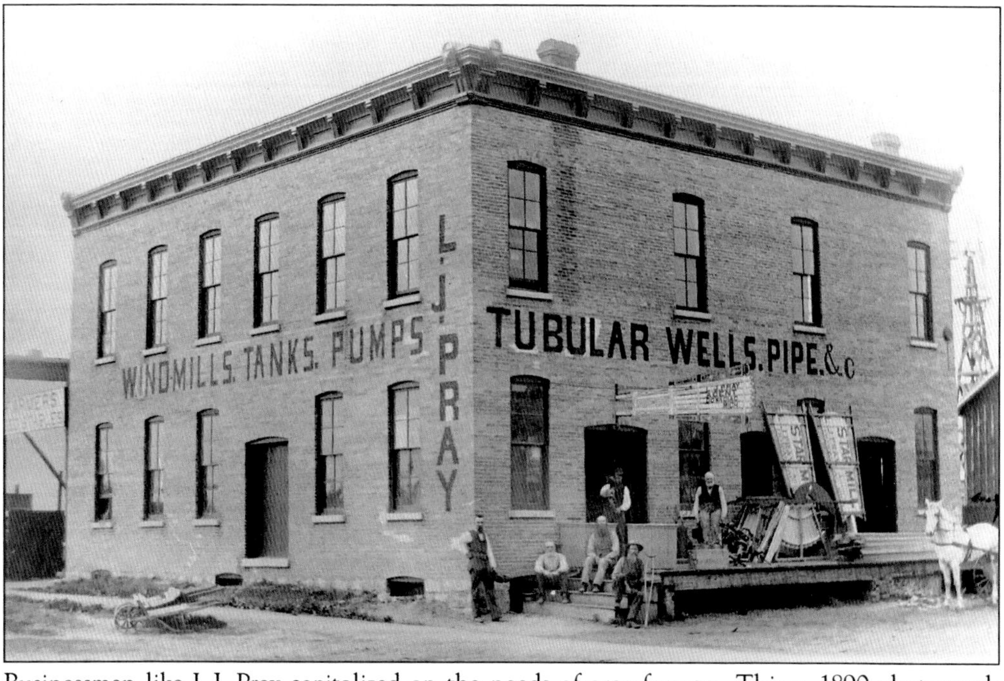

Businessmen like L.J. Pray capitalized on the needs of area farmers. This c. 1890 photograph shows the L.J. Pray Building on Park Place. Mr. Pray advertised that he was a dealer in windmills, a manufacturer of tanks of all kinds, and the sole owner of Jessup's Improved Washing Machine. His 1897 newspaper ad read, "It will pay you to see Pray for anything in the line of getting water and using it."

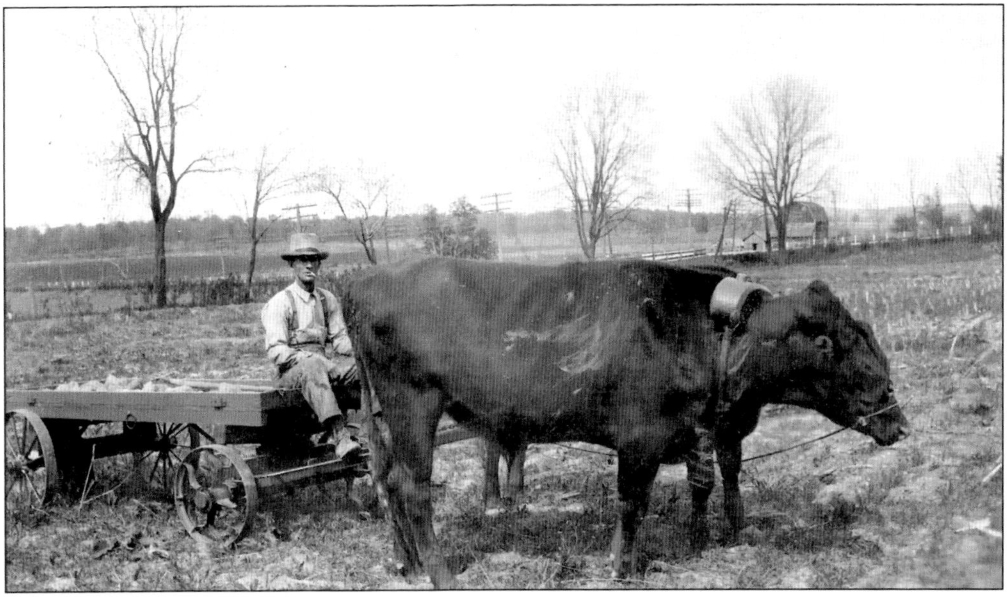

Clearing the land of rocks and trees was a major undertaking for farmers in the area. This c. 1930 photograph shows Frank Lanning with his two-year-old ox.

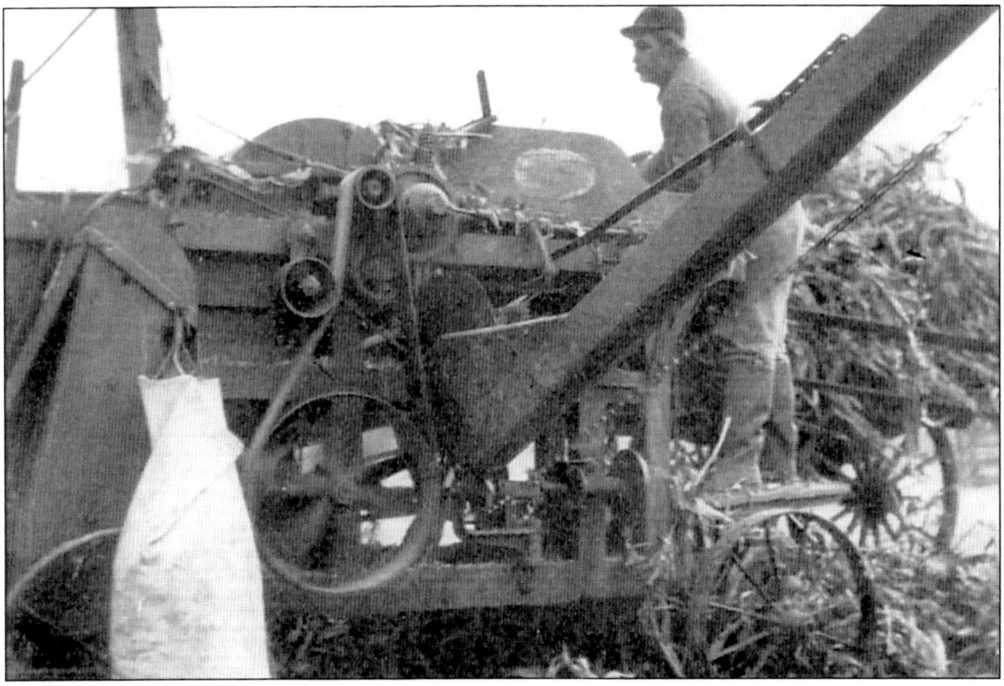

Grant Ridley is seen feeding a corn shredder, c. late 1920s. The corn shredder was used to husk the corn and cut stalks into little pieces for animal feed. The husked corn then was carried up the conveyer belt into a corn crib.

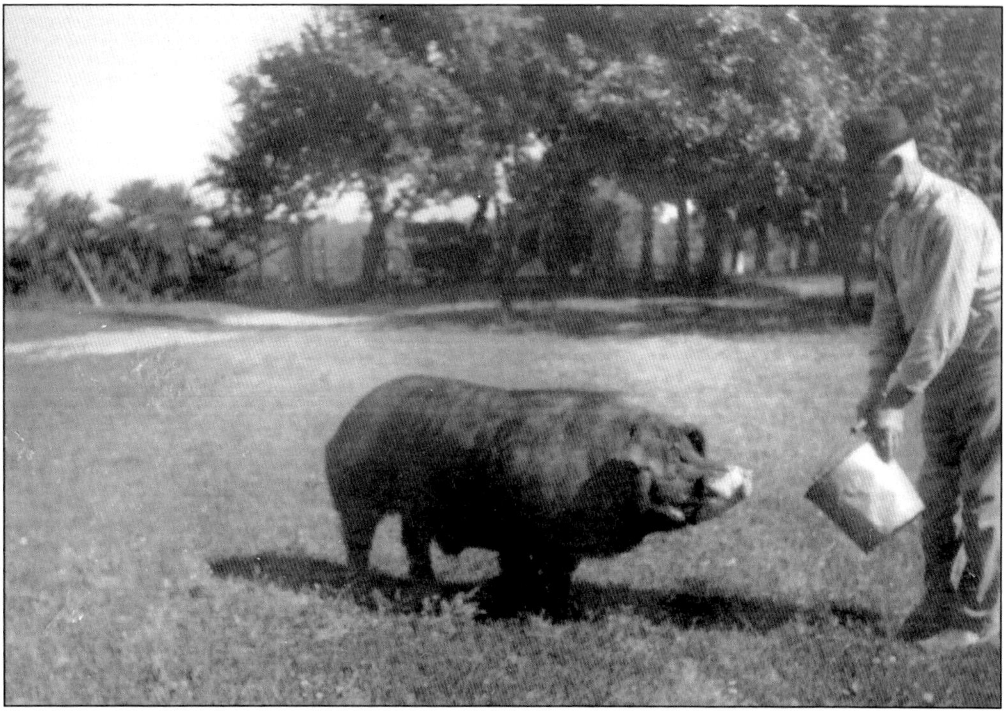

This fancy Poland China male hog is being fed by Clifford Taylor, c. 1915. Mr. Taylor farmed in Pokagon Township in the latter part of the century.

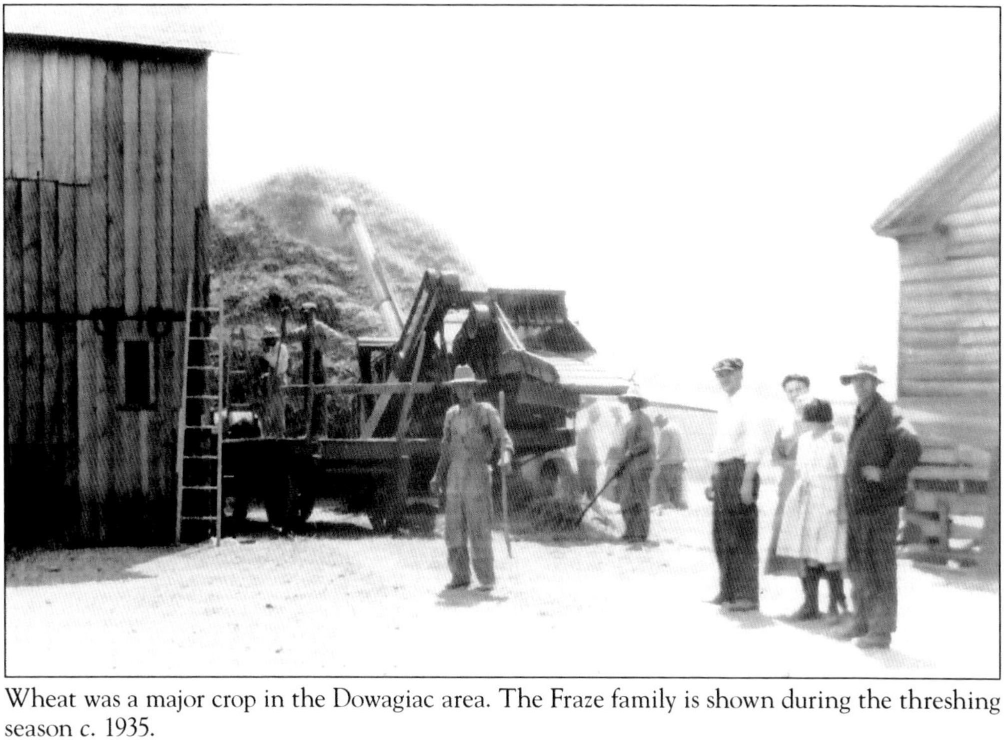

Wheat was a major crop in the Dowagiac area. The Fraze family is shown during the threshing season c. 1935.

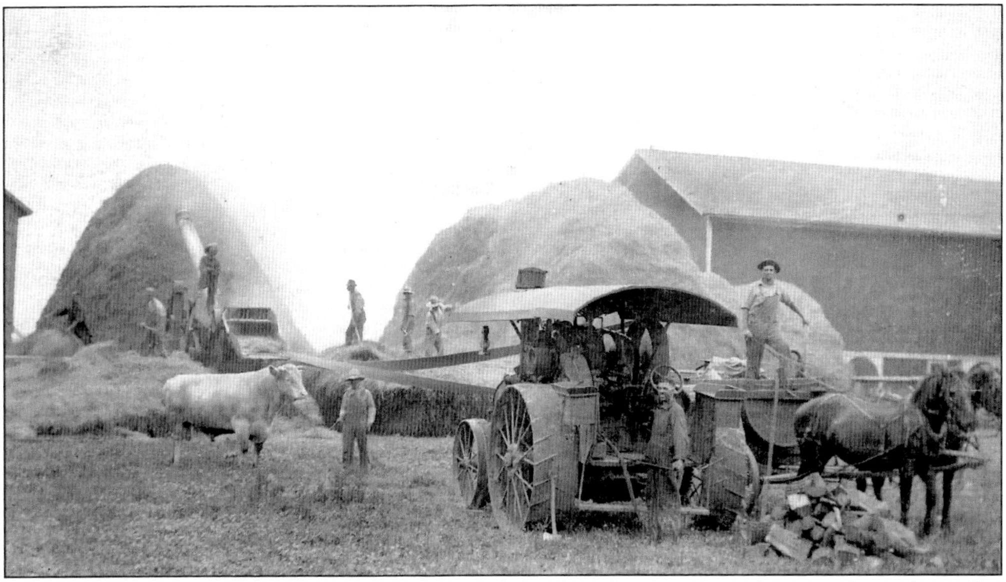

This 1921 postcard image shows a steam-operated thresher that separates the grain from the stalks. The wagon to the right of the steam engine was the water wagon, used to supply water to the engine. Threshing was a community event in which the thresher would move from farm to farm.

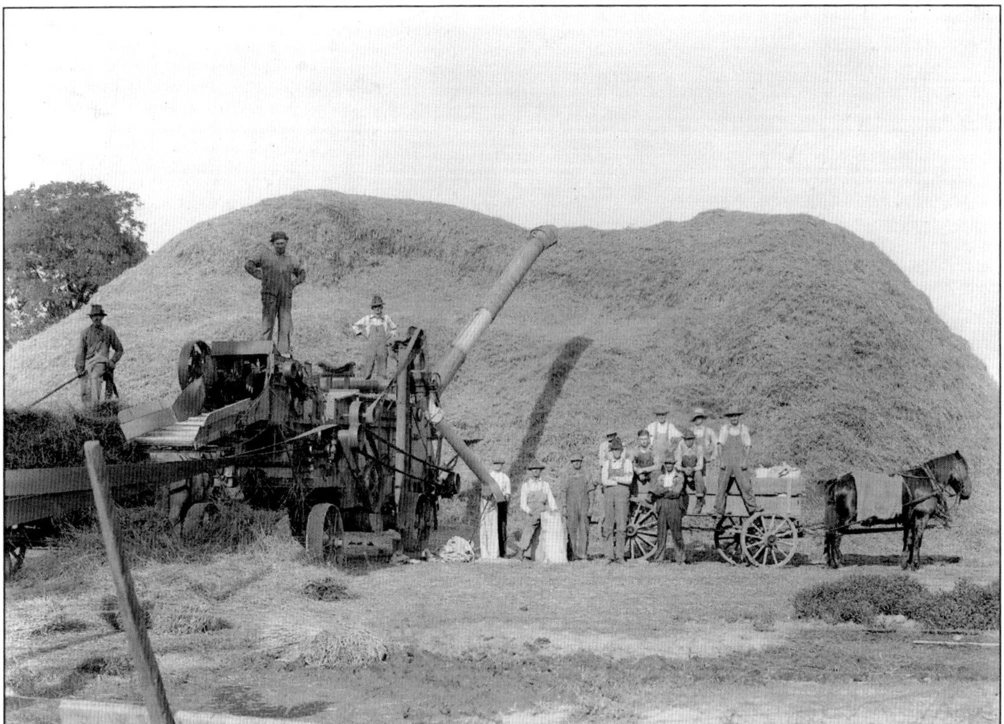

A final step in the threshing process was the sacking of the grain. This thresher has a chute on the lower right that would move the grain down so it could be sacked. The grain could be stored for use by the family or sold to a flour mill. This scene shows the Ed Emmons farm near Dowagiac. Second from left is Frank Taggart; third from left is Clarence Emmons.

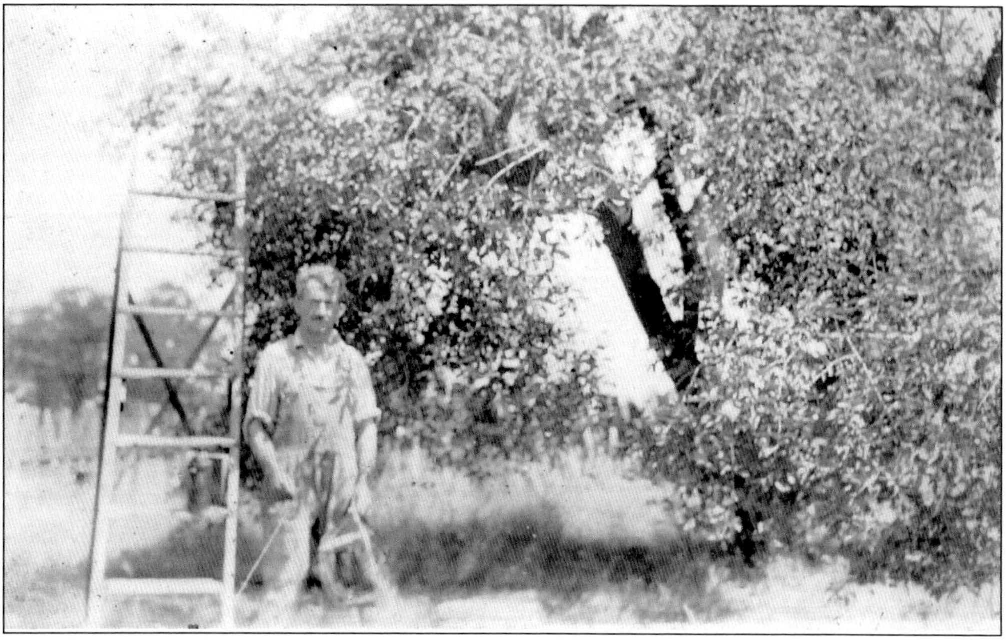

Jesse Corwin stands with beekeeping equipment, c. 1930. The Corwin Apiary was located off M-51 north of Five-Mile Corner. In the 1916 *Dowagiac Daily News*, it was reported that Ed Corwin (Jesse's cousin) secured nearly 5,000 pounds of honey and expected to secure an additional 3,000–4,000 pounds more before the season was over. The apiary had 250 colonies of bees that year, with the bees pollinating white clover and buckwheat blooms. The Corwin Apiary had been in operation since around 1883.

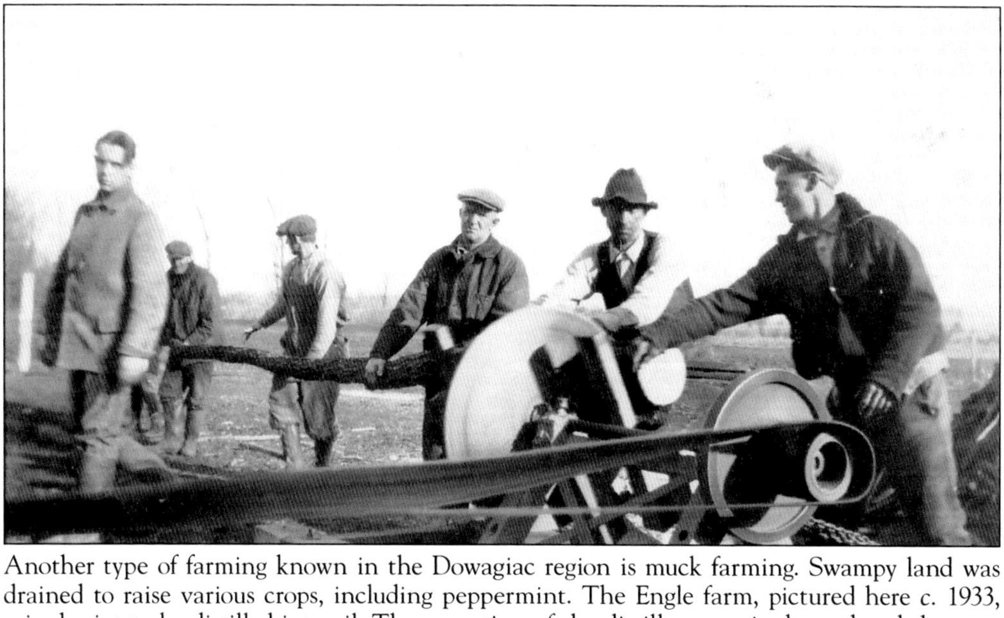

Another type of farming known in the Dowagiac region is muck farming. Swampy land was drained to raise various crops, including peppermint. The Engle farm, pictured here c. 1933, raised mint to be distilled into oil. The operation of the distillery required wood and the men in this photo are cutting trees from nearby woods for fuel. A steam engine (not pictured) was used to power the saw.

Three

Round Oak Stove Company

Dowagiac slowly grew after the railroad's arrival in 1848, but the village needed a manufacturer to provide jobs to fuel greater growth. That manufacturer turned out to be Philo D. Beckwith (P.D. for short), who arrived in Dowagiac in 1854. Beckwith was born in Eagle, New York, in 1825. He and his wife, Catherine Scott Beckwith, moved west in 1844 to join her family in Michigan. After stays in Battle Creek, Ypsilanti, and Niles, the Beckwiths settled in Dowagiac in 1854.

P.D. Beckwith opened a foundry on Front Street in Dowagiac and the business struggled for close to a decade. In search of a product to market, Beckwith first tried the roller grain drill—a revolutionary new planting implement. John Gage of Dowagiac patented the roller grain drill and Beckwith partnered with him in the 1860s. While this production improved his financial standing, he was not clear of his creditors and money was still tight.

To heat his foundry, Beckwith cast a heating stove around 1865. Upon seeing Beckwith's stove, a representative from the Michigan Central Railroad ordered one for the depot in Niles. This event would eventually lead to success for Beckwith and growth for Dowagiac. The railroad ordered hundreds more for depots and buildings between Chicago and Detroit, and Beckwith had a new business.

Beckwith proved himself to be an able marketer. The first stove he placed outside of railroad facilities was at the Dowagiac barber shop of Thomas Jefferson Martin. This was a shrewd move—most men in town (and visitors perhaps) had to visit the barber eventually. Beckwith reasoned that once they saw the stove, it would surely lead to more sales. In 1871, Beckwith officially started the Round Oak Stove Company.

The Round Oak stove was a great product—it was durable and also was supposedly the first heater to hold a fire overnight. Beckwith also produced fine advertising, further establishing his stove business, and Round Oaks were sold nationally. Modest success in the 1870s led to increased sales in the 1880s. Beckwith and his business impacted Dowagiac greatly. Round Oak was the largest employer in Dowagiac and it paid employees well. Beckwith built Round Oak Hall as an entertainment venue; he also sponsored a baseball team and served as mayor of Dowagiac for most of the 1880s.

Beckwith's death in January of 1889 shocked the city, but Round Oak continued to thrive. Beckwith's son-in-law, Fred E. Lee, became president, and in the 1890s, the company added furnaces and cookstoves to the product line. The new line expanded profits into the 1910s. In 1900, Round Oak introduced a mascot, a conceptualized Potawatomi Indian, Chief Doe-Wah-Jack, which appeared on advertising until the company's end.

In the late 1910s, after 40 years of steady growth, Round Oak started to misfire. Three competing furnace companies were founded in Dowagiac between 1915 and 1929, drawing on Round Oak's resources and sales. Poor management decisions in the 1920s, followed by the Great Depression, seriously damaged the company's standing. Round Oak stayed afloat and remained viable by handling government defense contracts during World War II.

In 1946, the company reorganized to liquidate its assets, selling its buildings to Kaiser–Frazer, an automobile parts manufacturer in 1947. The heating side of the company was sold to

Peerless Furnace Company of Indianapolis, which continued making stove and furnace parts. There was a brief resurgence from 1948–1951, when Round Oak produced heating and air-conditioning products in Dowagiac, but the company never reached the success of its first 50 years of business. The company's legacy, however, was already well established. It was the largest company in Dowagiac's history and had left its mark permanently on the city.

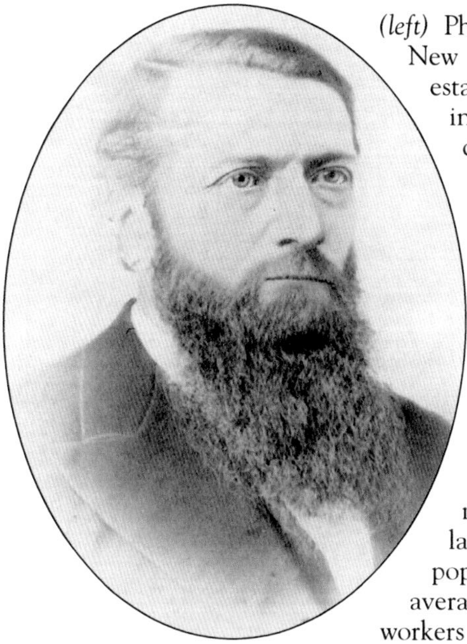

(left) Philo D. Beckwith (1825–1889), was born in Eagle, New York, and moved to Dowagiac in 1854. He slowly established his foundry business—an 1855 advertisement in the *Cass County Republican* showed that Beckwith cast many items, including plows, and he boasted, "In short, anything made of wood and iron can be had at the above establishment." He founded the Round Oak Stove Company in 1871.

(below) P.D. Beckwith was always popular with his workers, and is pictured here with part of his crew in the 1880s. Beckwith, with the long beard, is in the center of the second row; the other workers are unidentified. Beckwith served as mayor of Dowagiac for much of the 1880s, elected largely because of his stature at Round Oak and his popularity with his employees. He paid a higher-than-average salary, and it is said that he looked after his workers outside of the shop as well.

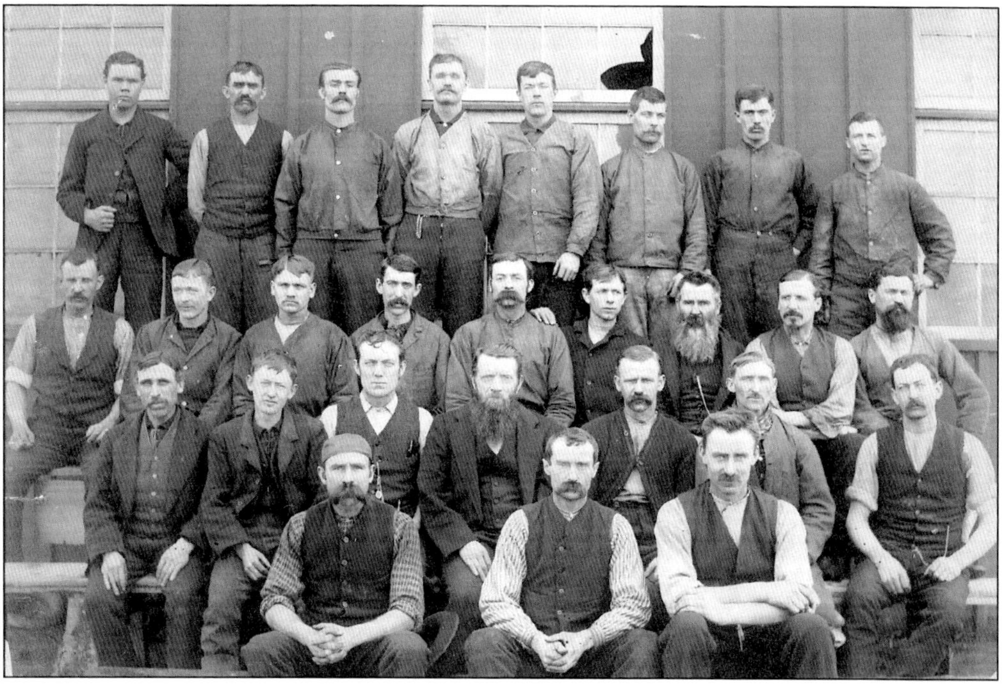

This has been identified as the first Round Oak parlor stove. If true, it would have been made around 1870 and placed in the barber shop of Thomas Jefferson Martin. At this time, the heater was strictly a utilitarian stove without any decoration—that would change over the next 50 years. Beckwith would also make modifications to make it more efficient and capable of sustaining a fire throughout the night.

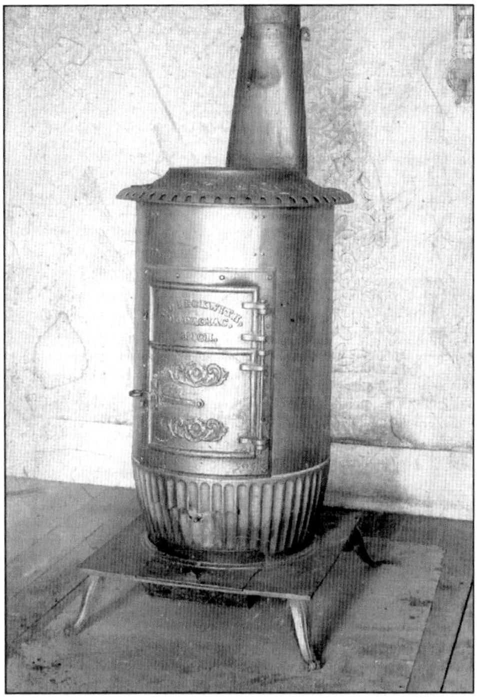

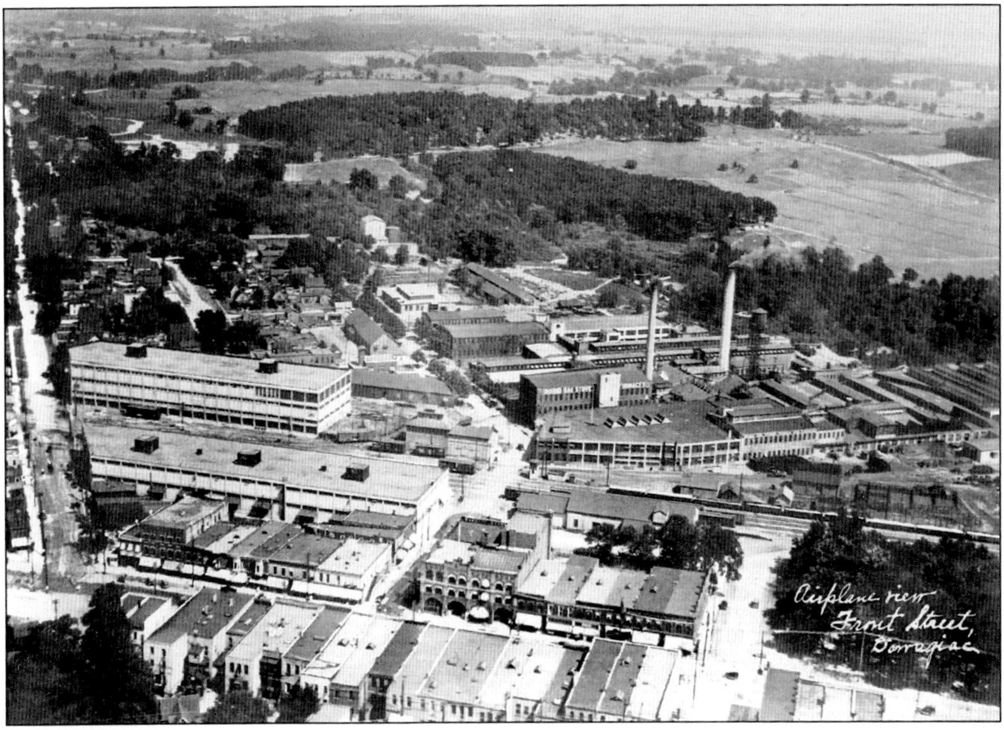

An aerial view of Round Oak in 1925 shows the factory's size and its proximity to downtown Dowagiac. Round Oak was a massive plant by this time and it truly dwarfed all the other Dowagiac businesses. In the foreground center is the Beckwith Memorial Building. The open space in the background is the Cass County Country Club golf course, today the Elks Club golf course.

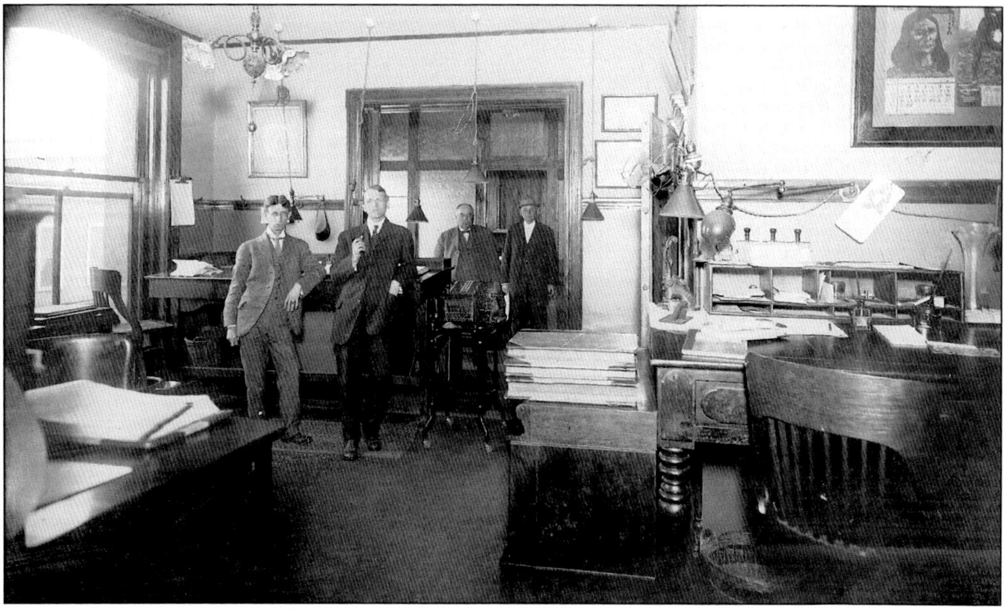

While the company expanded during Beckwith's lifetime, it was not until after his death that the company peaked. Beckwith's modest office at the factory was replaced by grander offices, located on the second floor of the Beckwith Memorial Building in 1893. This photograph shows part of the office area in 1913. Seen in the background are longtime secretary of the company, Julius O. Becraft (left), and Harry Mosher (right).

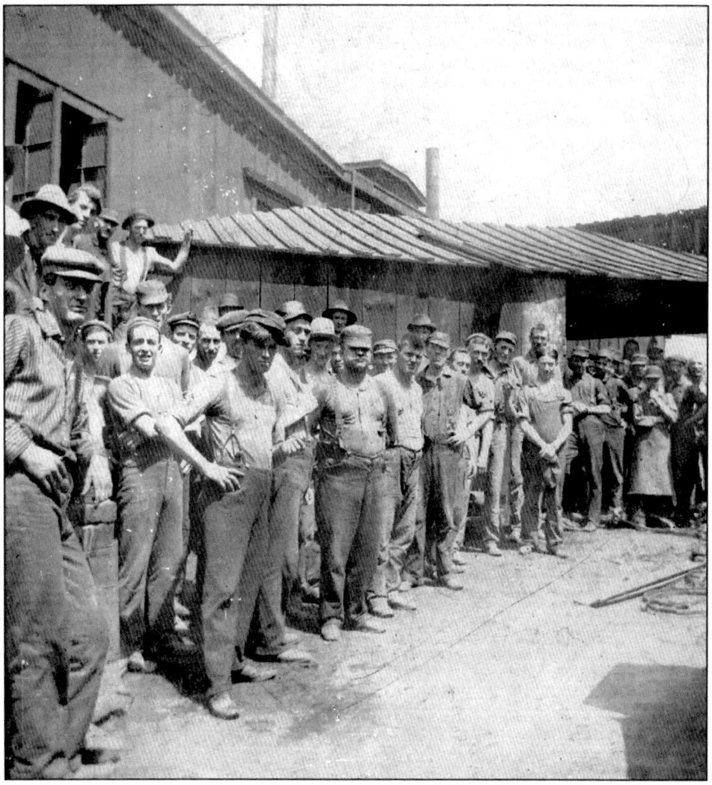

The Round Oak Stove Company work crew grew over the years. At the time this photo was taken around 1900, Round Oak employed about 500 men. From Beckwith's payroll of eight in 1869, Round Oak would expand over the next half-century and peak in the 1910s with over 1,200 employees. Dowagiac grew as Round Oak grew—from 2,349 residents in 1884 to 5,088 in 1910—and Round Oak was the biggest employer in the county. In the 1910s, Round Oak employed 25 percent of the entire city population and probably at least one in every two men in town.

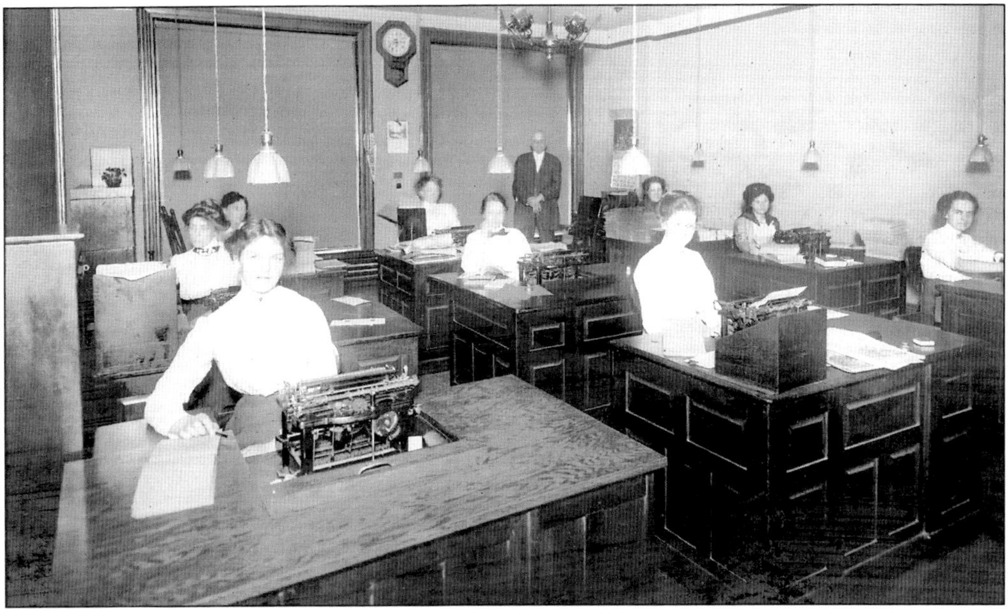

While the management and foundry were still men's clubs, women had employment opportunities at Round Oak too—they worked in the print shop and as typists in the office. In the pre-computer world, all company correspondence had to be typed on paper and offices like the one seen here were commonplace across the United States. This photo of the Round Oak typists was taken in 1913 in the Beckwith Memorial Building. Harry Mosher is seen in the background.

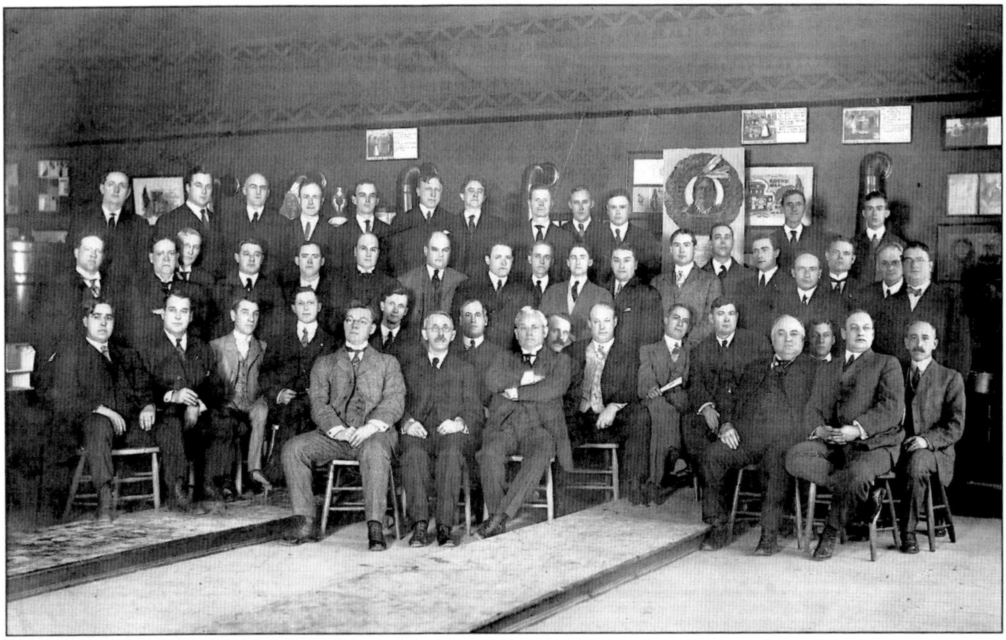

Round Oak's management and sales team pose in Round Oak Hall on January 6, 1910. This photograph is interesting for the people and the contemporary Round Oak advertising surrounding the group. In the front row center is the board of directors: Archie Gardner, Ormal G. Beach, and Fred E. Lee. To the right of that group is the company secretary, Julius O. Becraft, and an unknown executive.

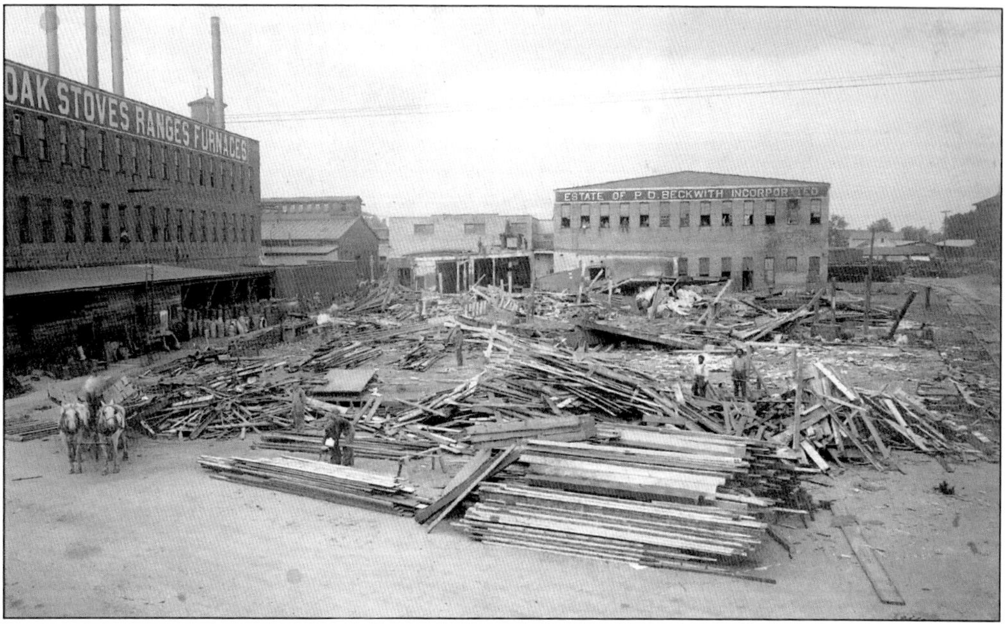

Progress and success brought the decision to tear down Beckwith's original foundry. In June of 1912, Round Oak tore down the last of the original Beckwith buildings, erected in 1866, and built the plant pictured in the photograph below. With that construction, Round Oak claimed to have a fully modern facility.

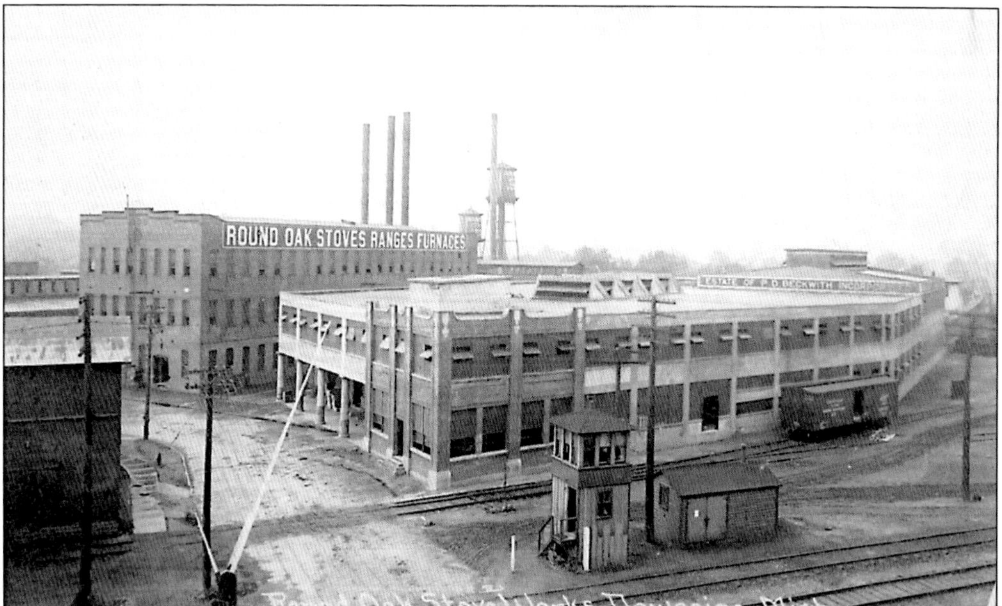

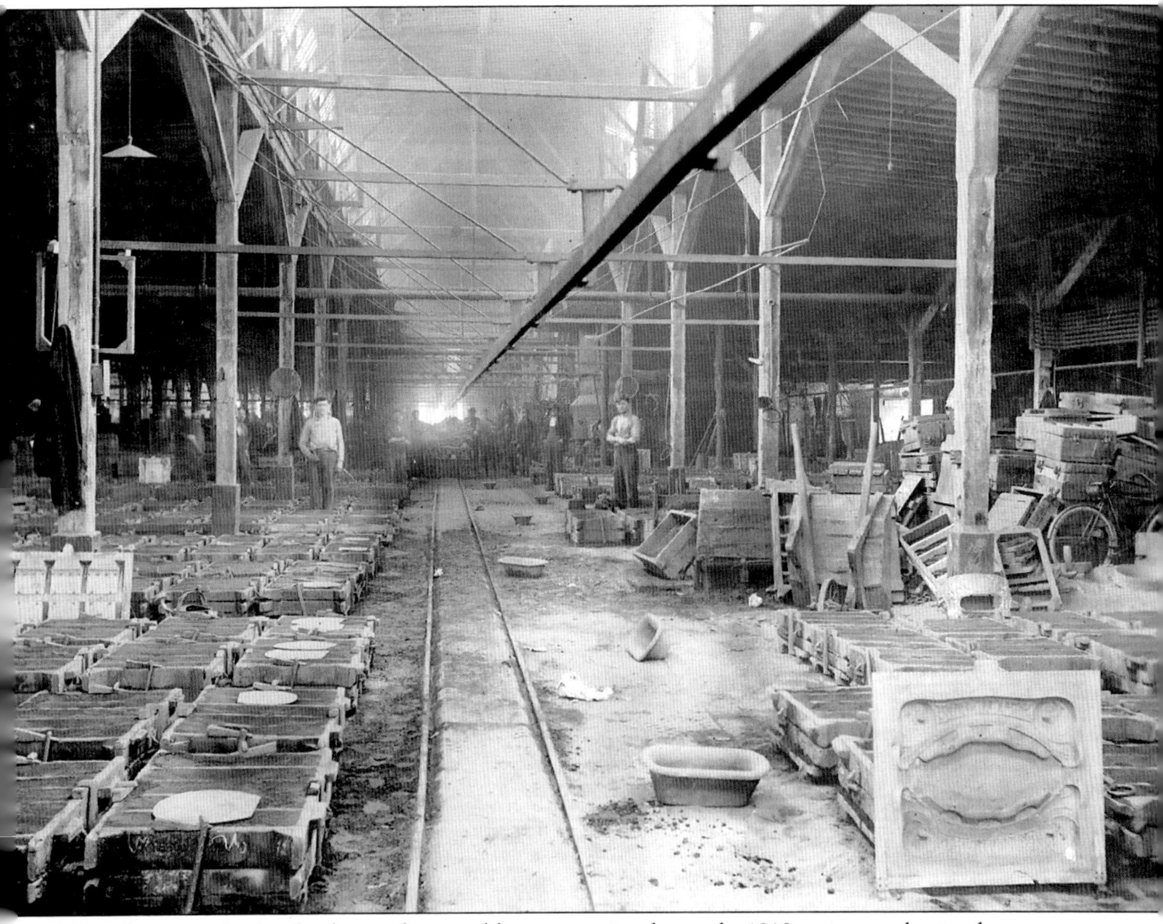

This photograph clearly shows the moulding room in the early 1910s—it may be in the new factory building built in 1912. The floor is lined with moulding flasks packed with sand and ready for molten iron to be poured into them. The tracks on the floor and overhead helped the moulders transport the molten iron from the cupola before pouring and facilitated moving the finished parts.The pattern in the foreground at right is for a piece of a baseburner stove and helps to date the photograph.

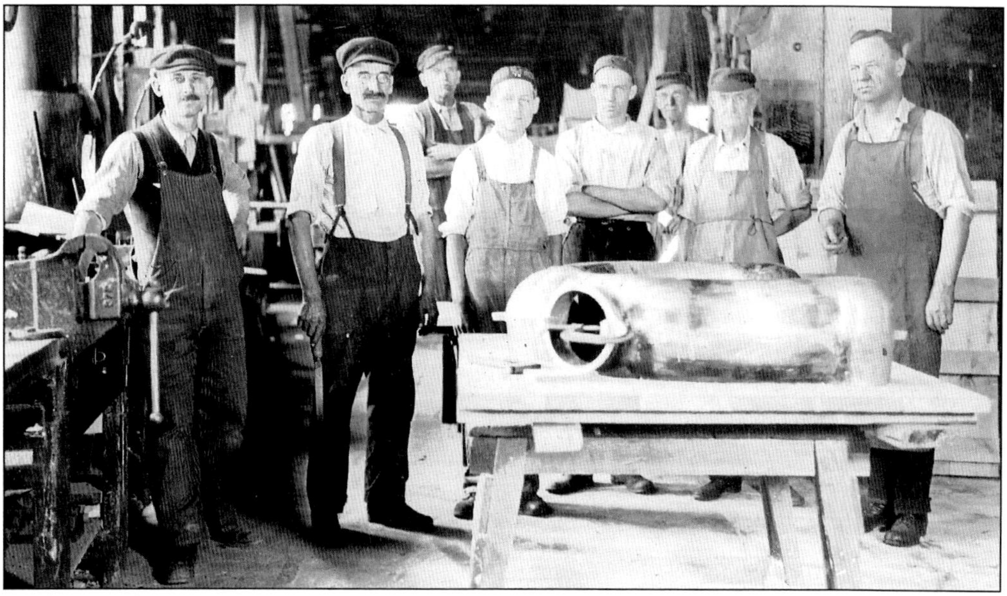

Workers in the pattern room are seen in this image from the 1910s. On the table is a pattern for a furnace part. The men in the front row are, from left to right: Oswald Wegner Sr., Herb Wade, unidentified, unidentified, Bill Weedo, and Jim Willis. Both men in the back row are unidentified. Wegner also invented stove parts, and was awarded a patent in 1911 for an improved stove door.

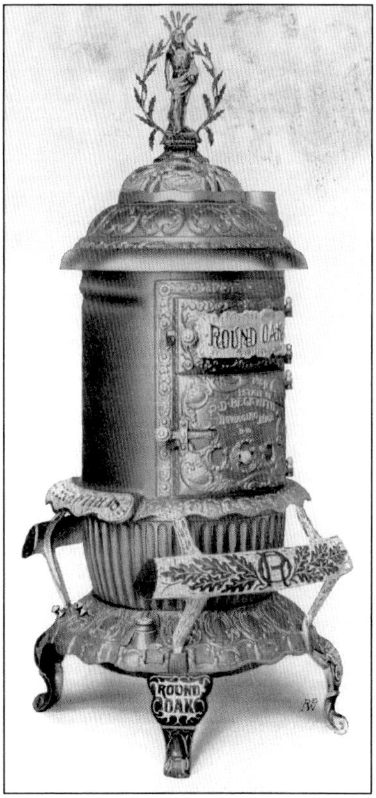

For 27 years, Round Oak produced a high quality utilitarian stove with little decoration. Beginning in 1898 with the B model, Round Oak stoves became more ornate while retaining their high standards of quality. This image of a D model stove, made from 1900–1904, is from a 1903 catalog.

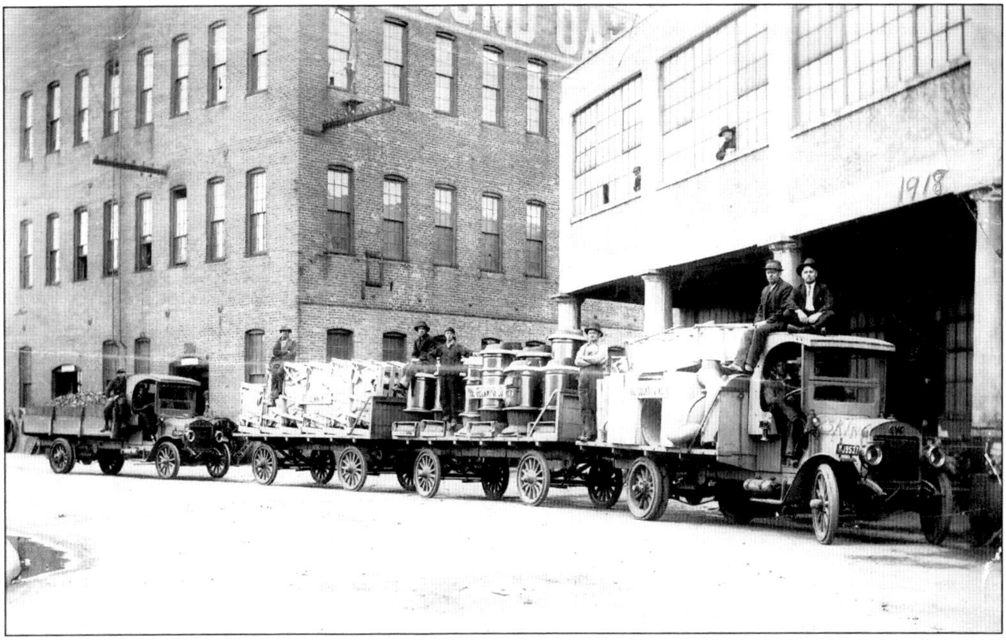

Round Oak Stove Company products are seen ready for shipment outside plant buildings in 1918. The flatbed trucks are loaded with the various products the firm manufactured, including heating and cooking stoves.

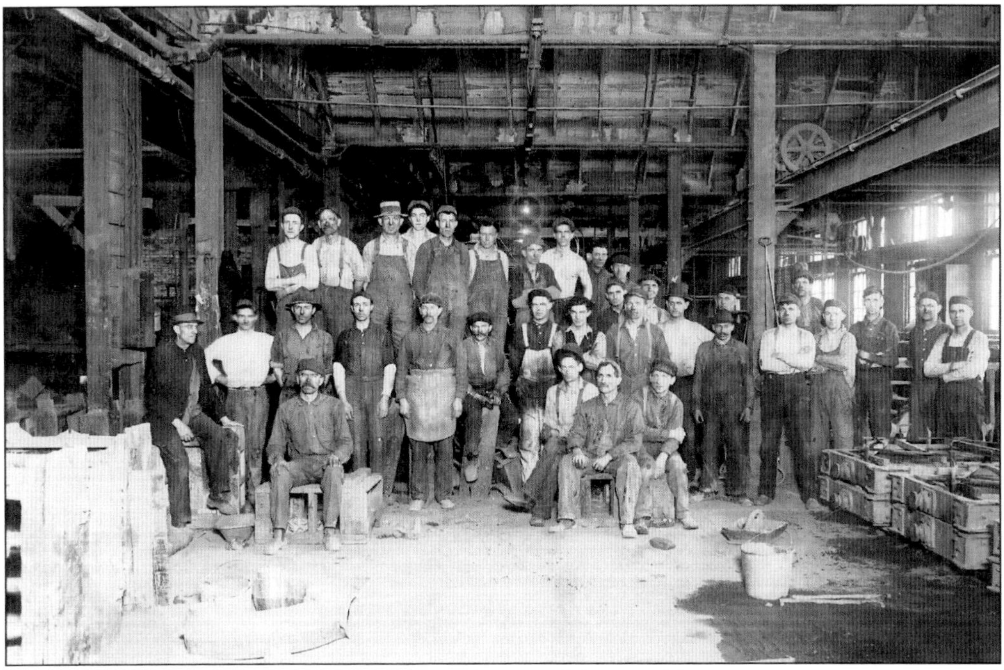

This is the inside of the moulding room, with part of the moulding room crew present, around 1910. Round Oak employed over 300 moulders at the time; this photo shows only one section of the large room. Most of the workers are unidentified, but it is known that William Bakeman is at far left; Roy Zelner is directly under the light; and Otto Behrman is in the back row at left with the rimmed hat.

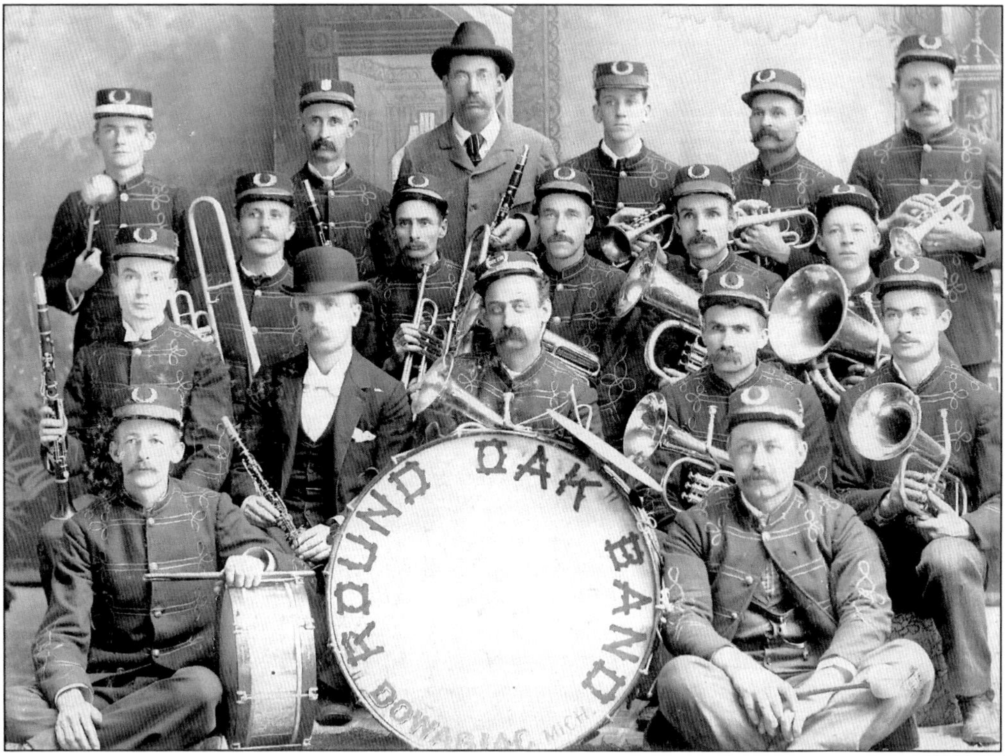

The Round Oak Band was formed in 1895 and was one of the most popular bands in southwest Michigan into the 1930s. William Schuchert, in the second row at far left, was the band leader throughout its history. This photograph is from the Round Oak Band's earliest years, possibly even 1895.

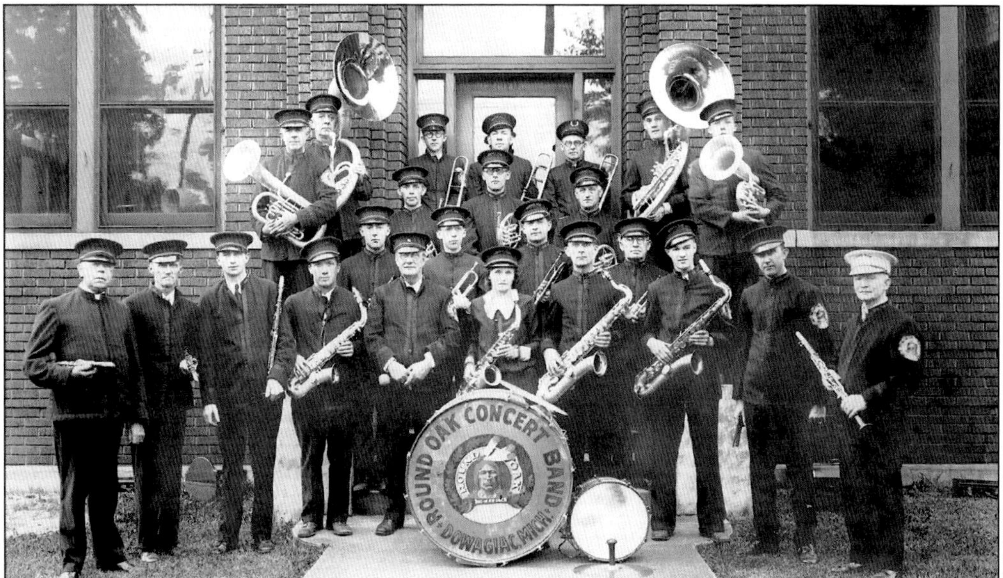

This is a later incarnation of the Round Oak Band, photographed in front of the new Round Oak office building in 1930. William Schuchert, at far right in the white hat, was still the bandleader.

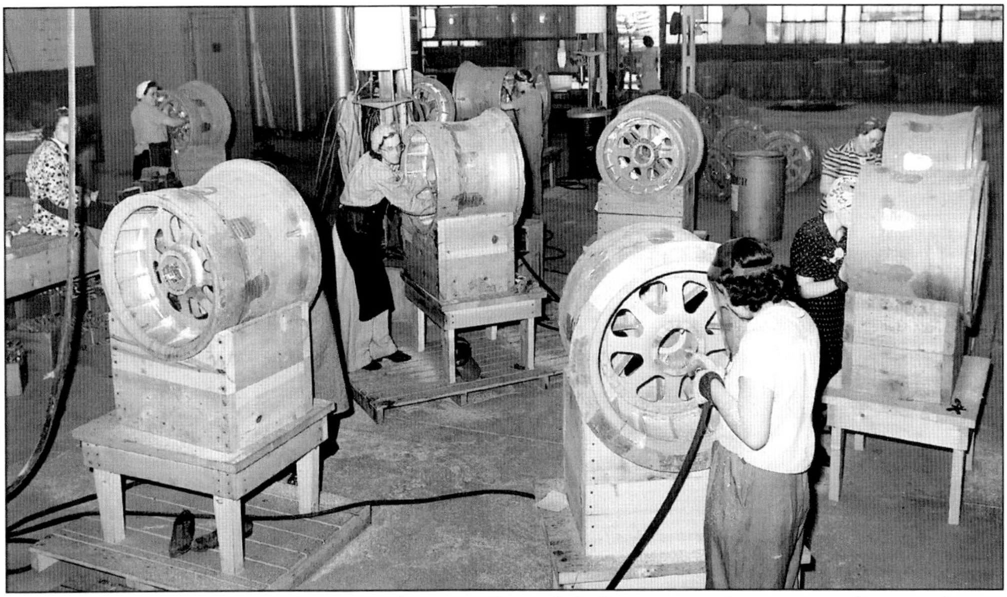

Like most factories across the United States, Round Oak converted to war production during World War II. The company made magnesium castings for the war effort and women workers replaced the men who were serving overseas. This photograph shows female employees, Round Oak's "Rosie the Riveters," smoothing magnesium castings of airplane wheels.

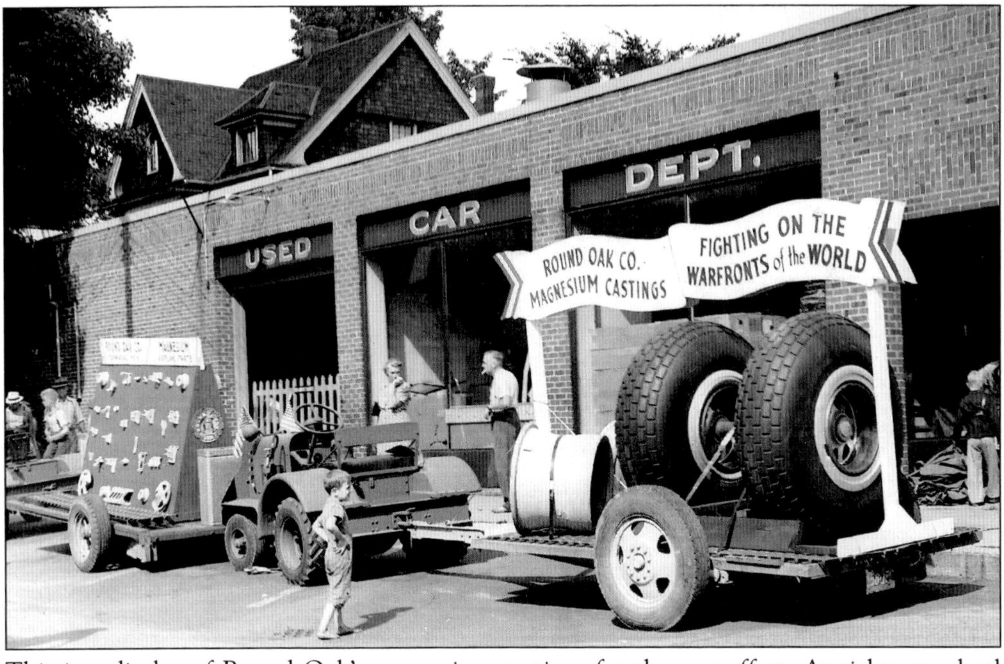

This is a display of Round Oak's magnesium castings for the war effort. At right are wheel castings that appear in the previous photograph, including two with the tires attached. While the magnesium castings kept Round Oak in business during the war, it represented an expensive transition from iron casting, and after the war, the company was stuck with magnesium casting equipment. The company lost money, and in 1947 sold its facilities to Kaiser–Frazer to manufacture engine parts.

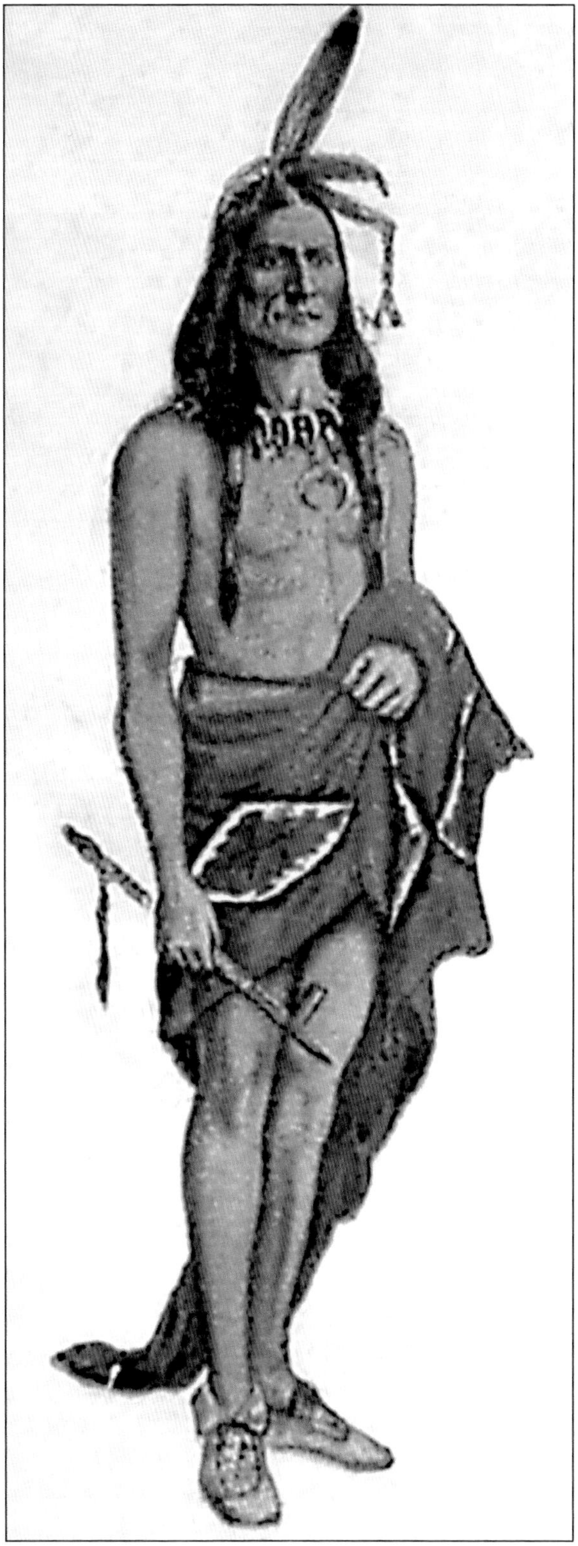

Round Oak introduced a mascot, a fictional Potawatomi named Chief Doe-Wah-Jack, around 1900. Legend claims that Round Oak devised the name to provide potential customers with the phonetic spelling of Dowagiac in an era when the telephone was spreading across the country. Customers, in theory, would know how to ask the operator for a Dowagiac connection. Chief Doe-Wah-Jack appeared in company literature and on premiums—like calendars, stickpins, watch fobs, matchsafes, and postcards—in any number of forms, including this standing pose. Despite an attempt to replace him with a Dutch boy around 1907, Chief Doe-Wah-Jack served as the company icon until Round Oak folded in 1947.

Four

Making a Buck in Dowagiac

Ezekiel Smith established Dowagiac's first business, a general store, at the corner of Main and South Front Streets shortly after the city was platted in 1848. An experienced businessman from Cassopolis, Smith did very well his first year and built a larger store in the lot next door in 1849. The first store became a saloon. Smith sold his business to Wells Atwood in 1850 and was later elected Dowagiac's first justice of the peace.

Smith's business venture, though brief, established Dowagiac's central business district along Front Street. Within one year of the erection of Smith's general store, a hotel, the Dowagiac House, had been built by A.J. Wares on Main Street. In 1851, the growing town already had several dry goods stores, general stores, leather goods shops, a tailor, carpenters, physicians, a clothing store, groceries, two hotels, and a hardware store.

Early manufacturing included gunsmiths (Dowagiac had two in the 1850s), blacksmiths, and foundries. The foundries led to the manufacturing base that fueled Dowagiac's growth in the late 1800s and early 1900s. Foundries in Dowagiac at this time did small casting jobs and specialized in plows.

Many businesses established in the 19th century remained viable well into the 1900s, with some families operating centennial businesses. They were also a reflection of a bygone era—many of the specialty shops in this chapter could not survive in small cities today due to growing pressure on the marketplace from national corporations.

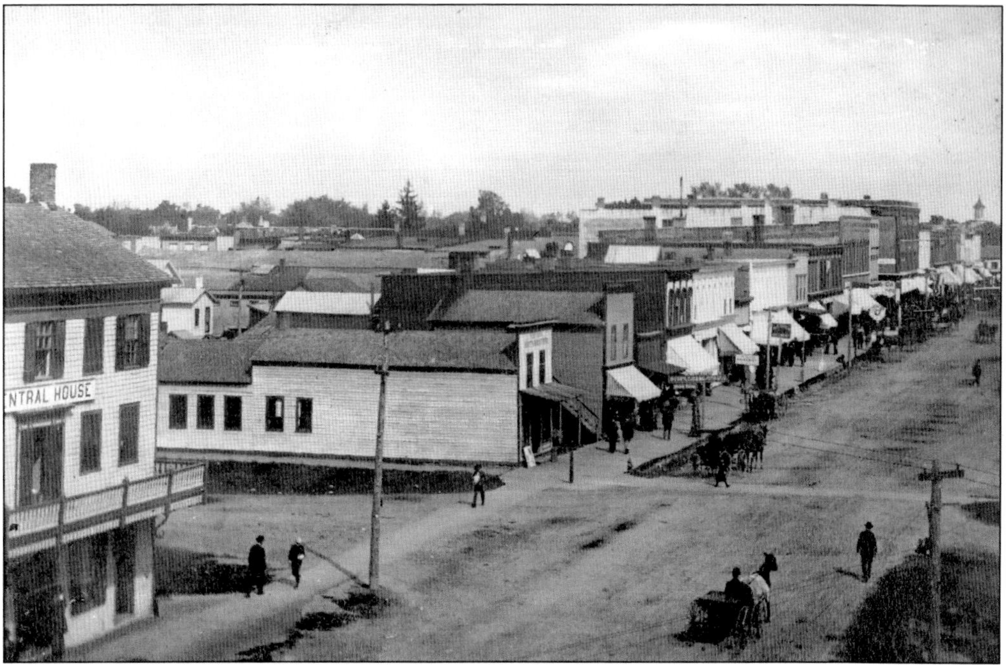

This photograph was taken from the L.J. Pray Building at the corner of Park Place and Front Street around 1892. The Central House, at left, was the first hotel in Dowagiac, built in 1848 as the Dowagiac House. Fire destroyed the Central House in 1895. The first commercial building, Ezekiel Smith's general store, is the small building across the street. The electrical poles were fairly new, having been installed in 1888–1889.

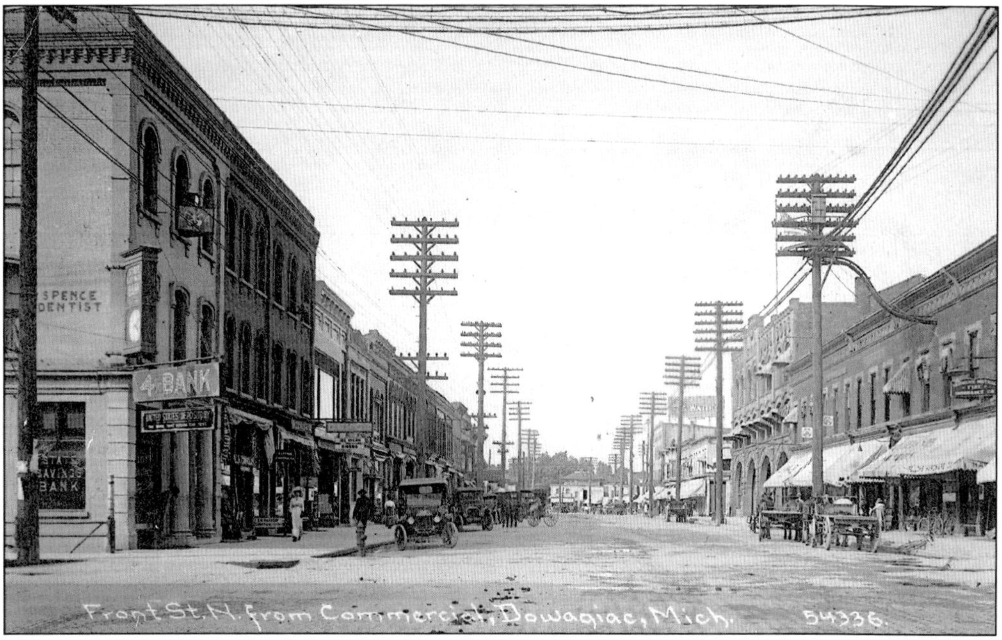

This view from Commercial Street looking north on Front Street shows a bustling Dowagiac in the early 1910s. According to *A Twentieth Century History of Cass County* (1906), the city paved Front Street with bricks in 1894. Horse-drawn carts had to deal with automobiles by this time.

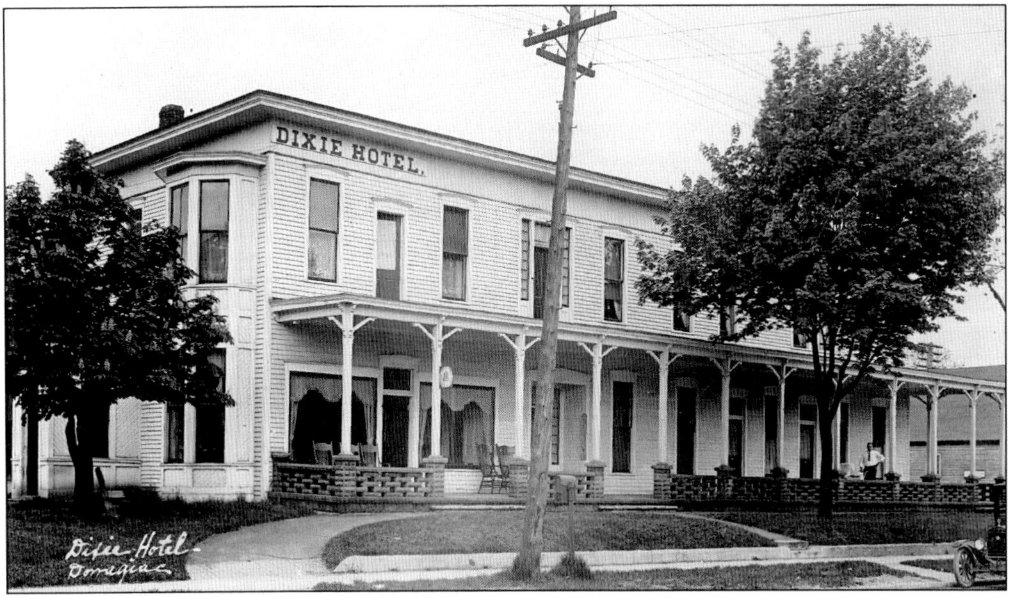

The Dixie Hotel, pictured here in 1931, was originally built as the Elkerton Hotel in 1885. Frank Elkerton, however, first had to overcome a fire that destroyed the original Elkerton Hotel one week before it was to open in October of 1885. Elkerton quickly built this structure on Park Place and it was open for business by Christmas of that year. It became the Dixie Hotel in 1923 and later was called Champ's and the Gaslight before being razed in the 1970s.

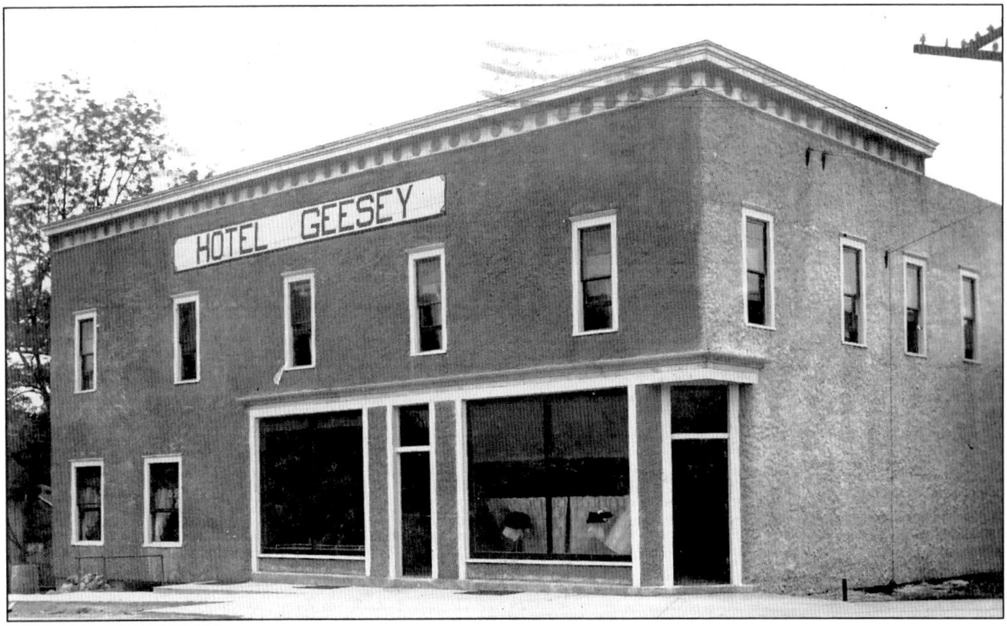

The Hotel Geesey is virtually unrecognizable from its original incarnation as the American House Hotel featured in Chapter 1. After changing hands many times, the hotel fell into disrepair until it was purchased by the Geesey family in 1909. They completely changed the building—the front porch was torn off, stucco replaced the wood siding, and the roofline was flattened. The Hotel Geesey became the Hotel Doe-Wah-Jack around 1912 and was torn down in 1920 to make way for a Standard Oil station after 70 years as a hotel site.

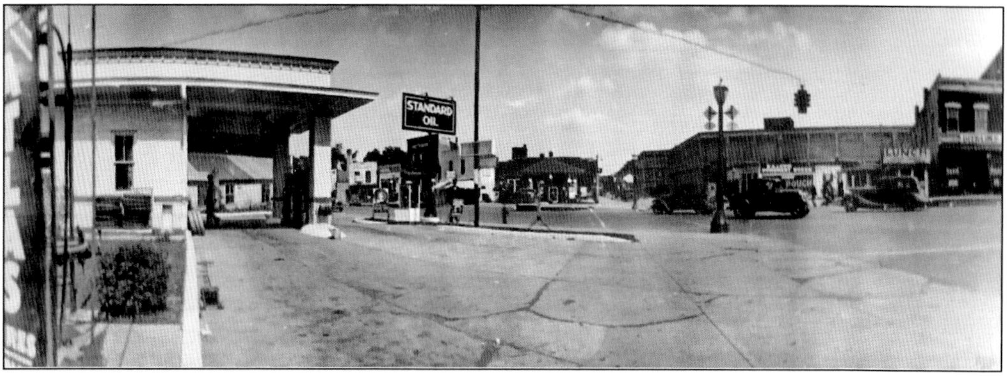

This Standard Oil station replaced the Hotel Geesey and a few shops along the west side of North Front and Division Streets in 1920. The Standard Oil Company operated the station, shown here c. 1930, until 1936 when March Durren purchased it. A gas station still occupies the site. This photo also provides a view of the east side of the street. A Shell station went in across the street in 1931—Steinman's Shell Station still occupies that site.

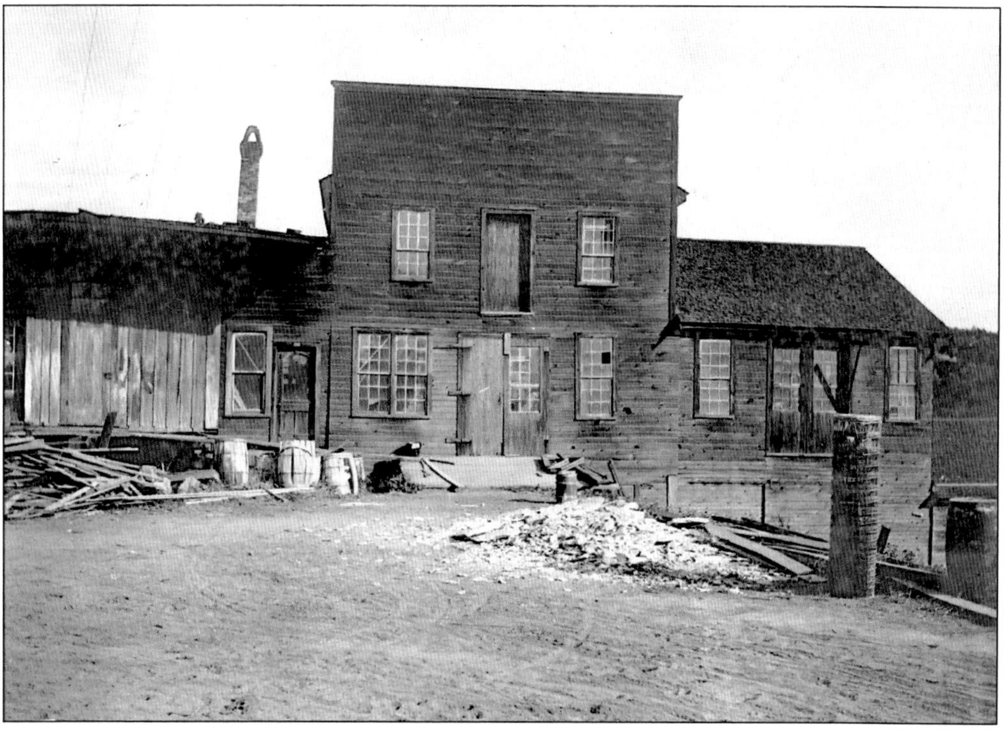

Judd Lumber Company is today the oldest continuously operated lumber business in Michigan and is still family-owned. Mark Judd built the original sawmill, shown here c. 1910, in 1859; he added a lumber yard in 1886. The two-story portion in the center was Dowagiac's original depot, which Judd moved to his mill for extra production space. These buildings were razed c. 1928 when Judds built a new mill.

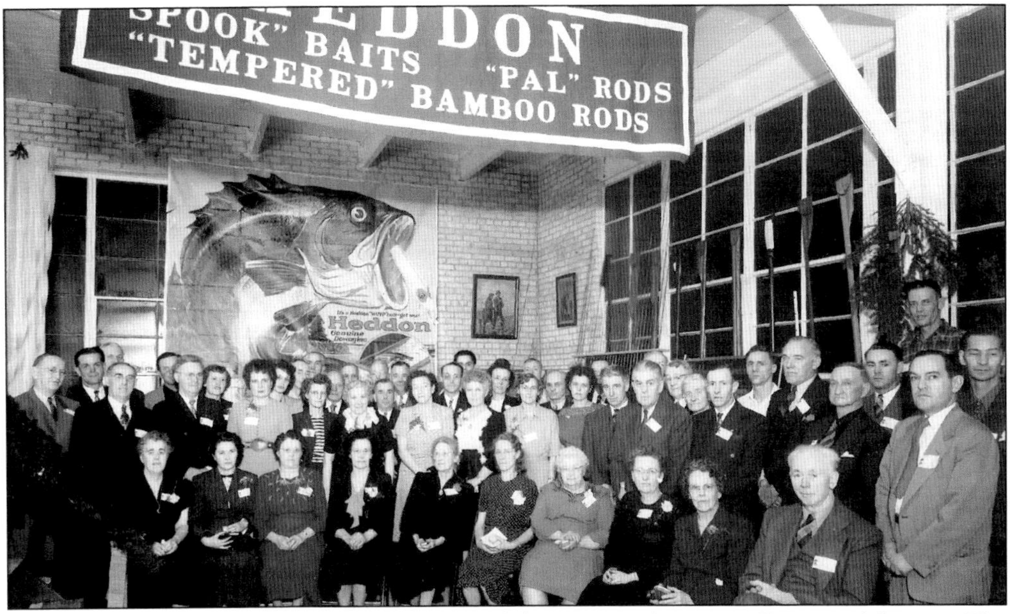

The James Heddon's Sons Company was one of the major industries in Dowagiac's history. The company, located on West Street, employed many Dowagiac residents over the years—primarily women whose nimble hands were often more suited for the necessary work. This photograph was taken in 1948 at a commemoration of the company's veteran employees who had 25 or more years of experience. John Heddon, the president at the time, is the third from the right in the first standing row.

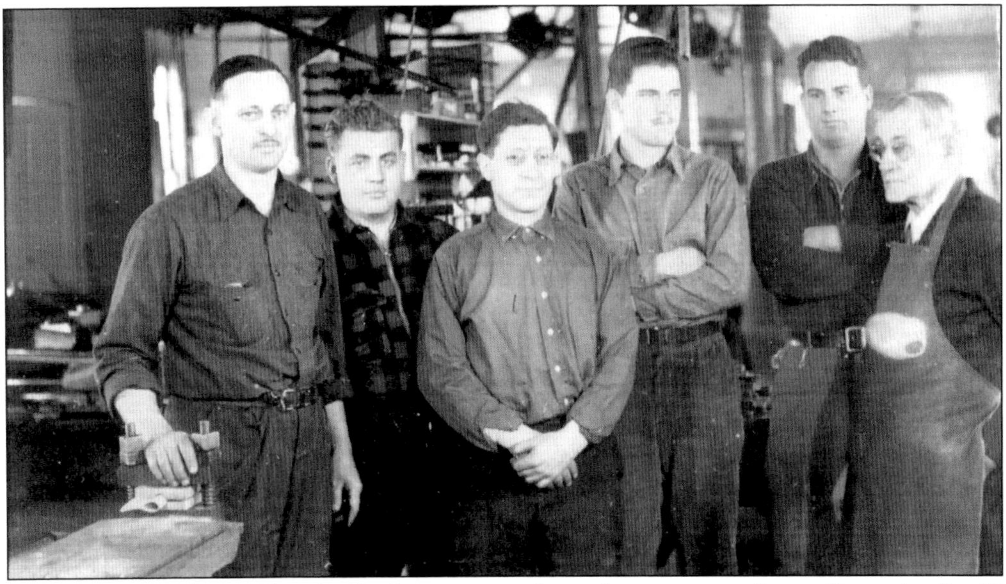

The workers at the Niedner Rifle Company made quality custom rifles in Dowagiac for 30 years. The workers are, from left to right: Vernor Gibson, Ray Langguth, Thomas Shelhamer, Lewis Dodd, C. Orville Behrmann, and Adolph O. Niedner. Niedner was already a well-known gunsmith by the time he was lured to Dowagiac in 1920. Shelhamer became one of the top gunstock makers in the world and he left Niedner to do his own work in the 1940s. The company went out of business shortly after World War II.

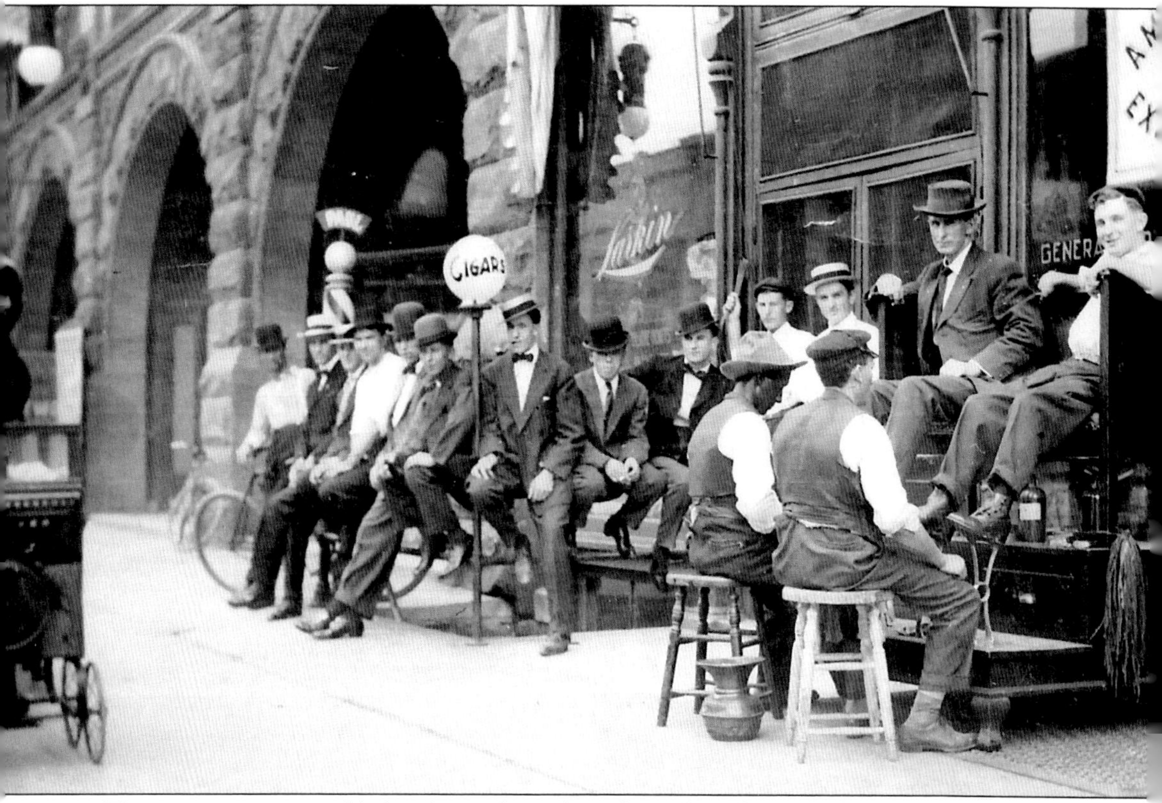

These men are presumably lined up to have their shoes shined outside the Larkin Store at 137 S. Front Street, c. 1910. This wonderful street scene reveals a lot about daily life in Dowagiac—the shoe shine stand and the barber shop below street level were obviously popular meeting places for the town's men, and the street vendor, at left, knew that well. The Larkin Store was a cigar and candy store that also housed Dowagiac's American Express service.

Workers pose outside the City Steam Laundry at 210 Commercial Street in the early 1900s. E.E. Alliger opened the laundry around 1903 and the building continued to serve as a laundry, alternating between the names Dowagiac Steam Laundry and City Steam Laundry, into the 1920s, when the business moved to a new location on Spruce Street.

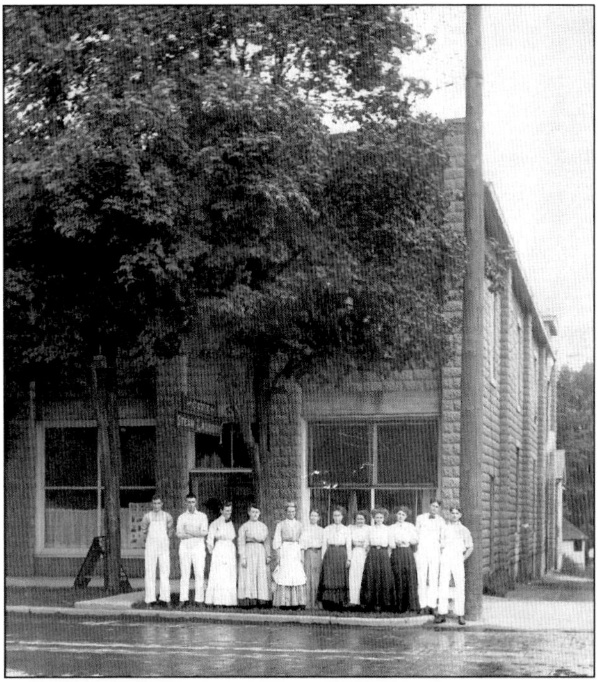

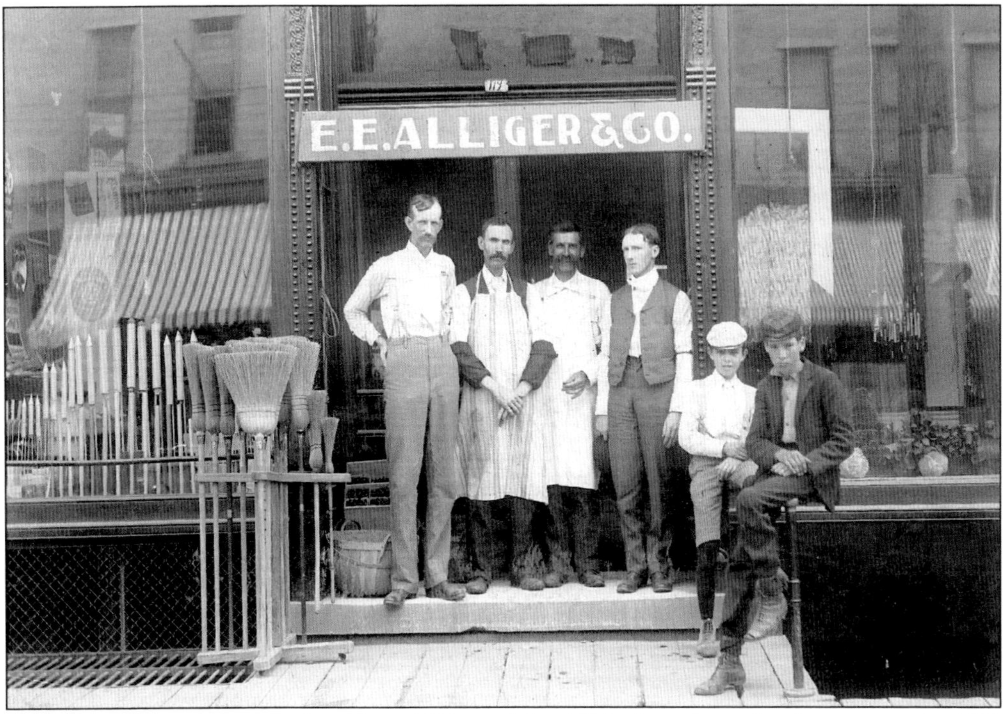

Edwin E. Alliger wore many hats from 1899 until the 1930s. Listed as a freight agent in the 1899 city directory, Alliger went on to start a dry goods store, open the City Steam Laundry, become manager of the *Daily Herald* newspaper, work as a bookkeeper at the Colby Mill, deal in real estate, and serve as justice of the peace. This photo of his dry goods store, at 117 South Front Street, is from the early 1900s.

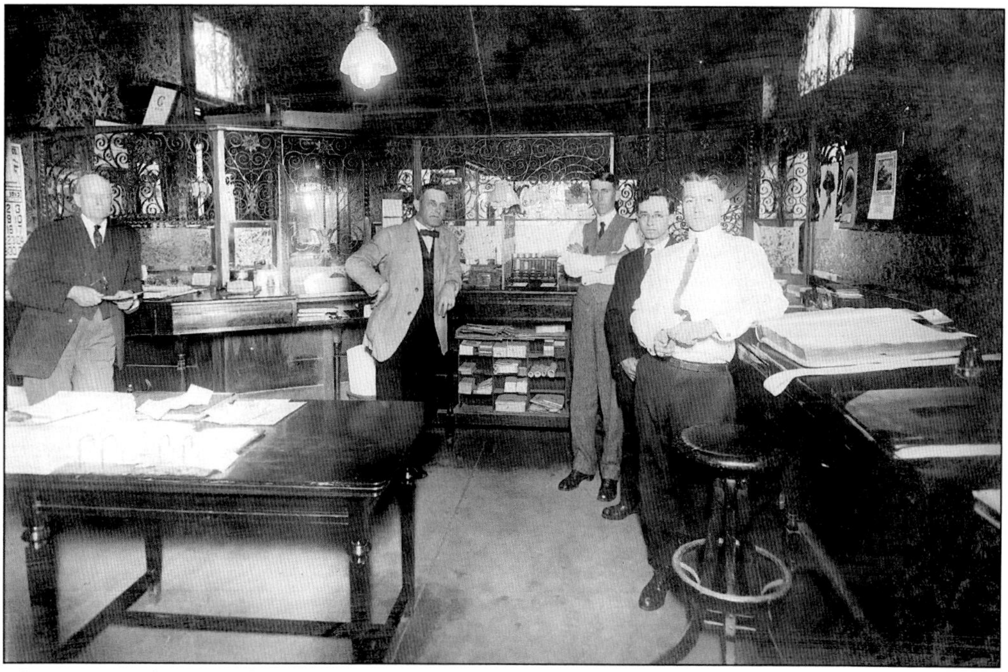

The Lee Brothers Bank was located in the Beckwith Memorial Building, where this 1913 photograph was taken, from 1893 to 1918. Chauncey Lee started the Lee family's Dowagiac banking business in 1875; his sons, Henry and Fred, followed him into the business and opened Lee Brothers Bank in 1887. It became Lee State Bank in 1917 and moved to the corner of Commercial and Front Street in 1918. Lee State Bank served Dowagiac until 1939.

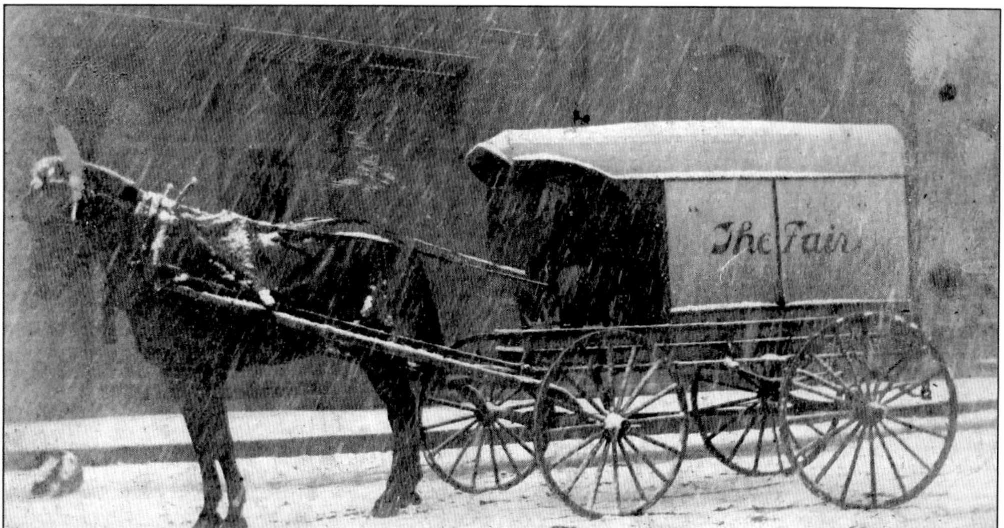

The Fair Store at 121–123 S. Front Street had two incarnations in its history. Founded in the early 1890s by Emanuel Tobias, the Fair Store was an early Dowagiac department store that enjoyed moderate success until closing in 1908. The building continued to serve as various department stores until the Shapero family once again named it the Fair Store in 1941. This photo from the 1890s shows its delivery wagon on Beeson Street on a snowy day.

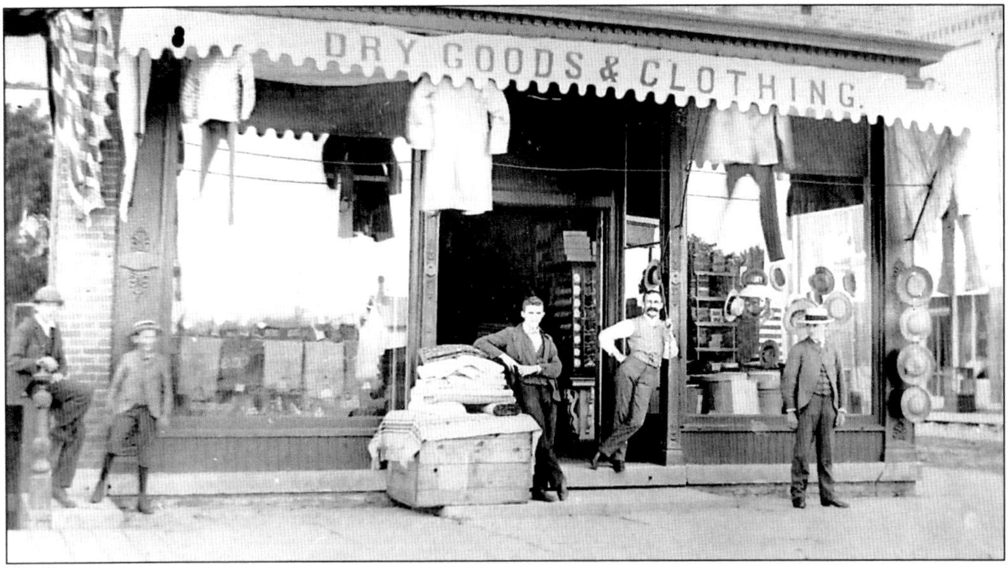

Mark Oppenheim, with mustache, stands in the doorway outside his dry goods store at the southwest corner of Commercial and Front Streets, *c.* 1900. A Russian immigrant who settled in Dowagiac in the 1860s, Oppenheim opened his store in 1871. The Oppenheim family operated the store, which eventually became a clothing store, for 123 years.

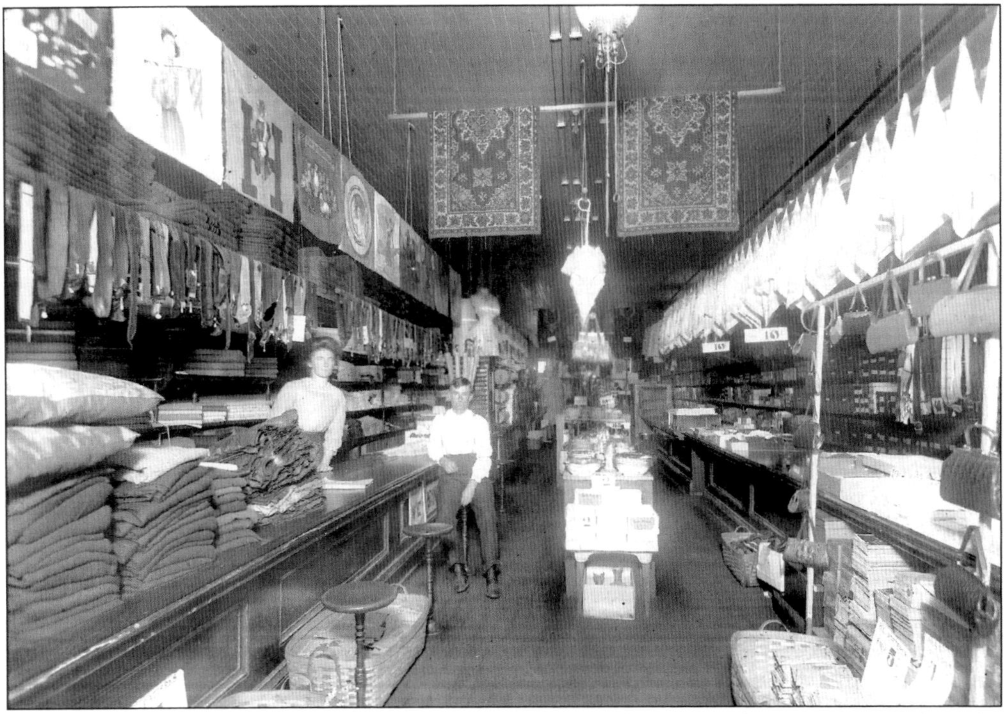

The Oppenheim Store, pictured here with Mayme Donahue and John Hartter minding the shop in 1907, became a clothing store some time after Mark Oppenheim sold his interest in the business to Israel and Ben Oppenheim in 1902. Israel's son, Maurice, took over the store in 1954 and ran it until closing in 1994.

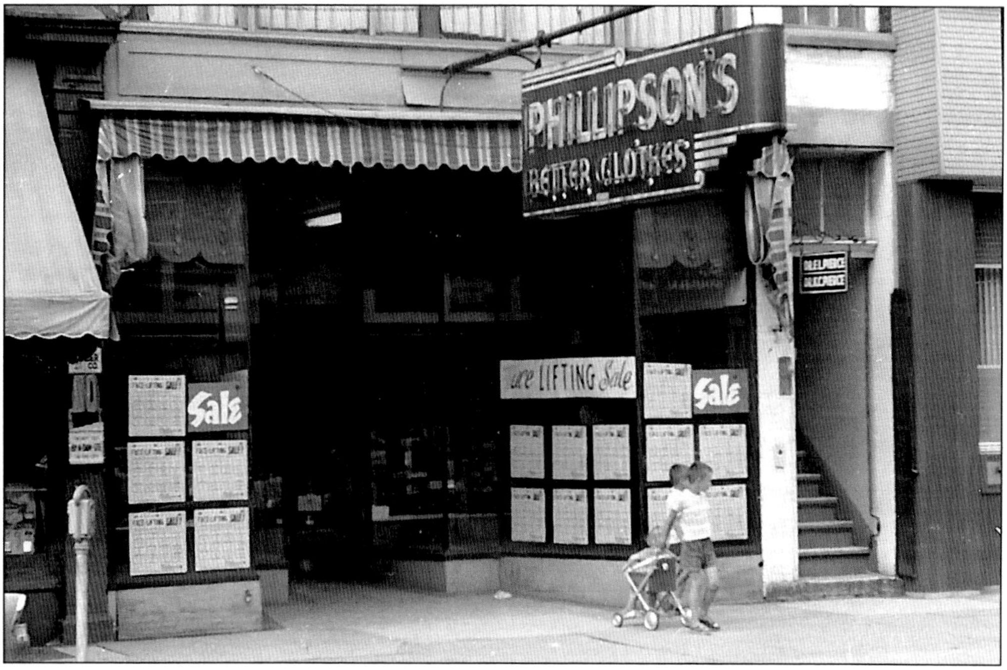

Jacob Hirsch opened a dry goods store in 1858 and in 1875 took on his brother-in-law, Emanuel Phillipson, as a partner. Hirsch & Phillipson became Phillipson's Clothing Store in 1905 when Emanuel's sons joined the business. The store stayed in the family until 1990 and featured fine men's clothing for most of the 20th century.

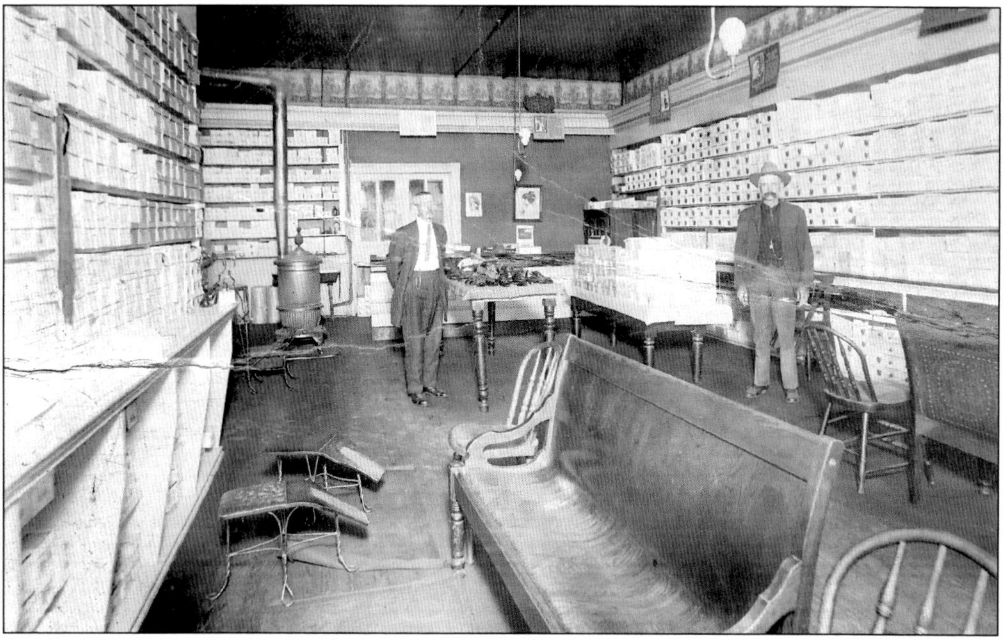

Jacob Gebhard, at left in the photo, was one of the German settlers who lived in the Dutch Settlement area. Gebhard opened Gebhard's Shoe Store at 220 S. Front Street in the early 1900s and ran it into the 1920s. Like any good Dowagiac shopkeeper, Gebhard heated his business with a Round Oak stove.

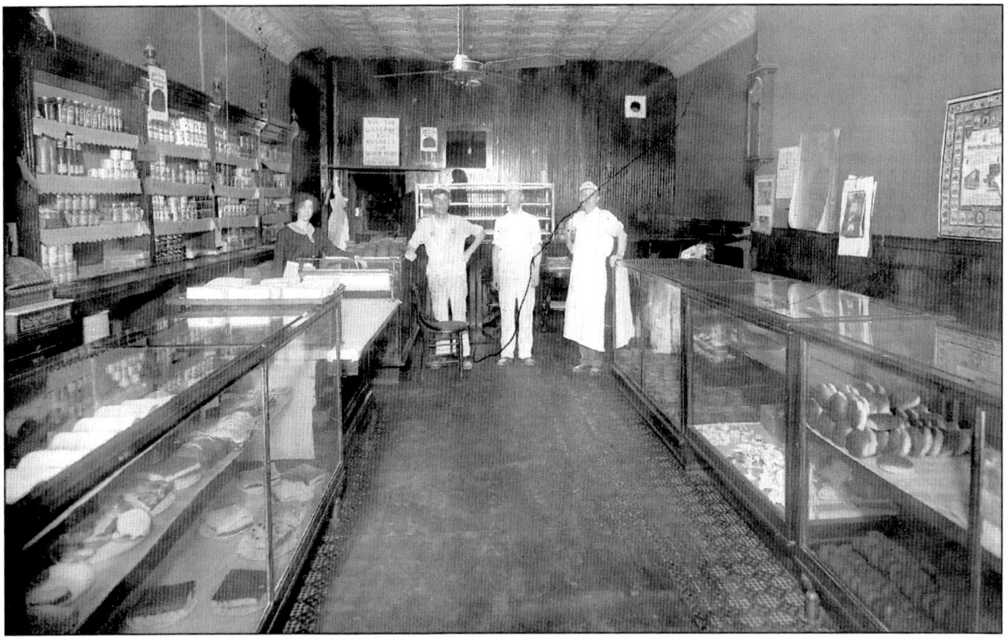

The building at 113 S. Front Street served as a bakery for the better part of 50 years in the first half of the 20th century. Called the City Bakery for much of its history, it was owned by several people, including Loren Eckert from 1910–1921, when this photograph was taken. The men in the picture are, from left to right, Arthur Skeeps, Harry Skeeps, and Loren Eckert. The woman at left is unidentified.

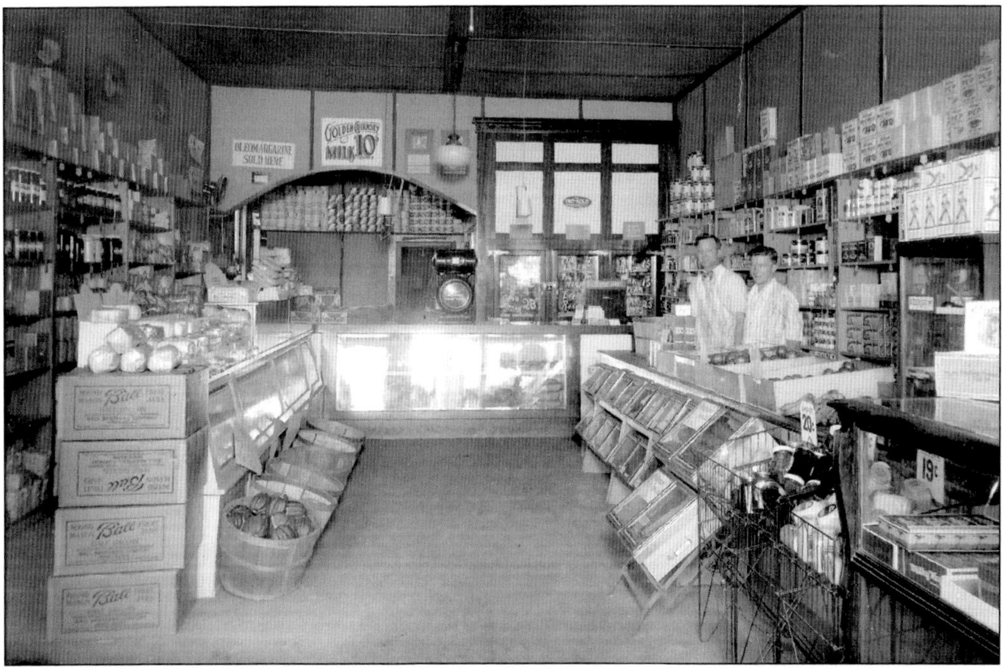

Before supermarkets changed the grocery industry, small grocery stores like this one could be found in most neighborhoods in cities like Dowagiac. This is the Sherb Dool Grocery Store on Main Street in the 1930s. Pictured are Otis Clark (left) and Raymond Powers (right).

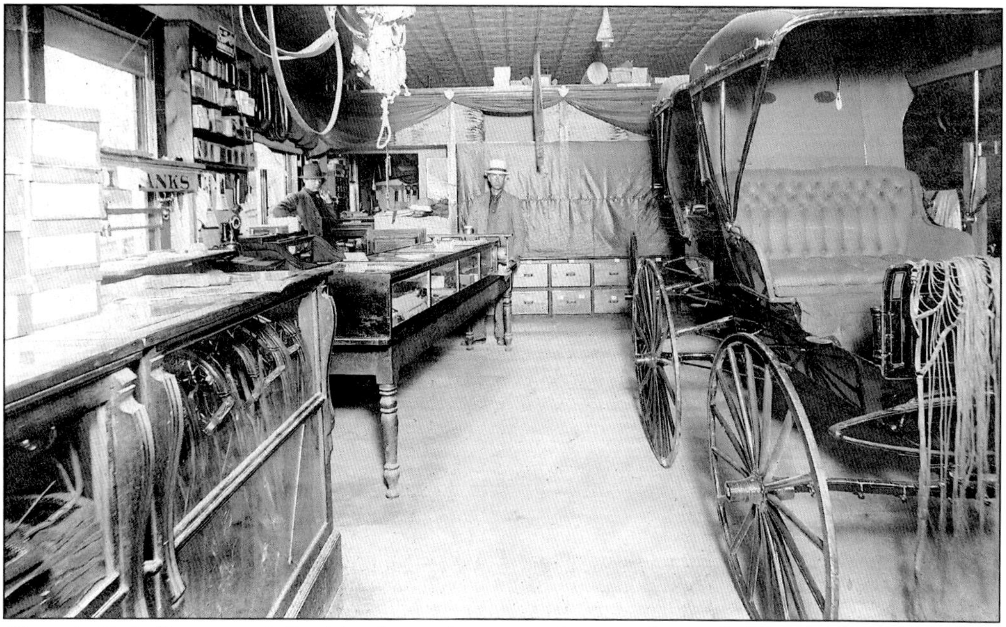

Claspy's Cash Store specialized in the wide range of materials needed for the care of buggies and horses. For most of its history, Claspy's Cash Store was located in the L.J. Pray Building but it had moved to 119 S. Front Street by 1908. Signs on the side of the building showed that it performed harness repair and sold "buggies, wagons, bobsleighs, cutters, harnesses, horse clothing, and farm gates."

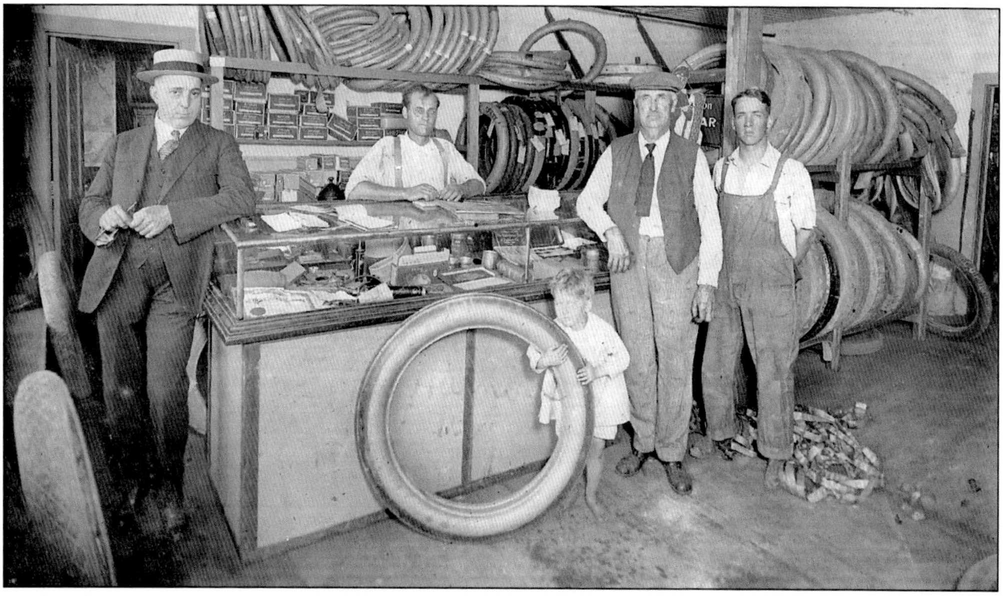

Technology was in the process of making Claspy's business obsolete, soon to be replaced by a business like Ferguson's Vulcanizing Works at 106 E. Division Street. Ferguson's was in the automobile tire business from 1914 into the 1960s. This photograph was taken shortly before World War I. Pictured are, from left to right: a Goodrich tire salesman, Harry Ferguson (owner), Harmon Ferguson (boy with tire), Mort Hadden, and Carl Dyer. Dyer enlisted in the service shortly after this photo was taken and died of illness during the war.

Five

FURNACE CITY

Possibly the biggest mistake Round Oak made in its history was letting Arthur Rudolphi leave the company in 1914. Rudolphi was a furnace salesman who worked his way up to manager of the furnace sales division. He left Round Oak, however, due to a dispute with President Fred E. Lee. While it hurt Round Oak, his departure would greatly influence Dowagiac and lead to its unofficial title as "The Furnace City."

Rudolphi had a sharp business sense and formed the Rudy Furnace Company (the future was furnaces, not stoves) in 1915. His partner in this venture was Harry Wood, also from Round Oak. Production began on October 11, 1915, and because of its experienced work crew and leadership (many came from Round Oak), Rudy succeeded immediately.

After Rudolphi's death in 1929, his wife, Phebe Rudolphi, took over as president of the company, with Charles Biek, Walter Frazee, and Sidney Tremble overseeing the day-to-day operation. Rudy's output of furnaces and water heaters maintained high levels through the Great Depression, but World War II changed the company's focus. Defense contracts forced the company to change its plant, and after the war, it never returned to full-time furnace manufacturing. It became the Rudy Manufacturing Company in 1948 and completely eliminated its line of furnaces in 1950.

That did not leave Dowagiac without a furnace company, however. Harry Wood left Rudy in 1920 to form a competing firm, the Premier Furnace Company; Ralph McNaney left Premier in 1929 to form the Dowagiac Steel Furnace Company. This meant that Dowagiac had four major furnace manufacturers in the city from 1929 through World War II.

Premier enlisted the financial help of William and Richard Judd, members of the Judd Lumber Company family, to get off the ground. Due to failing health, Wood stepped aside almost immediately after starting the company, but nonetheless Premier quickly made a name for itself in the furnace industry. Financial troubles in the 1920s gave way to unexpected success during the Great Depression. This strengthened Premier, with members of the Judd family serving as president of the company throughout its 40-year history. Faced with either expansion or a merger in 1960, the Premier Furnace Company decided to merge with Consolidated Industries and left Dowagiac in 1962.

Ralph McNaney had a vision of furnaces different than the cast-iron models that were being manufactured in the 1920s. He wanted to make sheet-steel-bodied furnaces that would be more compact and lighter weight. McNaney tried to persuade Premier to work on his ideas, but when he was rebuffed, he left and formed the Dowagiac Steel Furnace Company with Allie Greer and Bob Phillips.

The problem was that technology had not yet caught up with McNaney's ideas. Early Dowagiac Steel Furnace Company furnaces look remarkably similar to the other Dowagiac models. Many parts were still cast-iron, especially the workings, but McNaney was making modifications.

While the Dowagiac Steel Furnace Company enjoyed modest success, it did not succeed on the levels of the other companies and its history is fairly short. In the 1950s, it contracted with a Kalamazoo company to manufacture industrial laundry equipment in addition to furnaces.

That move spread the company's resources in too many directions and it started losing money. In 1962, the Dowagiac Steel Furnace Company was sold to the Hall–Neal Company of Indianapolis, ending Dowagiac's 90-year history in the heating industry.

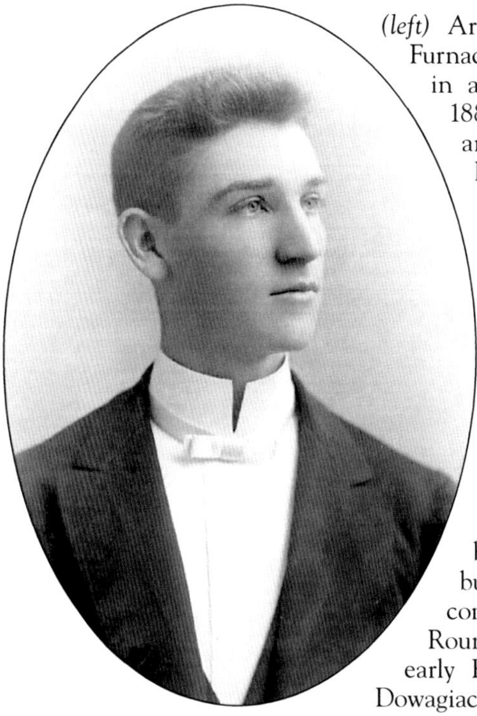

(left) Arthur Rudolphi (1869–1929) founded the Rudy Furnace Company in 1915 after leaving Round Oak in a dispute with Fred Lee the previous year. In 1886–1887, Rudolphi studied music in Chicago and this photograph was taken at that time. After he completed his studies, Rudolphi returned to Dowagiac and taught music and played locally; he also took a job as a salesman for Round Oak. Rudolphi was manager of furnace sales at the time he left Round Oak in 1914.

(below) This photograph shows the construction of the original Rudy Furnace Company foundry in 1915. It was located on Prairie Ronde Street along the railroad tracks just north of Round Oak's plant. The new furnace company proved to be competition for Round Oak not only in sales, but also in the labor force. Rudy (and later furnace companies) drew experienced workers away from Round Oak, which enabled immediate success—an early Rudy logo featured the expression, "Made in Dowagiac by Those Who Know How."

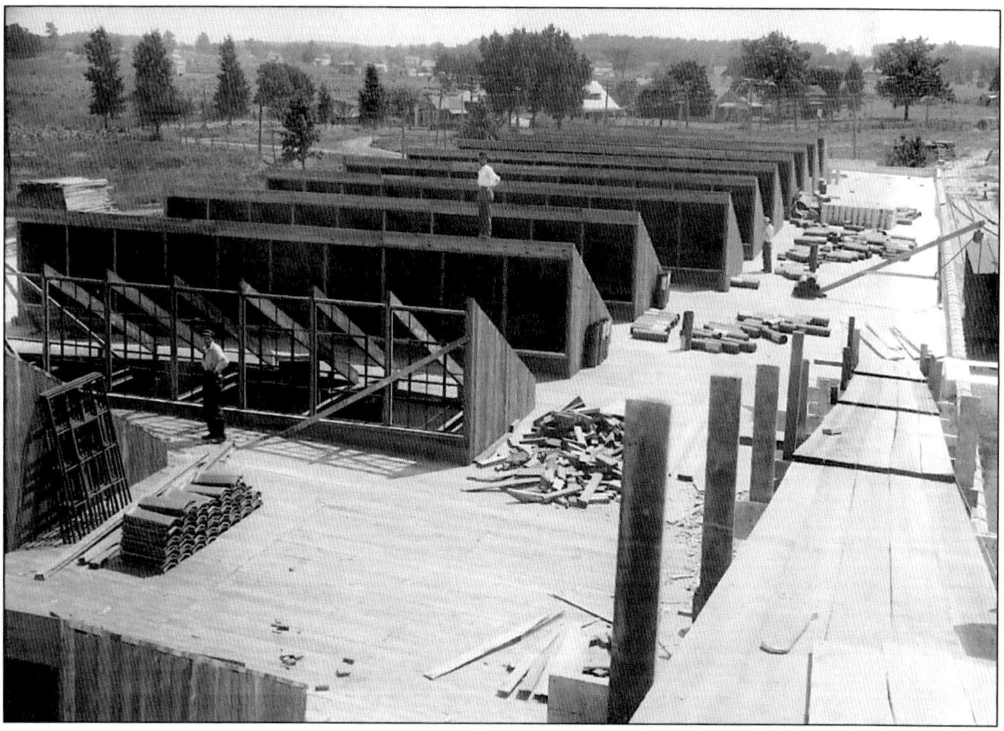

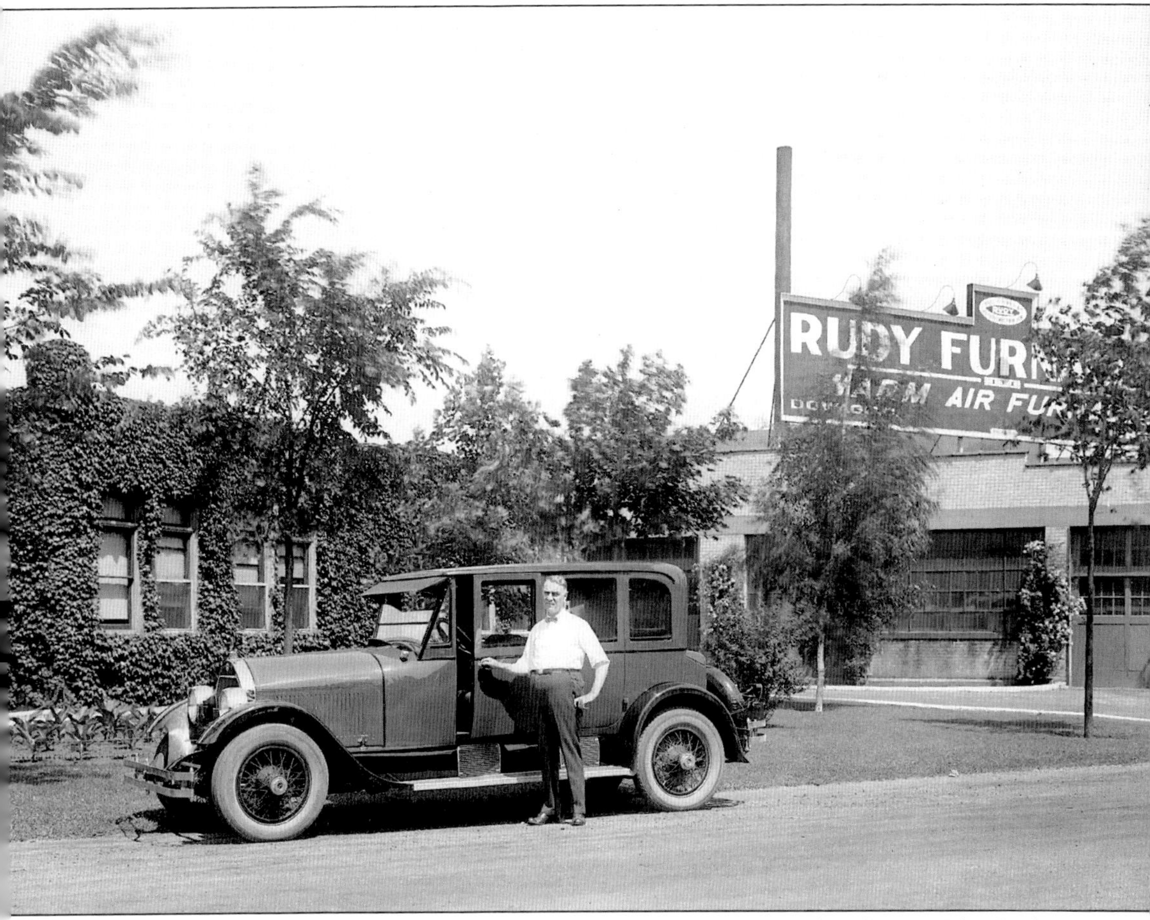

Arthur Rudolphi stands outside his successful furnace company in July of 1924. The Rudy Furnace Company succeeded almost immediately, due to a good product and Rudolphi's connections in the industry. Rudolphi died in 1929, but the company continued to make cast-iron furnaces and water heaters until World War II, when it shifted to war production.

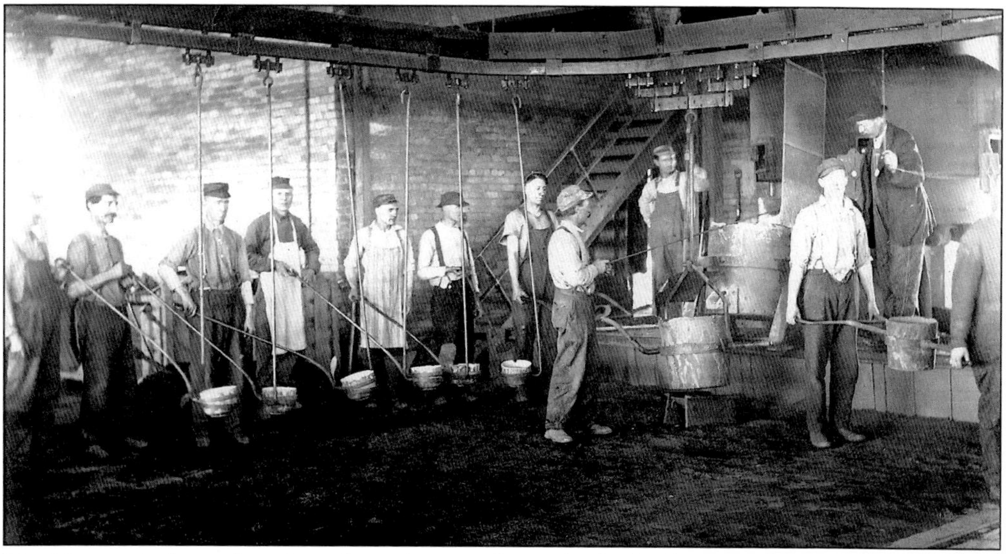

Moulders wait for molten iron from the cupola at the Rudy Furnace Company in the early 1920s. This photograph and the next two were used in a Rudy advertising booklet, *Visiting with Rudy*, which took the reader through the factory and the moulding process. The title of this photo in the booklet is, "Where Iron Runs Like Water." The iron in the cupola was heated to 2,500 degrees Fahrenheit, and the large ladle under the cupola, called a "bull-ladle," held 500 to 2,000 pounds of iron.

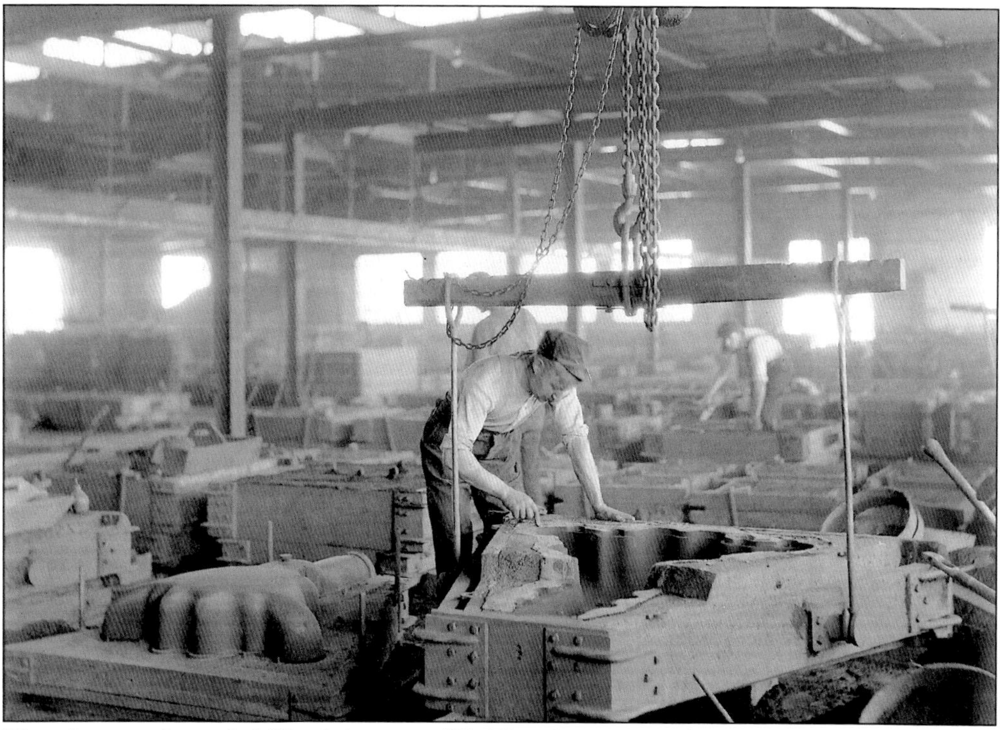

This photograph is titled "Sand Artists at Work" and appears in the *Visiting with Rudy* booklet. The moulder has removed the wood pattern (on the ground at left) from the moist sand and is inspecting the imprint to ensure there are no errors before pouring iron into the sand mould.

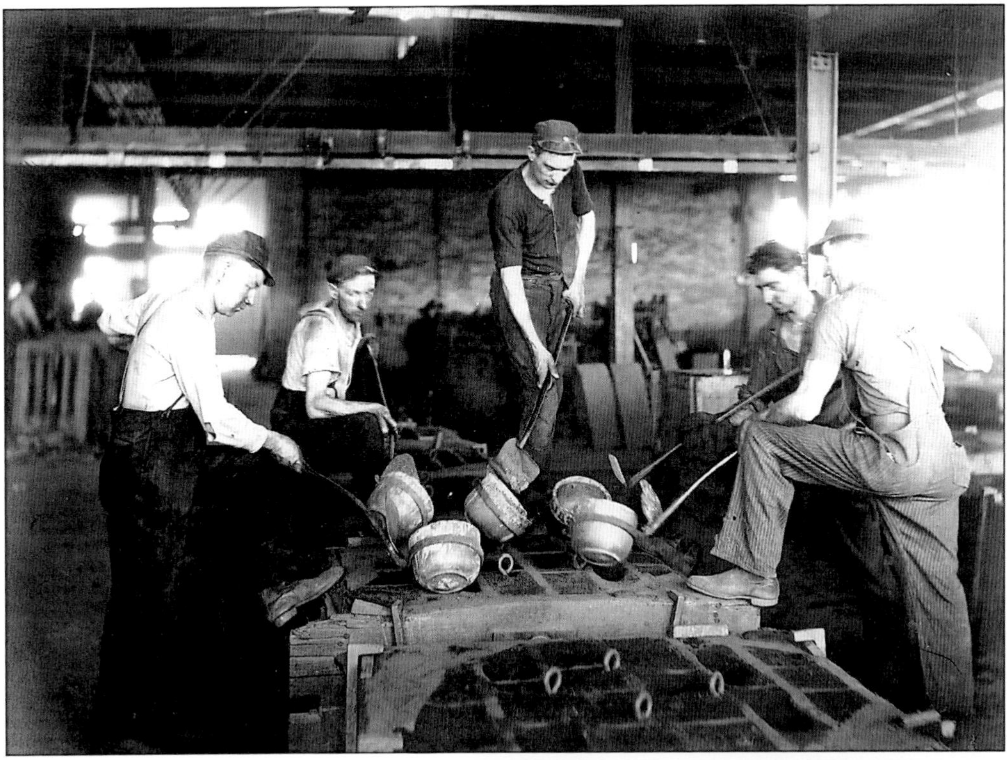

(above) This photograph is titled "Five Minds With But a Single Thought." The caption for this photo reads, "It must be remembered that the iron 'sets' in from three to five minutes after it is poured, and the casting is ready for removal from the mould." For this reason, several moulders would pour one large casting simultaneously—this allowed the iron to cool evenly to prevent cracks. Each hand ladle held 50 to 60 pounds of metal and could be filled directly from the cupola or from a bull-ladle closer to the mould.

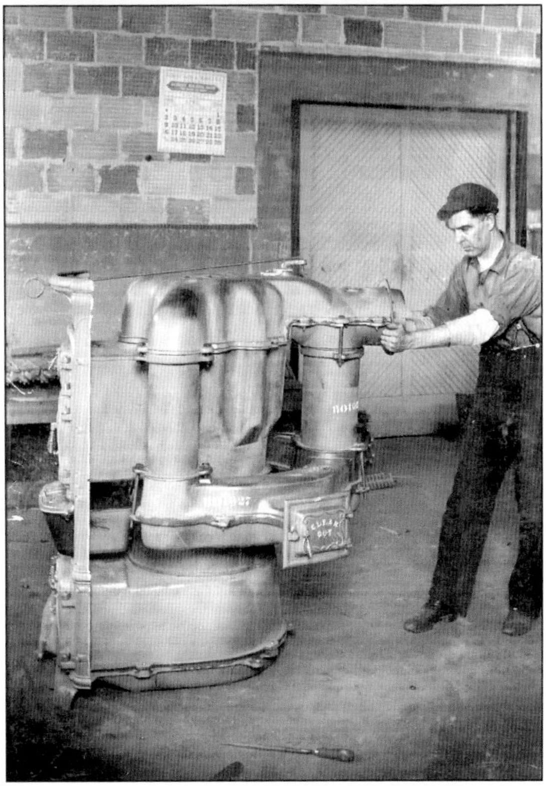

(right) An unidentified worker assembles a finished furnace at the Rudy Furnace Company in 1916. Workers fully assembled furnaces in the set-up room to ensure proper castings. They then disassembled the furnaces for shipment. Rudy was a worldwide company by the 1920s, with orders from as far away as South Africa.

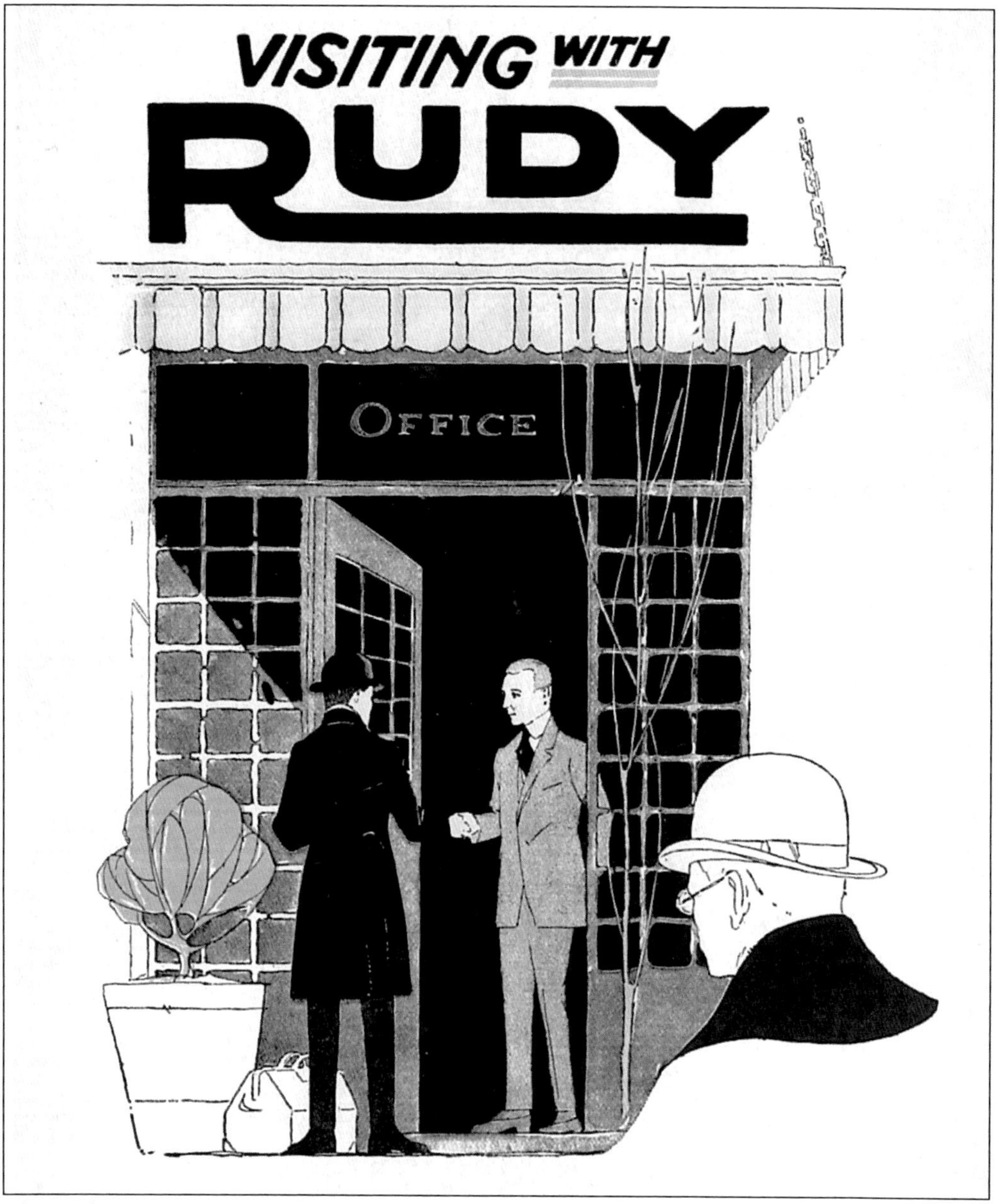

This is the cover of the *Visiting with Rudy* booklet, c. 1920s.

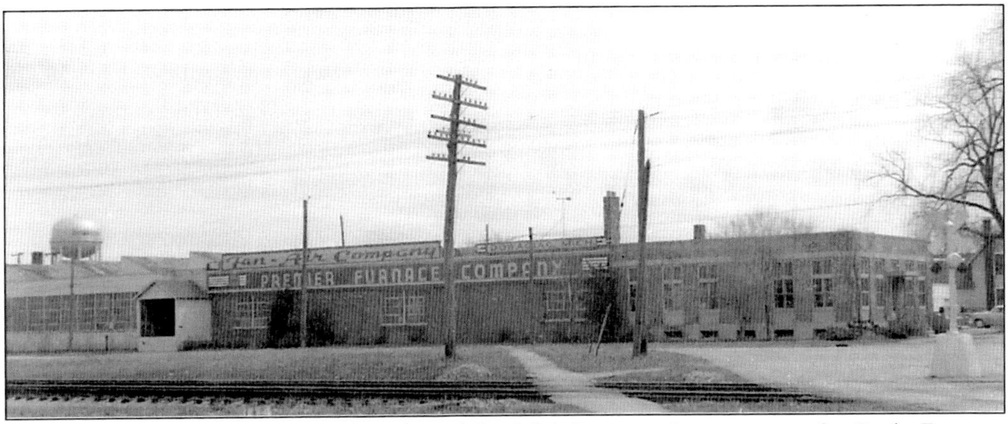

Harry Wood, formerly of Round Oak and Rudolphi's original partner in the Rudy Furnace Company, looked for investors for a new furnace company after World War I. Once he secured the funding in 1920, with the Judd family playing a key financial role, the Premier Furnace Company became Dowagiac's third furnace company. Premier was located along the railroad tracks between Round Oak and Rudy. Premier started slowly but remained in the furnace industry for 40 years.

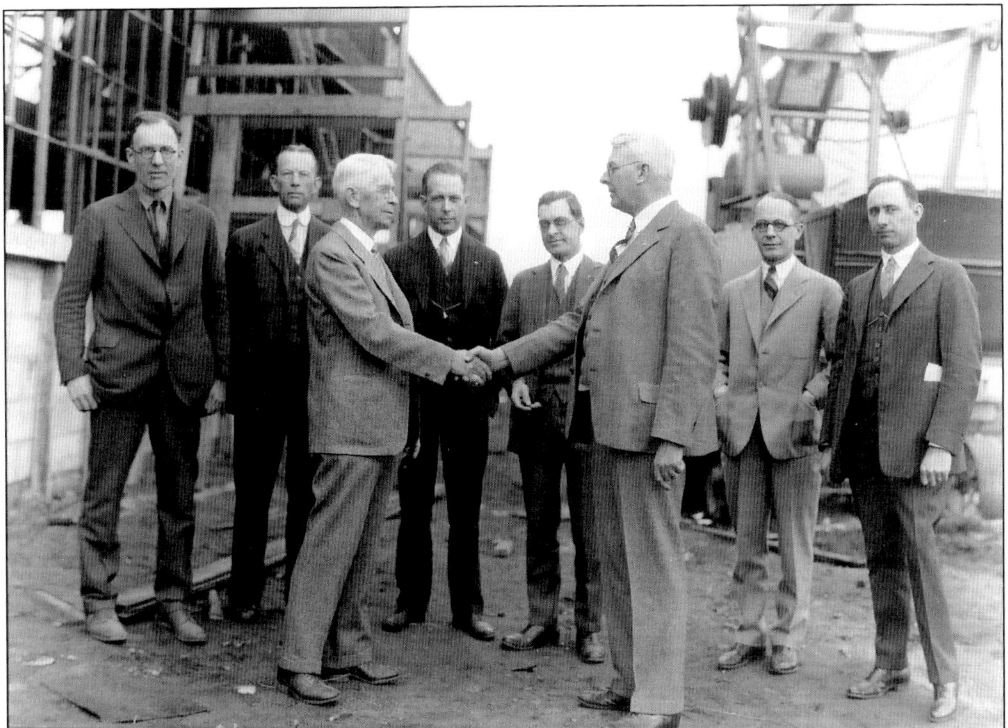
The Premier Furnace Company completed its new addition on May 2, 1927. In the foreground shaking hands are William Judd (left) and Dowagiac Mayor E.P. Platt. In the background are, from left to right: Clint Voorhees, Dr. William Cory, E.L. Taylor, Richard M. Judd, E.B. Loring, and W.E. Legalt. William Judd was president of the company at this time, but he died the following year. His death resulted in Richard Judd becoming the majority stockholder and company president.

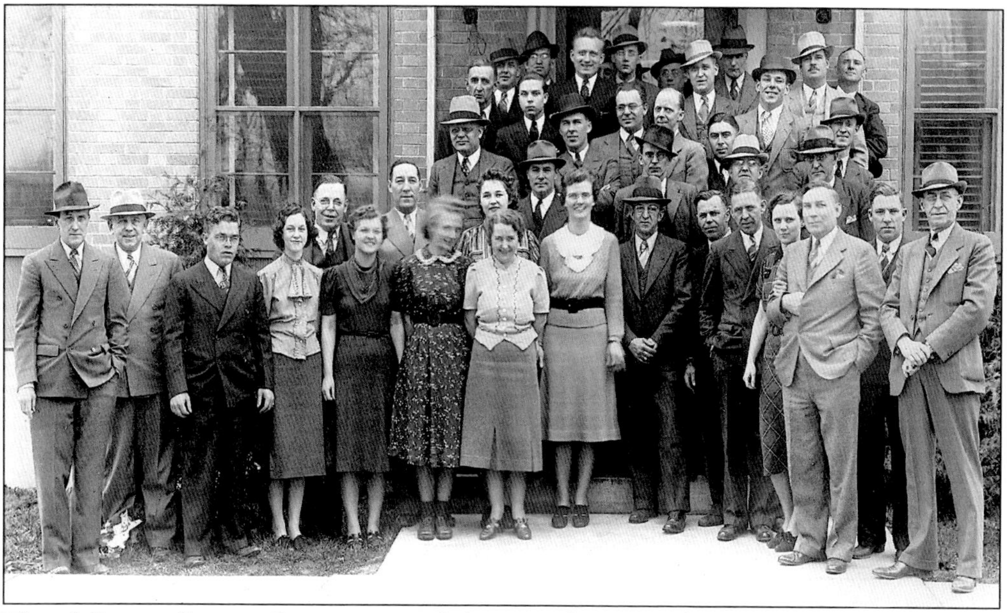

Though Premier Furnace Company struggled in its earliest years, by the late 1920s it had started to thrive. According to Richard Judd, the business really accelerated in 1932, while the nation was in the middle of the Great Depression. This photo of the Premier Furnace Company office staff was taken in the late 1920s to early 1930s.

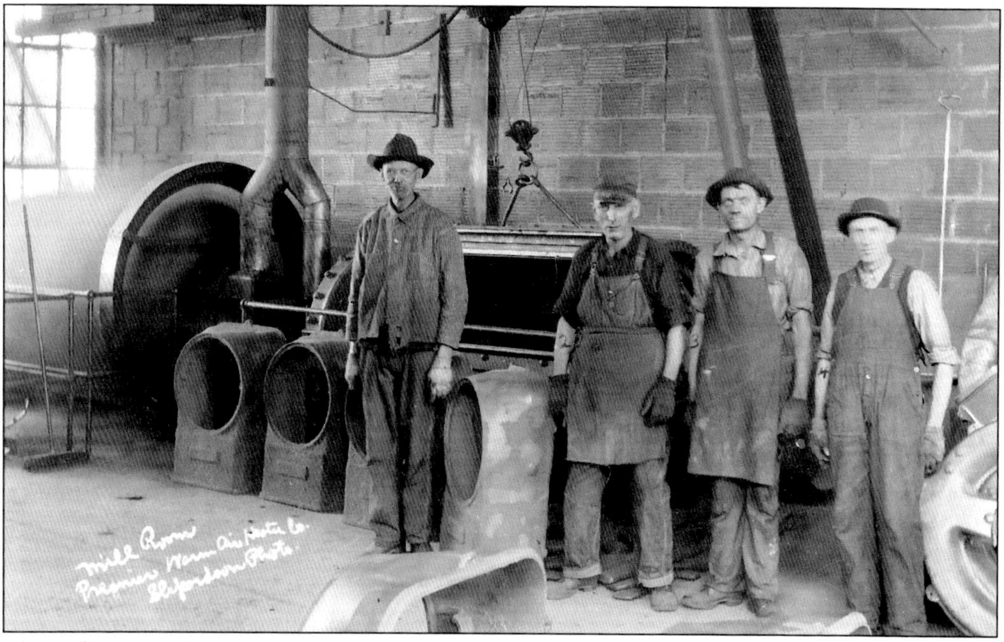

The mill room (also called the rattler), was the noisiest room in the foundry. All castings had to go through the rattler, the large machine behind the men posed here. They are, from left to right: Seymour Price, Clyde Peck, Bert Rowe, and Fred Rowe. Workers set the castings inside the rattler along with small pellets of iron. The rattler then spun around creating friction between the castings and the small pieces of iron. This process took off excess sand and smoothed out the parts—and made a lot of noise!

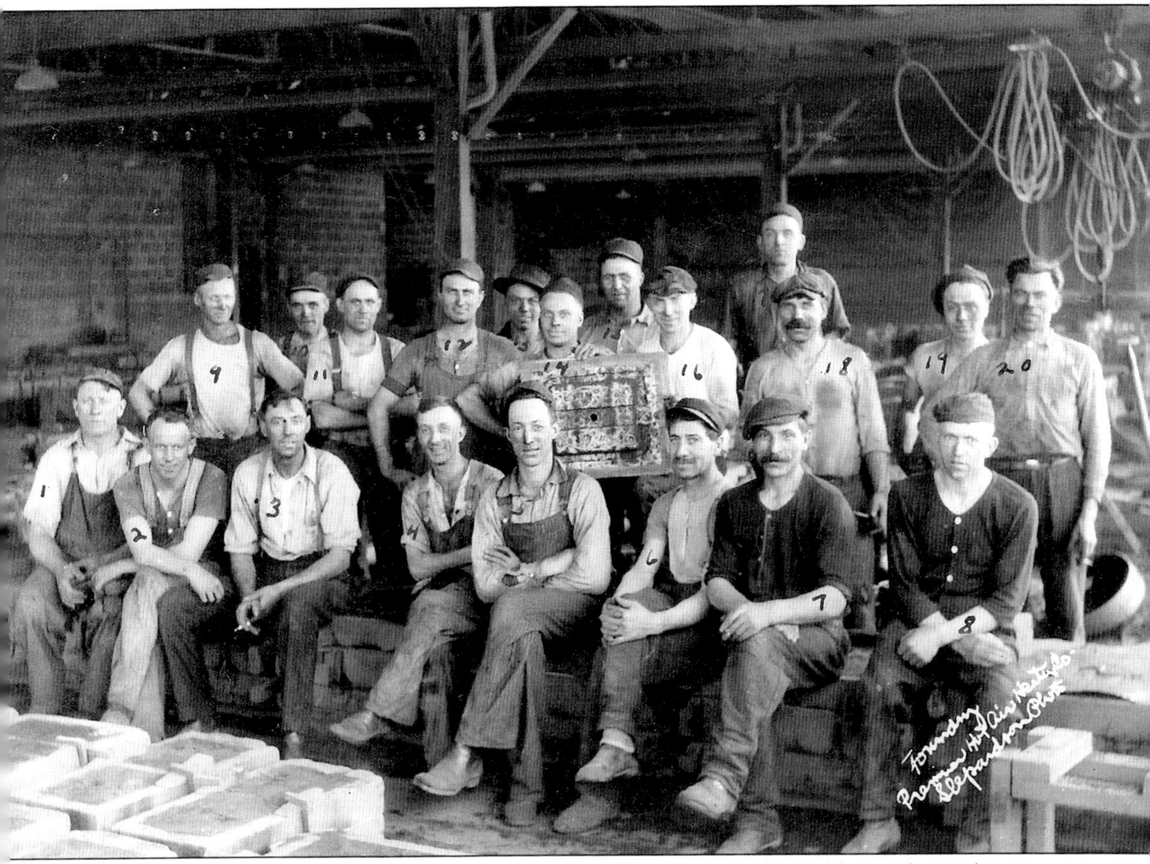

Like Rudy, Premier boasted of its practice of employing experienced moulders—shown here in the 1920s. Pictured from left to right are the following: (front row) Charles Grayson, Horace Laverick, Jay Patterson, Glenn Morford, Herman Bower, Jess Dokey, Mike Frontczak, and Joe Walczak; and (back row) Clyde Smith, Jim Delaney, Fred Dunkleberger, Clyde Huff, Lee Cox, Eugene Clinton, Fred Hodge, Walter Ingram, John Fernham, Walter Frontczak, Leonard Cox, and George Pietron.

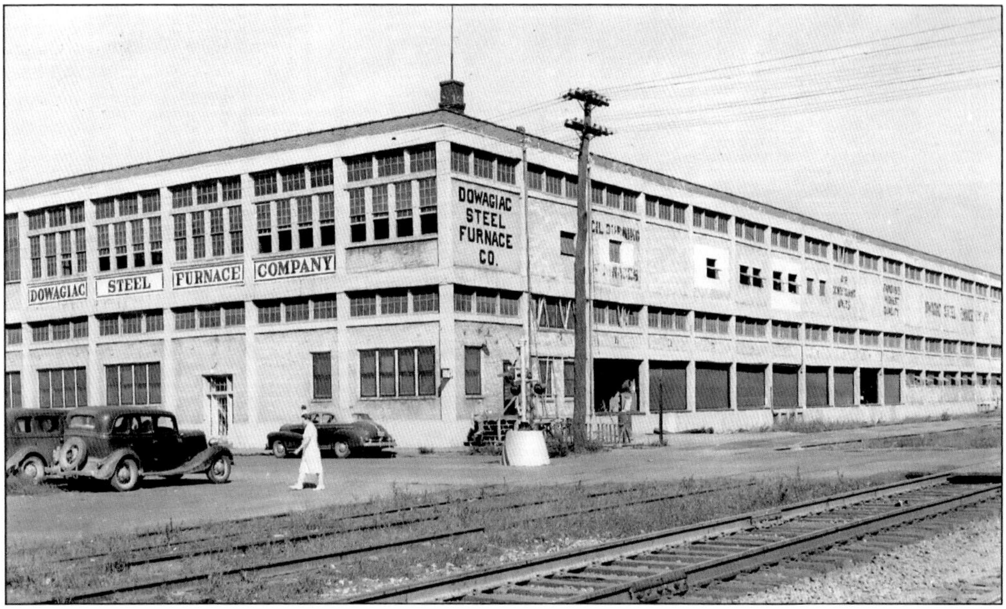

The Dowagiac Steel Furnace Company was the last of the Dowagiac furnace companies. Ralph McNaney, formerly of Premier, had an idea for steel-bodied furnaces and founded the company in 1929. His ideas were a bit ahead of their time and would not materialize until after World War II. Dowagiac Steel Furnace bought buildings from Round Oak, like the one in this 1930s photograph.

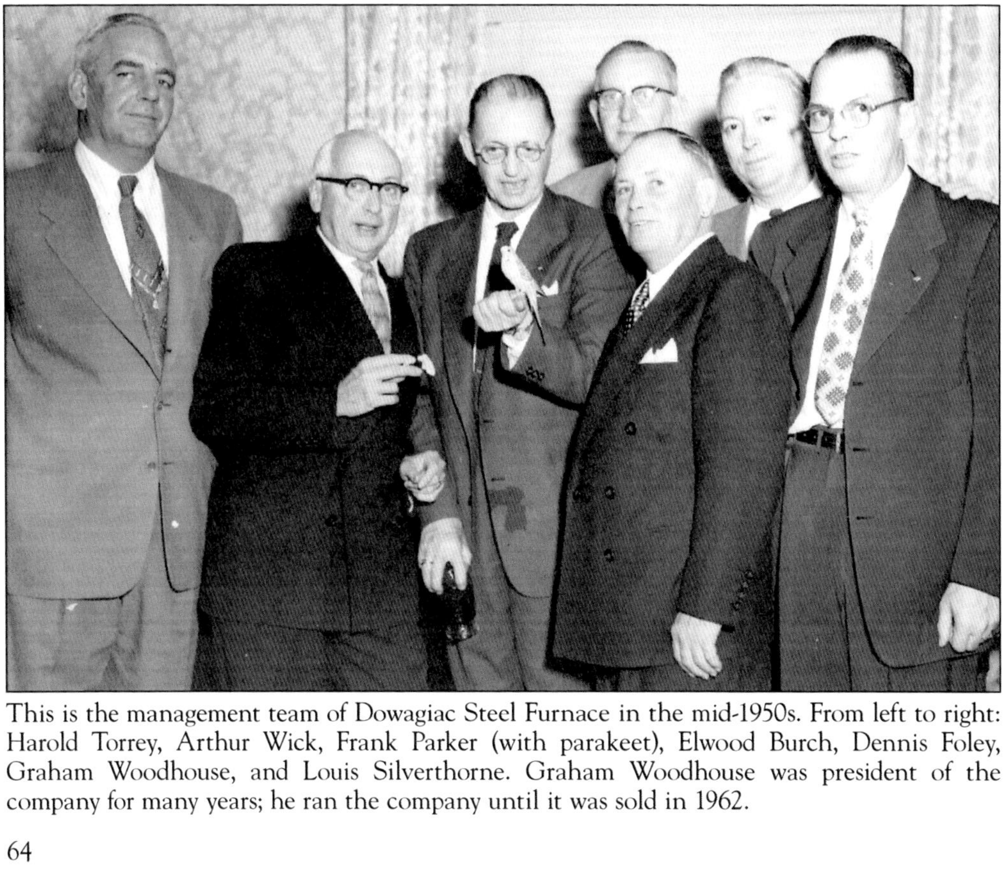

This is the management team of Dowagiac Steel Furnace in the mid-1950s. From left to right: Harold Torrey, Arthur Wick, Frank Parker (with parakeet), Elwood Burch, Dennis Foley, Graham Woodhouse, and Louis Silverthorne. Graham Woodhouse was president of the company for many years; he ran the company until it was sold in 1962.

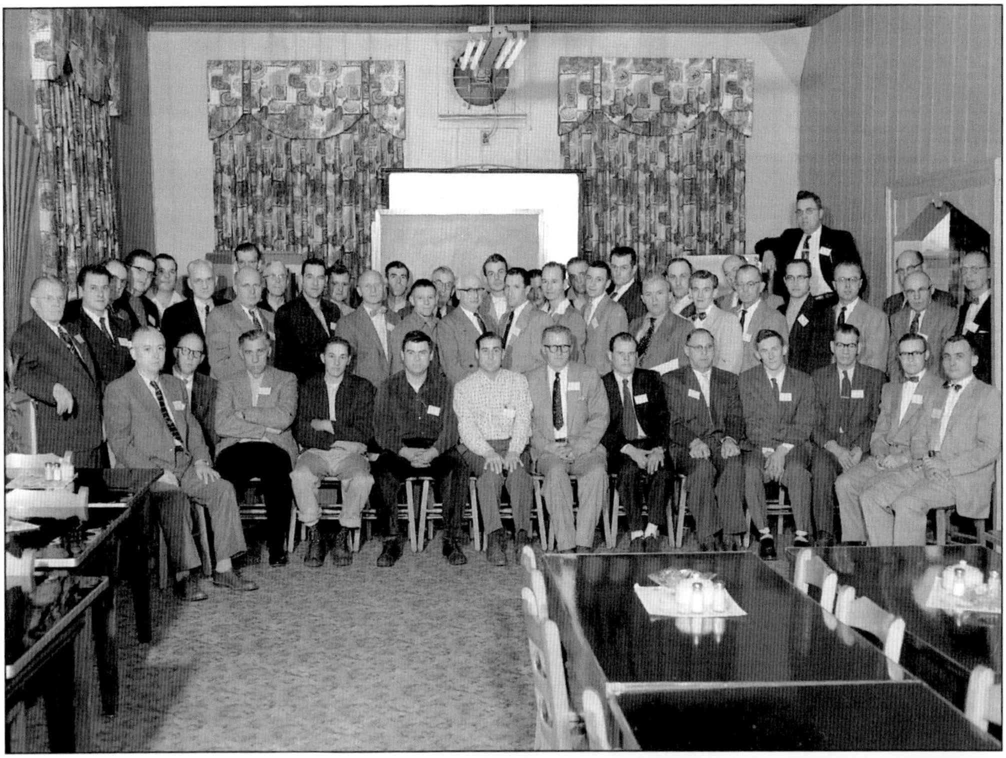

(above) This photograph shows a Dowagiac Steel Furnace Company sales team meeting in Champ's Hotel in Dowagiac, *c.* mid-1950s. The company held training sessions throughout the sales region—salesmen had to be acquainted with their product. Many times the firm took the school on the road and taught the salesmen on their own turf. Graham Woodhouse, company president, is seated at far left.

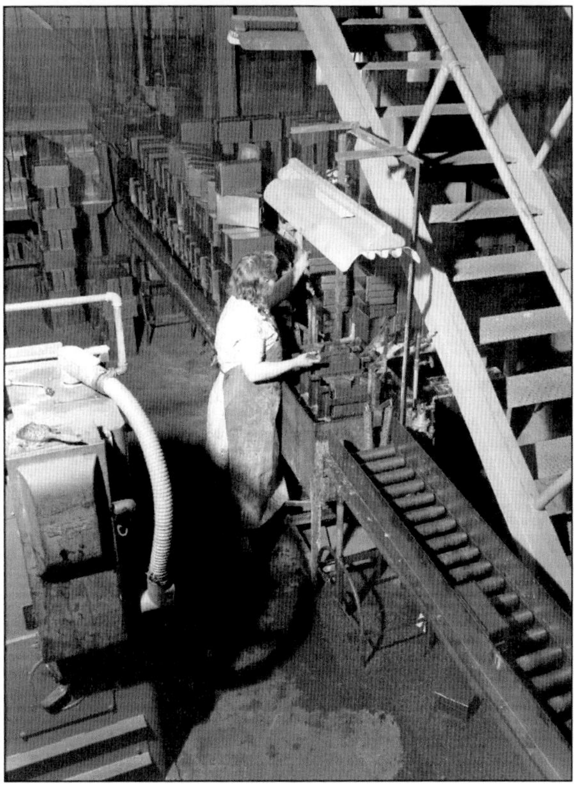

(right) Rudy never went back to making furnaces full-time after World War II. In 1948, the company became the Rudy Manufacturing Company and by 1950 it had ceased furnace production altogether. Instead, Rudy built air conditioning equipment, heaters, and water heaters, and also continued to work on defense contracts, including parts for bombs. This photograph shows the production of M-19 ammunition boxes in 1948.

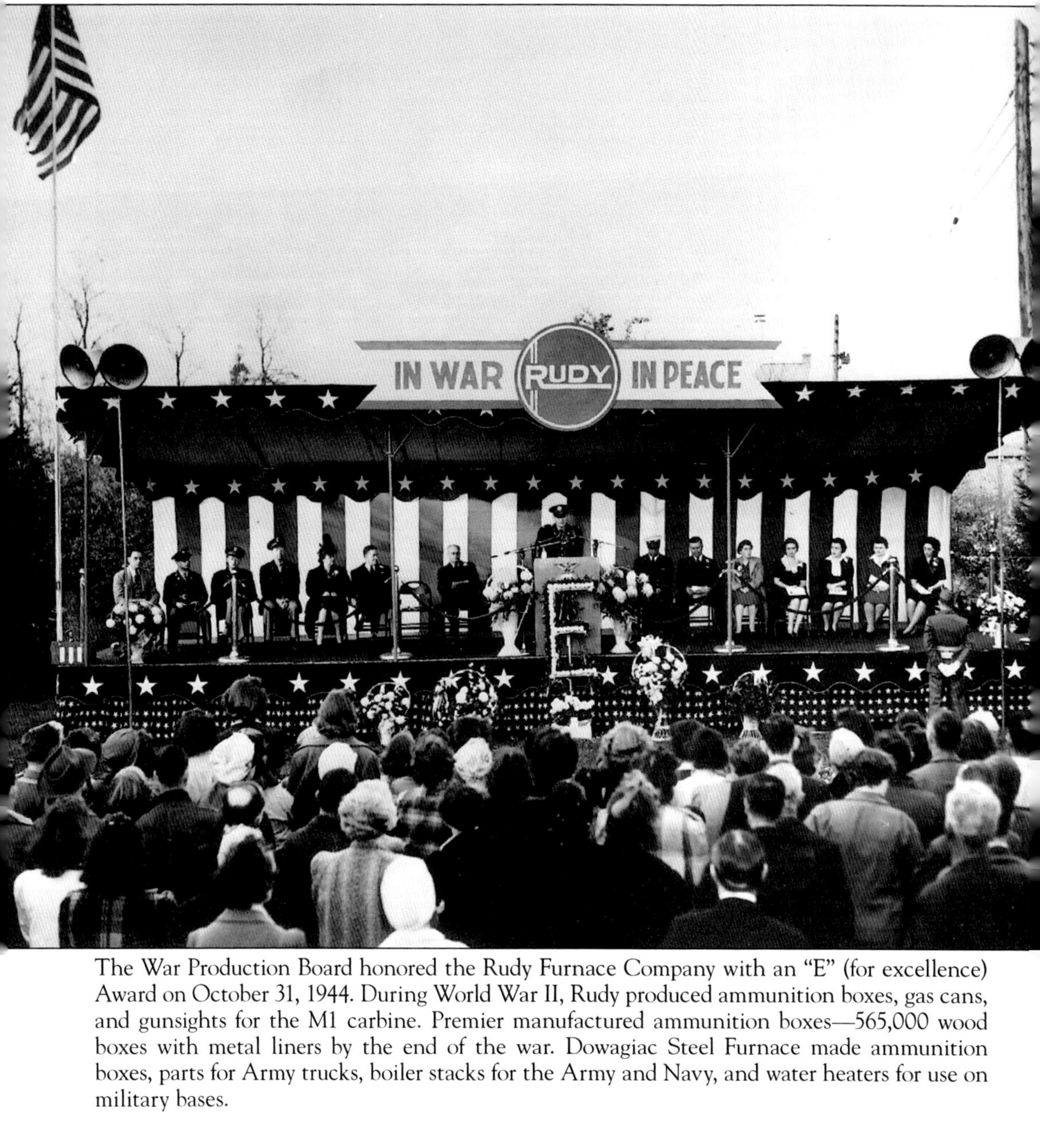

The War Production Board honored the Rudy Furnace Company with an "E" (for excellence) Award on October 31, 1944. During World War II, Rudy produced ammunition boxes, gas cans, and gunsights for the M1 carbine. Premier manufactured ammunition boxes—565,000 wood boxes with metal liners by the end of the war. Dowagiac Steel Furnace made ammunition boxes, parts for Army trucks, boiler stacks for the Army and Navy, and water heaters for use on military bases.

Six

Friends and Families

What better way to understand a community than through its people? The photographs in this chapter represent not necessarily the movers and shakers of Dowagiac, but individuals who capture the essence of the city's character. Few photographs document Dowagiac's earliest people, the Pokagon Band of Potawatomi Indians and its earliest settlers. There are many photographs, however, of Dowagiac's other residents engaged in everyday activities: working, playing, or gathering for special occasions. It is these experiences that are documented here.

Dowagiac has been home to a variety of immigrants, reflecting a microcosm of America, as the necessity or romance of western migration captured the hearts of those living in more settled areas of the nation. Two unique experiences also shaped Dowagiac's population. One was in 1854, when a trainload of orphans from New York City arrived. Part of the nationwide effort to place urban children in rural homes, the "orphan train" made it first stop in Dowagiac, where 45 children were placed in area homes. A second phenomenon was Dowagiac's proximity to Underground Railroad routes that brought escaping slaves to the area in the first part of the 19th century.

Our study of the lives of those who lived here before us enriches our own experience. Although each photograph captures only a moment in their lives, it does provide an interesting history lesson, and consequently, a better understanding of the present.

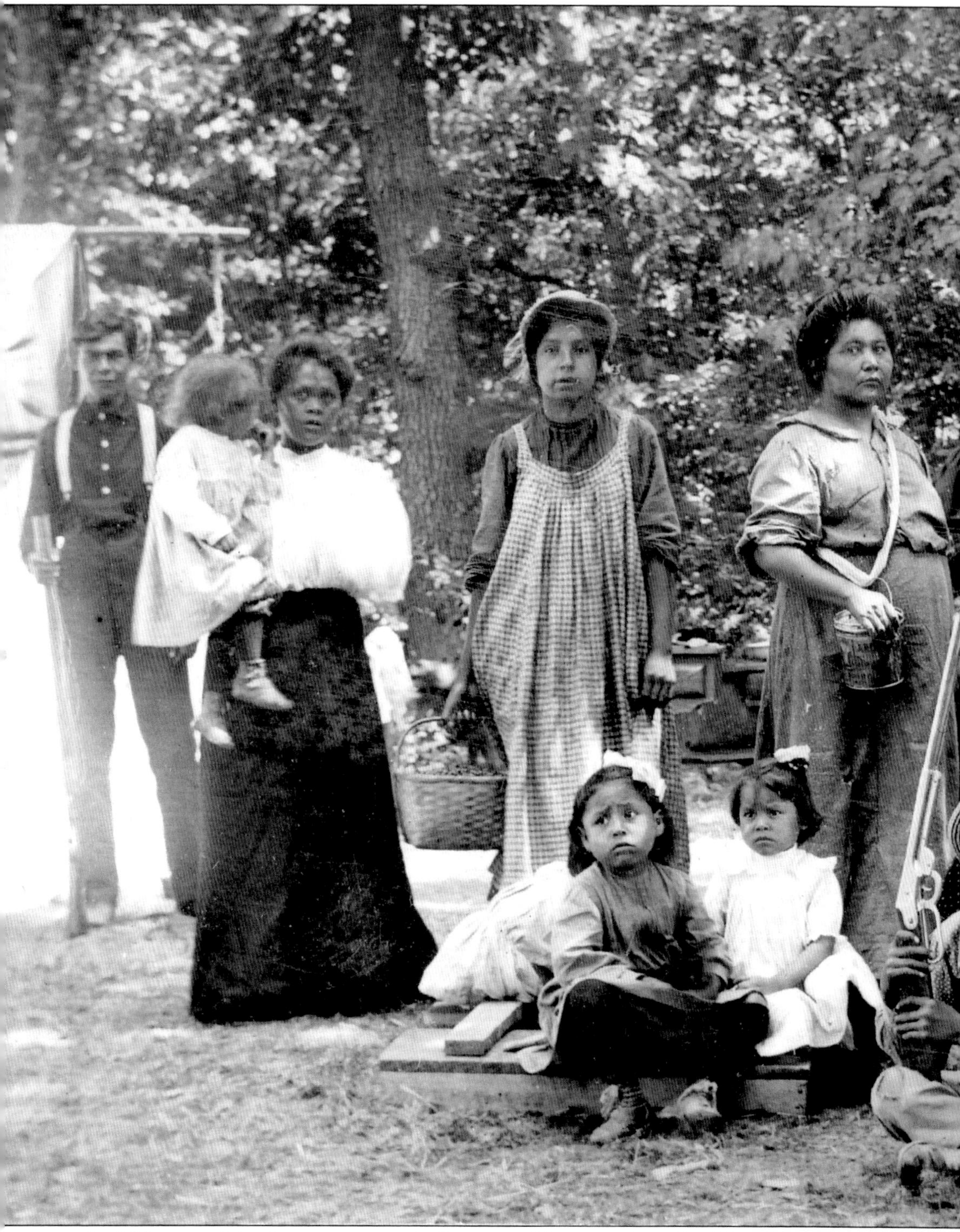

In 1838, most of the Potawatomi people (known as "Keepers of the Fire") living in southwestern Michigan were forced to leave by the U.S. government. The exception was the Pokagon Band, which owned land and had converted to the Catholic faith and remained in the area. Today the

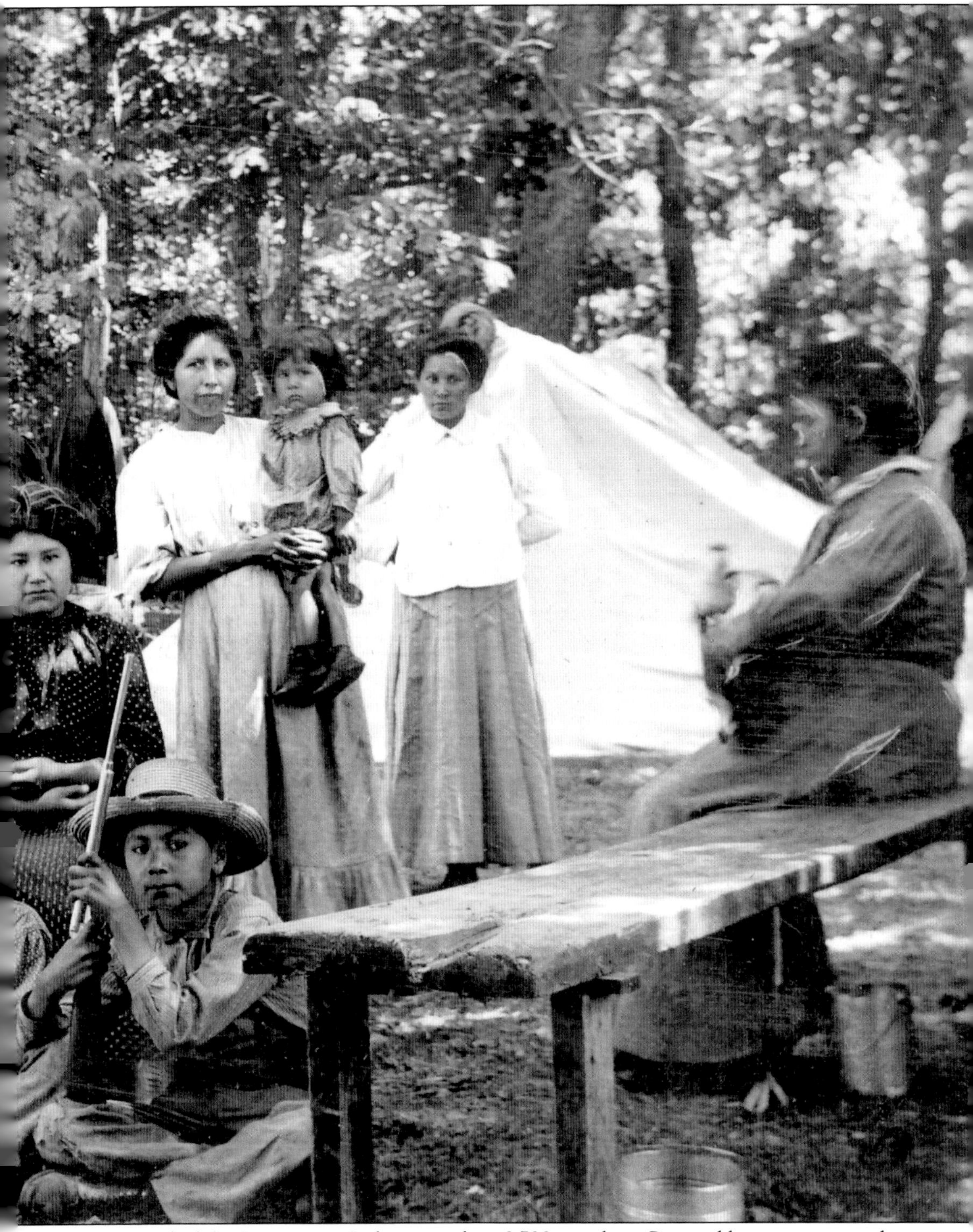

Pokagon Band of the Potawatomi Indians numbers 2,700 members. Pictured here in a postcard image from around the turn of the century are a group of Potawatomi Indians camped at Dewey Lake near Dowagiac.

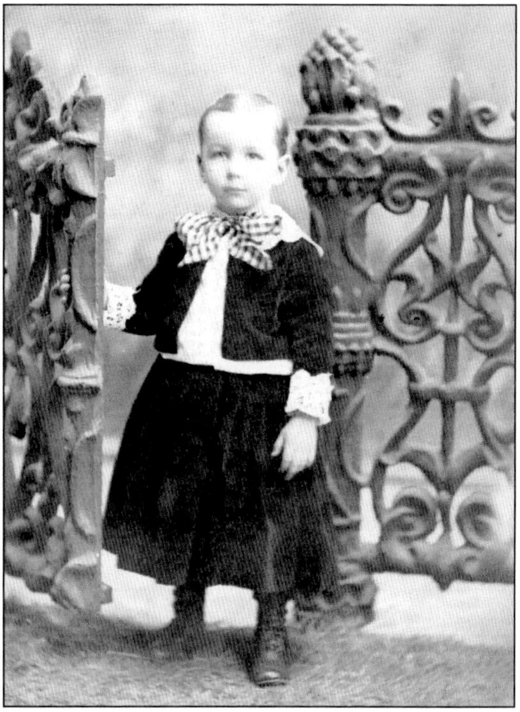

Ralph McNaney, pictured c. 1890, founded Dowagiac Steel Furnace Company in 1929. At the time of its founding, it was the only company in Michigan using steel to make furnaces. Mr. McNaney and his wife had one child, a daughter named Ruth who died at the age of 14. The McNaneys established a memorial foundation in her name to assist with community projects.

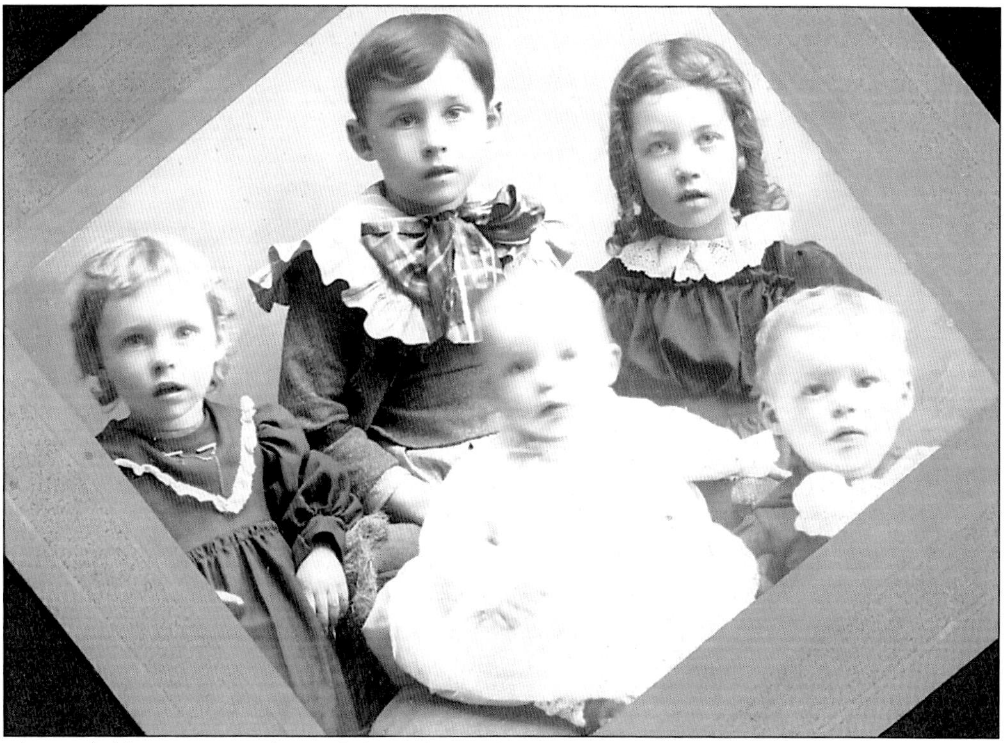

These children are members of the John and Marcella Biek family. From left to right are Gertrude, Charles, Phoebe, Bernadette, and Arthur. Mr. Biek was a moulder and stove builder with the Round Oak Company.

These children are assembled for Mary Lee's birthday party, *c.* 1895. Mary is standing and her guests, seated, are from left to right: Helen Lee, John Conkling, Owen Ball, Dick Gardner, and Paul Hackstad. Mary was the daughter of Fred and Kate Lee, and the granddaughter of P.D. Beckwith, founder of the Round Oak Stove Company. The Lee family was very prominent in Dowagiac, living in the Rockery, a Romanesque-style mansion inspired by architect Henry Hobson Richardson.

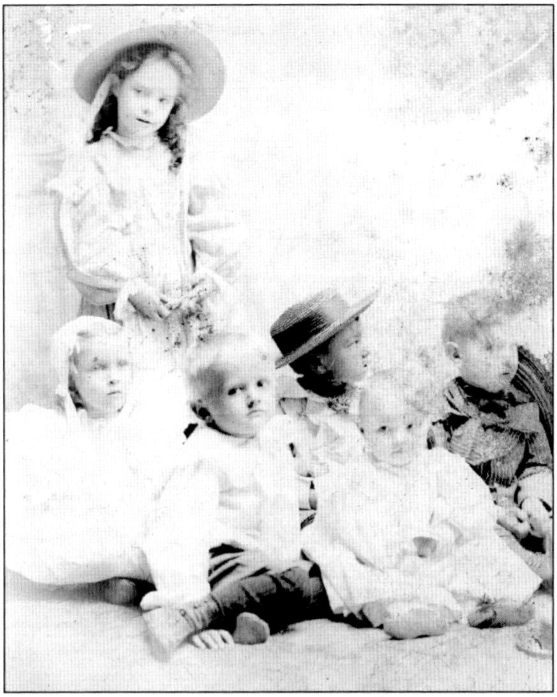

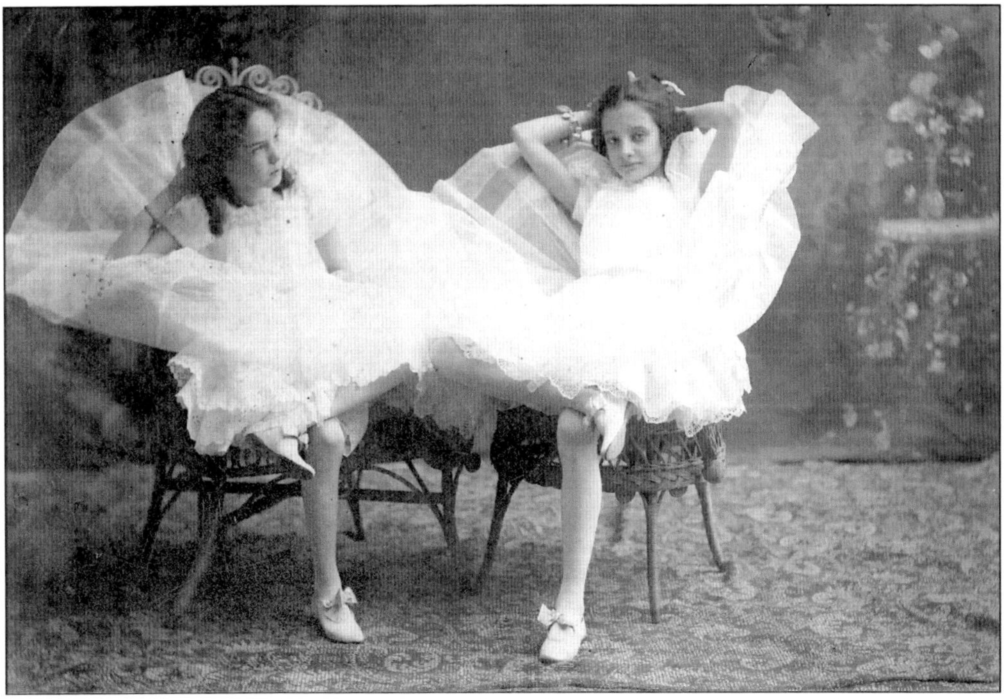

Mary Lee, left, is pictured with her friend, Cecil K. Hatfield, *c.* 1900. Cecil Hatfield married Charles Mosher, who worked with the Round Oak Stove Company around 1910. The couple eventually had ten children. Mary Lee married Dickinson Bishop, who later survived the *Titanic* disaster. Mary Lee Bishop gave birth to their only child, Pauline, in 1910—Pauline died ten minutes after her birth. Mary died 13 days later at age 22.

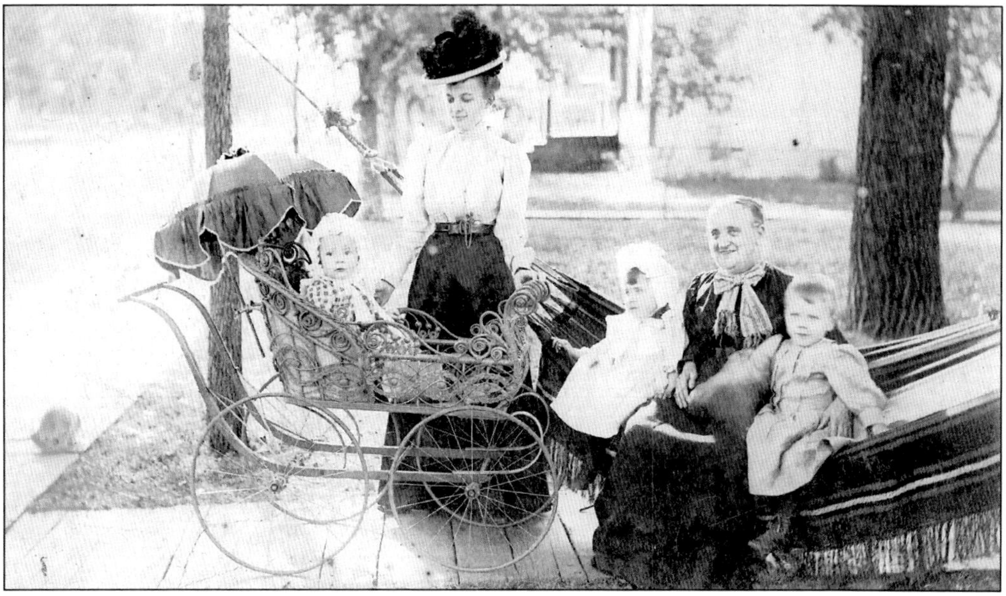

This family scene, c. 1903, features members of the Frank W. Richey family. The baby in the carriage is probably Alma, accompanied by her mother, Mary (Mrs. Frank W. Richey whose nickname was Birdie), and Mary's mother-in-law, Charity Richey. Frank Richey was a miller for the Colby Mill and was a distinguished member of the community, serving as mayor and alderman, and was a member of the Masons, the Knights Templar, and other fraternal organizations.

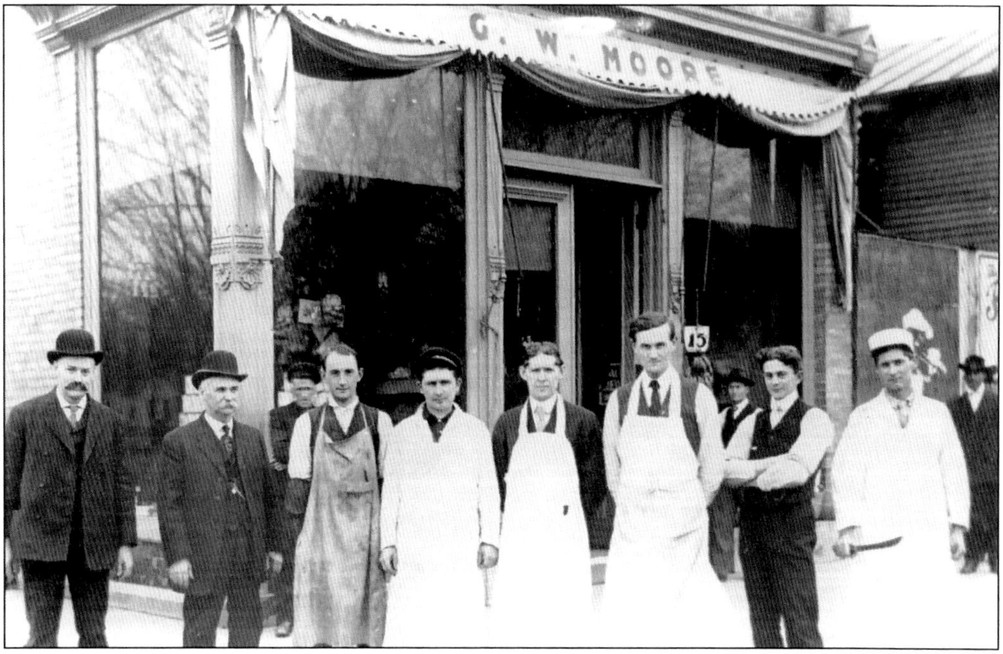

George W. Moore (left) and his staff pose for a photograph outside his grocery store, which he operated from 1897 to 1907. The store was located at the corner of Main and Front Streets. George Moore arrived in Dowagiac in the 1860s on an "orphan train" from New York. Homeless and orphaned children were sent west from the years 1854 to 1929 in the hopes that rural families would take them in and give them a better life.

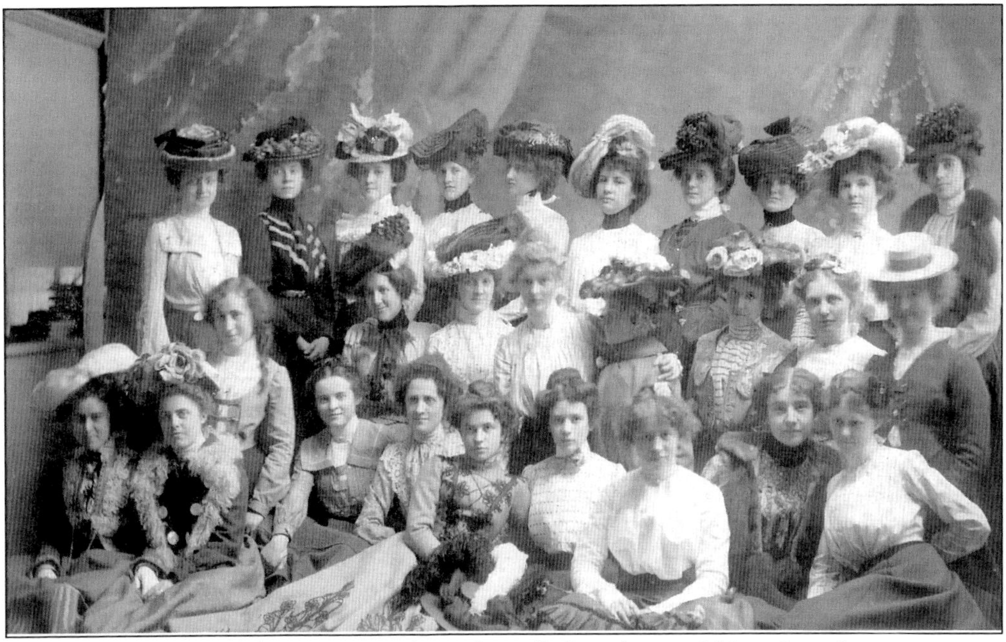

These young ladies of the 1890s are dressed in all their finery. Although each person is not specifically identified, notable family names of Dowagiac are represented including Defendorf, Phillips, Oppenheim, Lake, and Conklin.

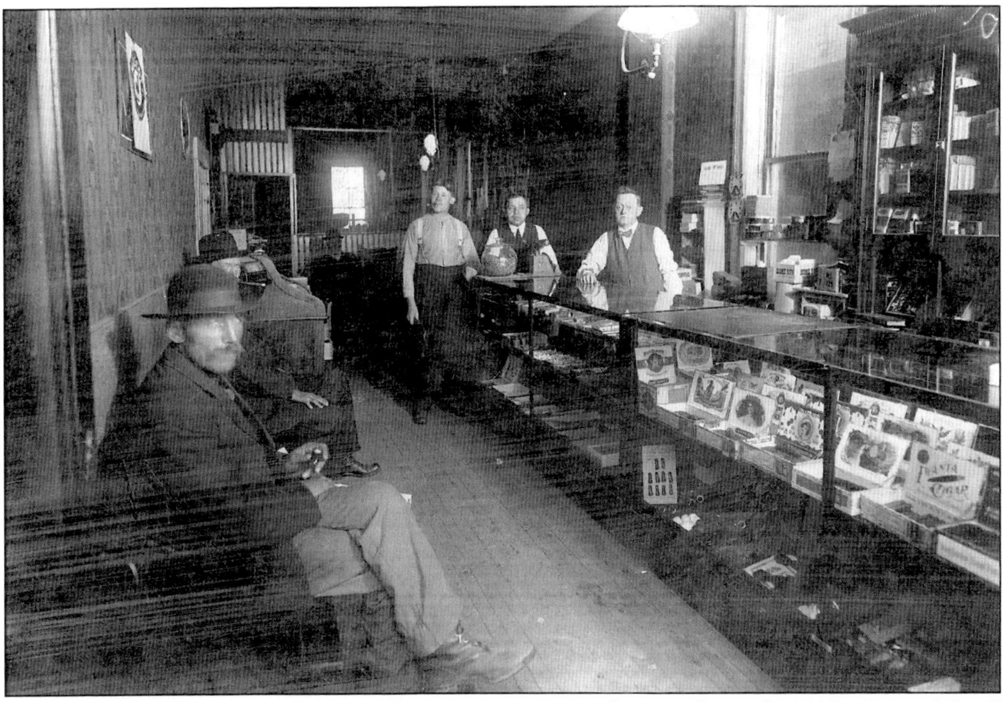

This interior photograph of the Snell Cigar Store was taken in the early 1900s. Samuel Snell was a cigar manufacturer and owned this store on Beeson Street. Standing (from left to right) are Frank Snyder, Mike Tabias, Samuel Snell.

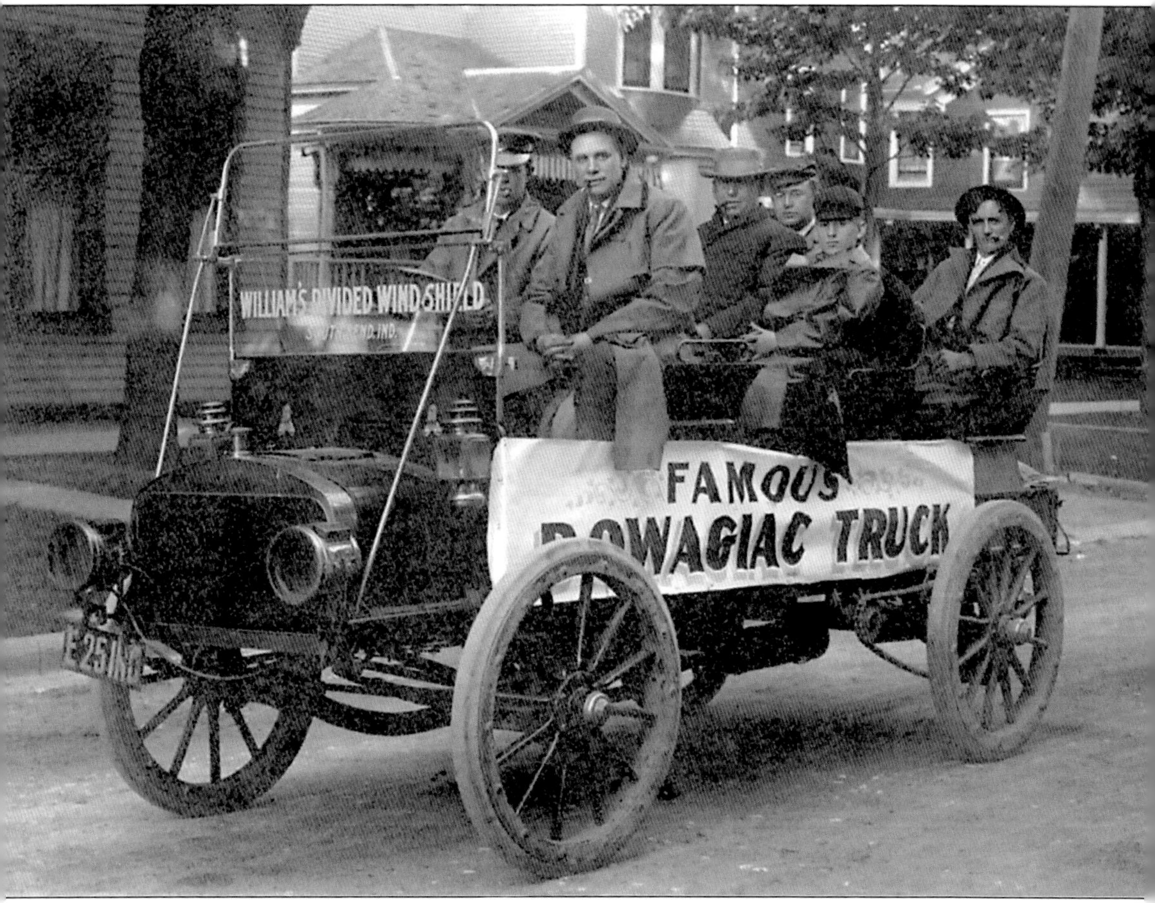

This photograph was taken in LaPorte, Indiana, one day before four of these individuals were killed in an automobile/interurban railroad accident in 1909 near Chesterton, Indiana, as they returned to Dowagiac from Chicago. Frank Lake and Leon Lyle were co-owners of Dowagiac Motor Car Company. In the front seat are Frank Lake (left) and H.H. Huston; in the middle seat are Robert Atkinson (left) and Harry Huston; and in the back seat are Leon Lyle (left) and Frank Barber. Those spared in the accident were Atkinson and Harry Huston (middle seat) because they finished their journey to Dowagiac early by taking the Michigan Central Railroad.

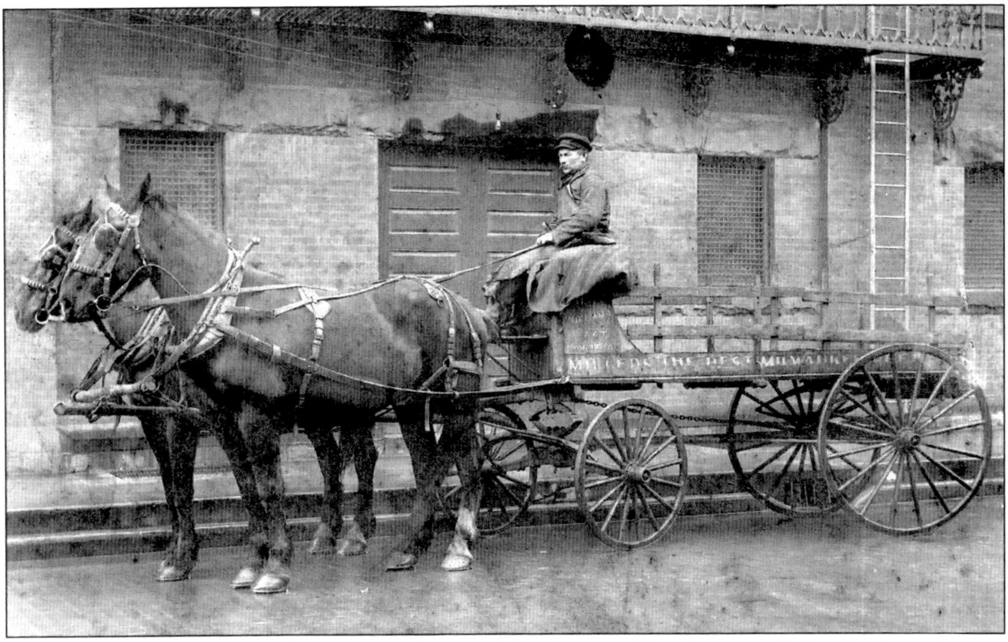

This beer delivery wagon, driven by Adam Stahl, was owned by August Weiland, saloon keeper in Dowagiac at 120 E. Railroad Street. He was a wine and liquors agent for Miller Brewing Company. This photograph was probably taken around 1900.

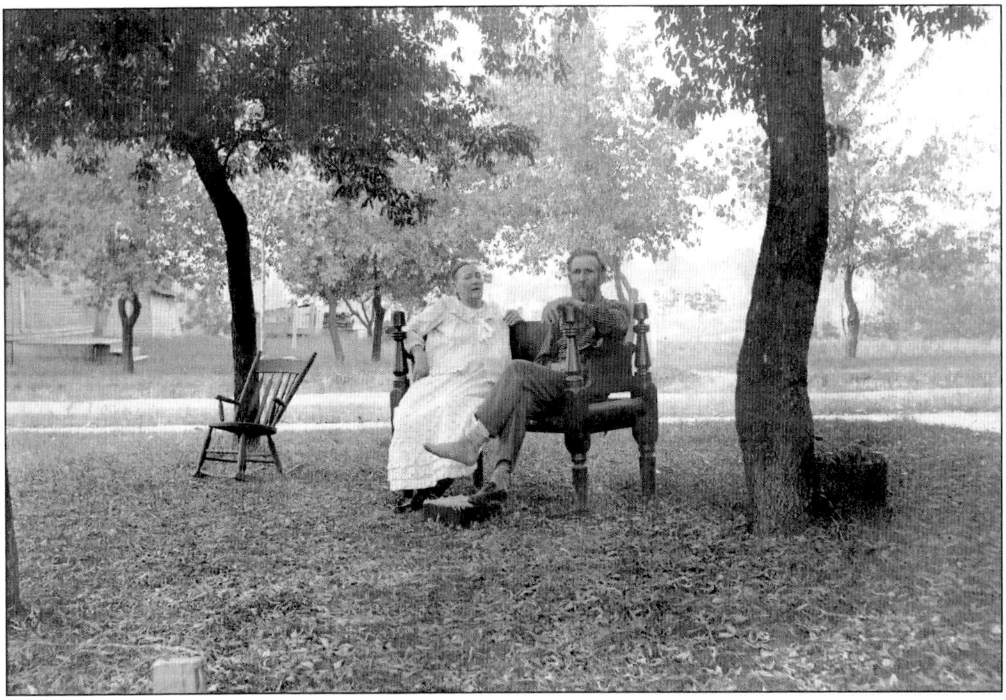

Melissa and Thomas Kirkwood were married in 1858. This photograph is from a postcard invitation that reads: "1858–1908: You are invited to the fiftieth wedding anniversary of Mr. and Mrs. Thomas Kirkwood. November 4, 1908 at 209–211 Jefferson Avenue, Dowagiac, Michigan. Hours from 10 a.m. to 4 p.m. Dinner at 12 o'clock." The Kirkwoods farmed for a living.

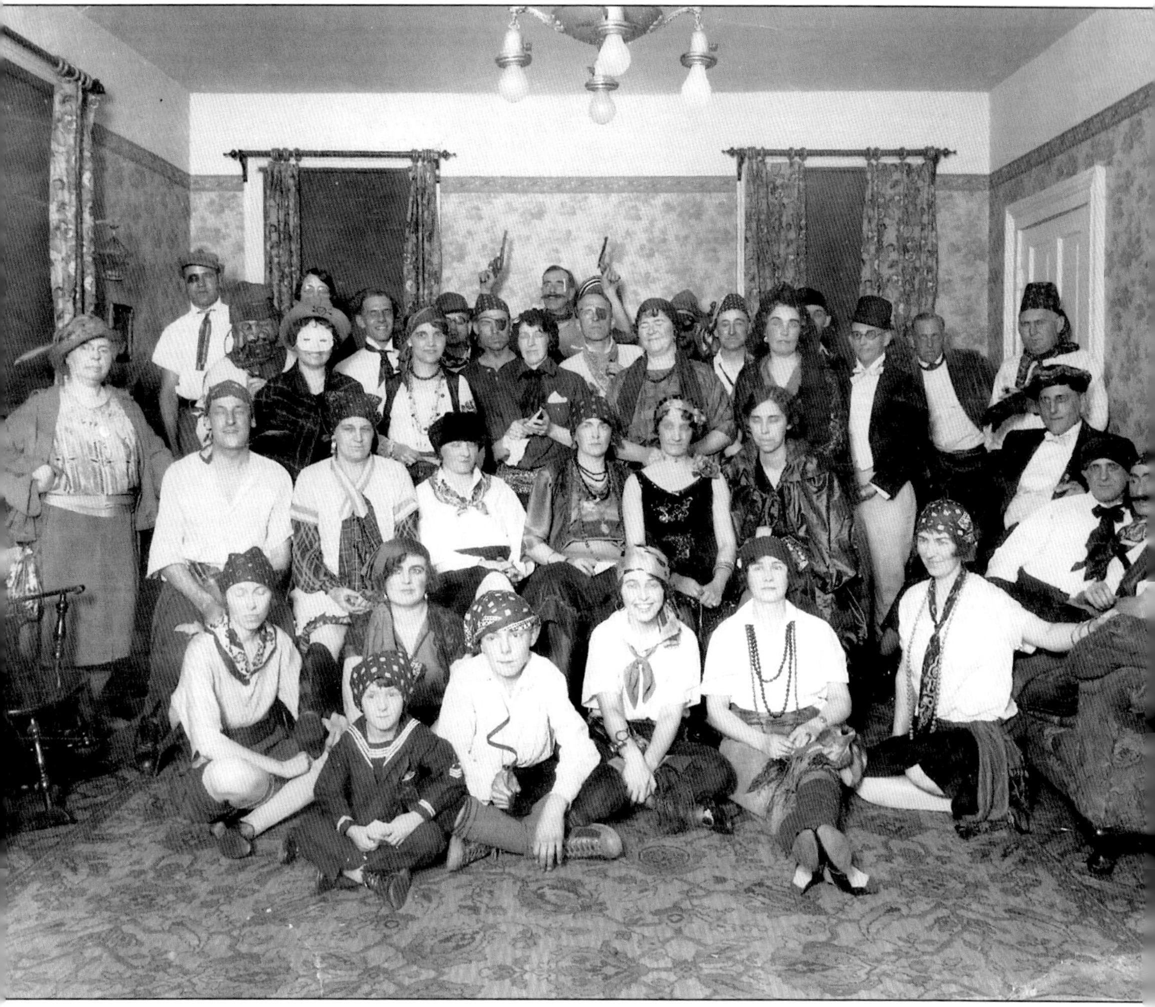

This 1927 photograph features many prominent Dowagiac citizens dressed in pirate and gypsy costumes at the Lyle Wooster home at 210 Indiana Avenue. From left to right, they are pictured as follows: (front row) Elizabeth Wooster Singer, Betty Wooster, Evelyn Conklin, Jack Wooster, Josephine Mersereau, Jess Mosher, and Nita Wooster; (second row, seated) Lyle Wooster, Ruth Mosier, Hazel Parker, Ethel Whitely, Cecil Mosher, and Lucy Frazee; (men on couch) Arthur Frazee, vernon Redner, and Harry Whitely; (third row, standing) Lena Green, unidentified with mask, Tillie Carey, Carl Mosier, Margurite Walker, Robert Mersereau, Stella Welch, Harry Mosher, Lena Weir, Paul Conklin, Rosamond Jamar, Dr. George Green, Charles Mosher, and William Carey; and (back row) Jack Welch, Florence Redner, Rene Walker, Mitchell Jamar (with guns), Edward Weir, and Frank Parker.

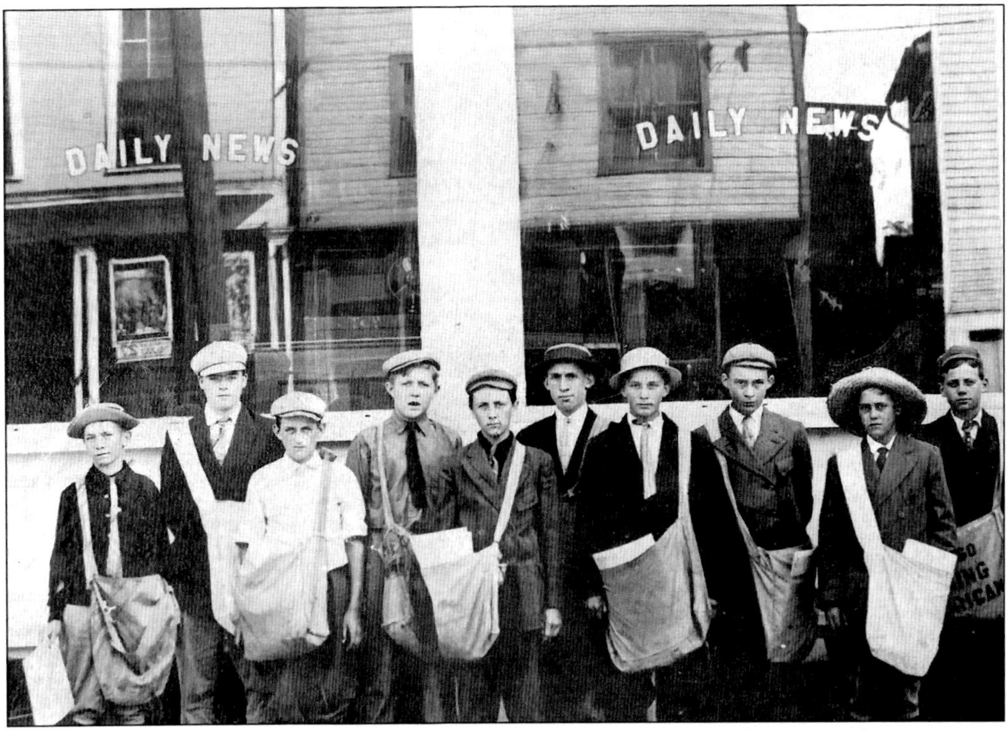

These newsboys worked for the *Dowagiac Daily News* c. 1920. At this time, the newspaper office was located at 203 Commercial Street. It was first published in 1897 and remains in publication today.

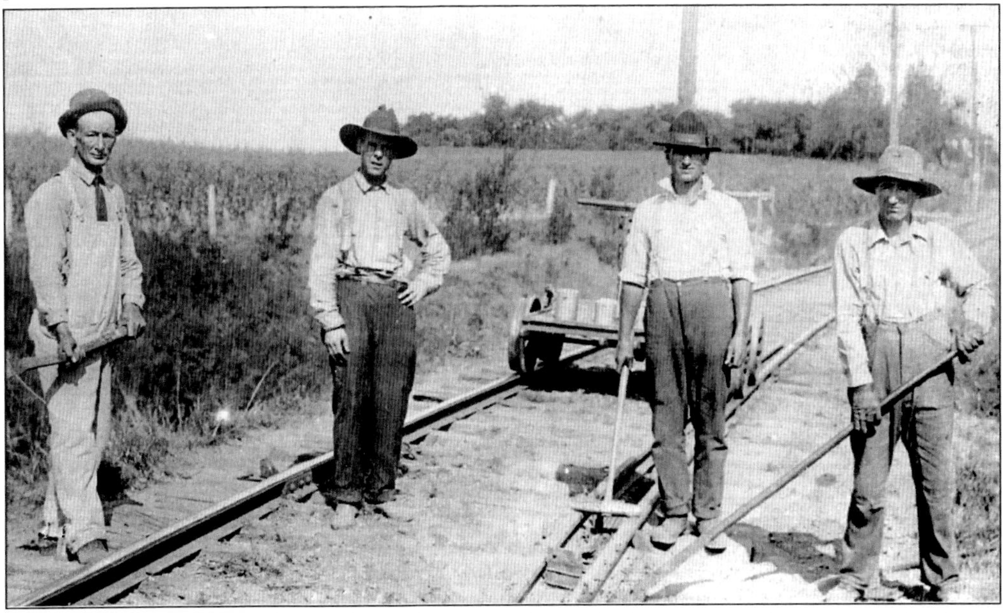

This crew is at work on the tracks of the interurban, which ran through southwest Michigan from Benton Harbor to Dowagiac, 1911–1928. It made stops at Eau Claire and Indian Lake before arriving in Dowagiac. This photograph shows Tom Rupert, Jacob Mangold, and two unidentified men at work on tracks west of Dowagiac c. 1920s.

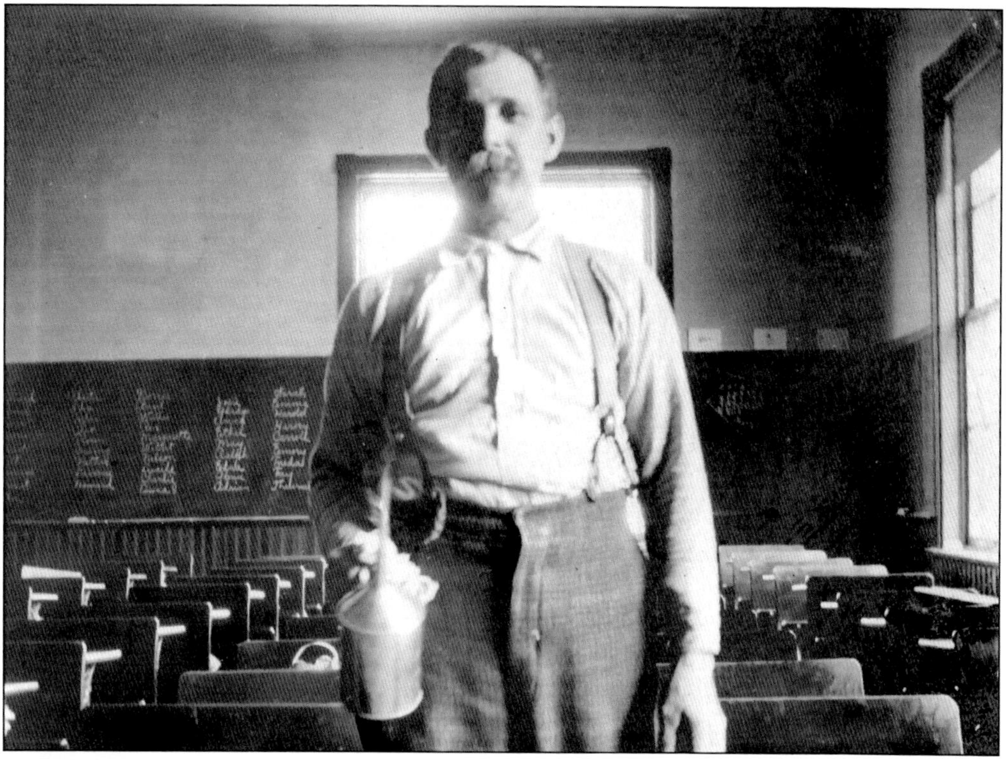

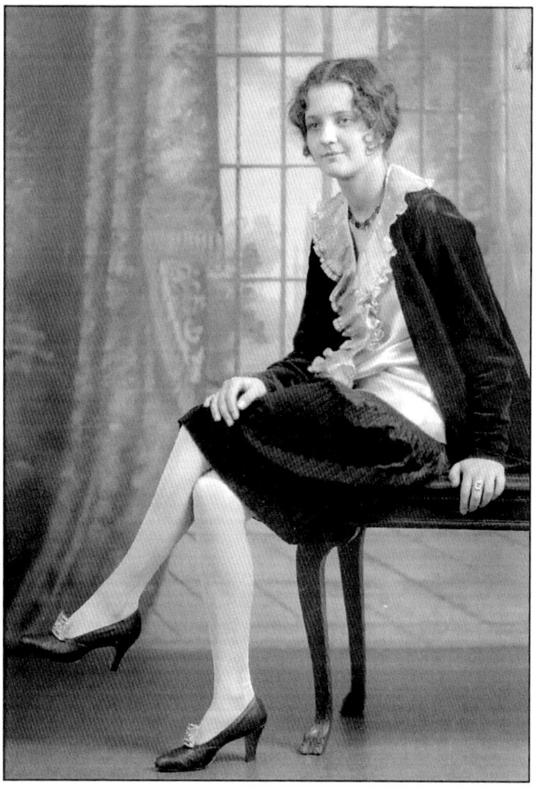

(above) Walter Crowel is pictured at Oak Street School. The school served as both high school and grade school until 1926 when the new high school was built. Mr. Crowel was the school janitor and also worked in one of Dowagiac's fishing lure factories.

(left) Velma Lason is pictured at about age 18, *c.* 1930. Miss Lason worked in the office at Premier Furnace. The back of the photograph includes the photographers' notes to be used for hand-tinting the image, stating that Miss Lason's hair was reddish brown and her eyes were blue.

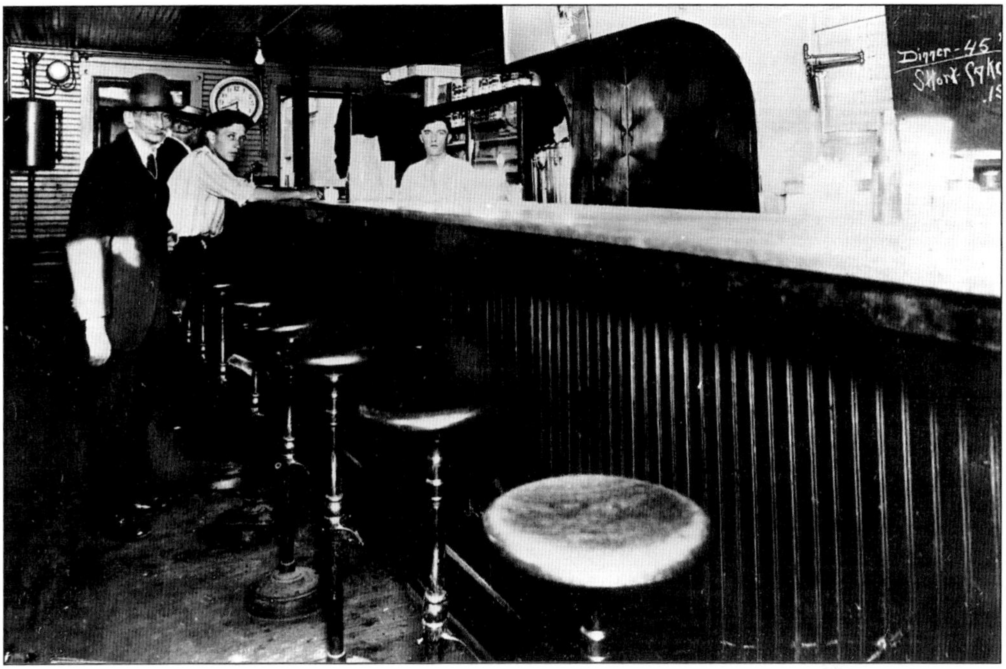

The Lunch Car, located at the corner of Division and Front Streets, operated from the 1920s into the 1950s. Pictured in this photograph are Nelson Anderson, Short Holliday, Bob Hanley, and James Kinnane.

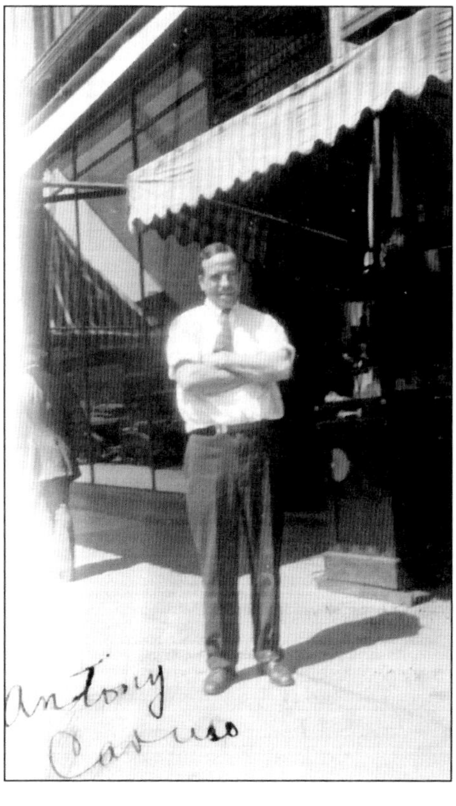

Antonio Caruso is pictured outside his candy store in 1930. The Caruso store featured homemade candy and a soda fountain, still in operation today.

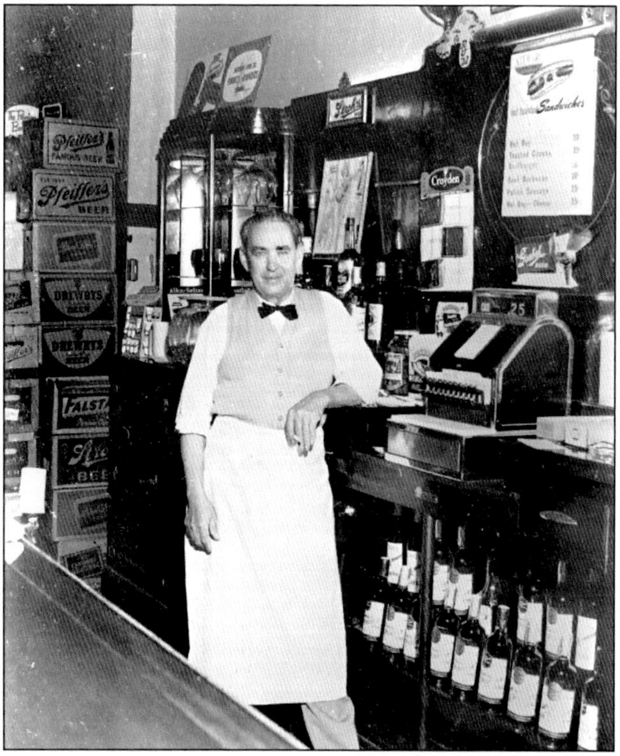

(left) George Klapchuck is pictured behind the bar at his tavern at 105 Beeson Street.

(below) Posed inside the Dowagiac train station are 16 Dowagiac men on their way to service during World War II. This photograph was taken January 5, 1942, less than a month after the attack on Pearl Harbor. The men are identified, from left to right, as follows: (kneeling) Les Hyatt, Dick Sifford, John Jurgensen, Lisle Borders, and Gerald Laylin; and (standing) Jack Reed, Glenn Andres, Clare Lee, Charles Moden, Jack Hunsburger, Jim Jewell, Mike Bobik, Lyle Hunt, Howard Allison, John Callahan, and Ed Geisler.

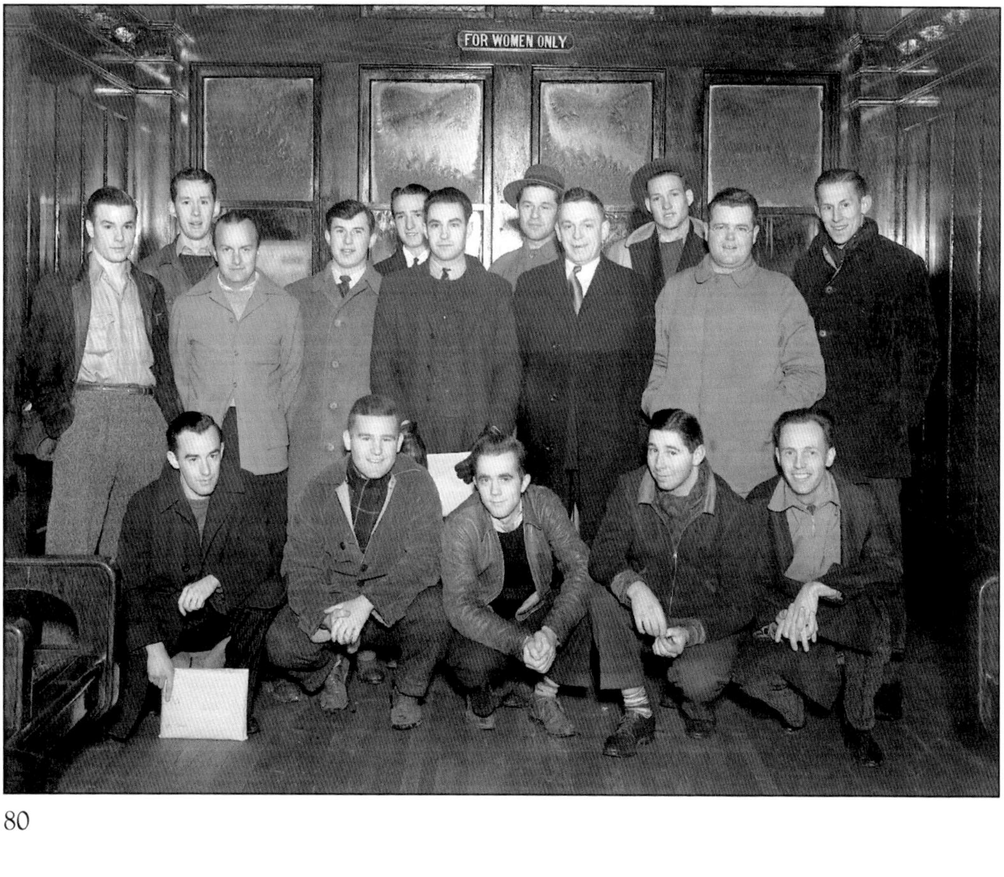

Seven

At Home

The houses of early Dowagiac reflect a great deal about the lives of the people who lived in them and serve as a microcosm of the architectural styles that were popular in America throughout the years. From the factory worker's house to the opulent mansion on the hill, each house has a story to tell.

Not surprisingly, the growth of Dowagiac was linked directly to the growth of the Round Oak Stove Company. As the city grew, new neighborhoods sprang up. By following the history of new residential construction, it is possible to track which neighborhoods were becoming the "better side of town." Generally, workers' houses were located closer to the railroad tracks and the factories, while wealthy business owners tended to build their houses farther away from the noise and soot of steam engines and factory chimneys.

Some of the houses pictured here retain their original features today. Others have been remodeled to the extent that they would be unrecognizable by their original occupants. Some are simply gone. But whether the buildings themselves survive, or only images of them, we can learn a great deal about the people who occupied them and their aesthetic sense.

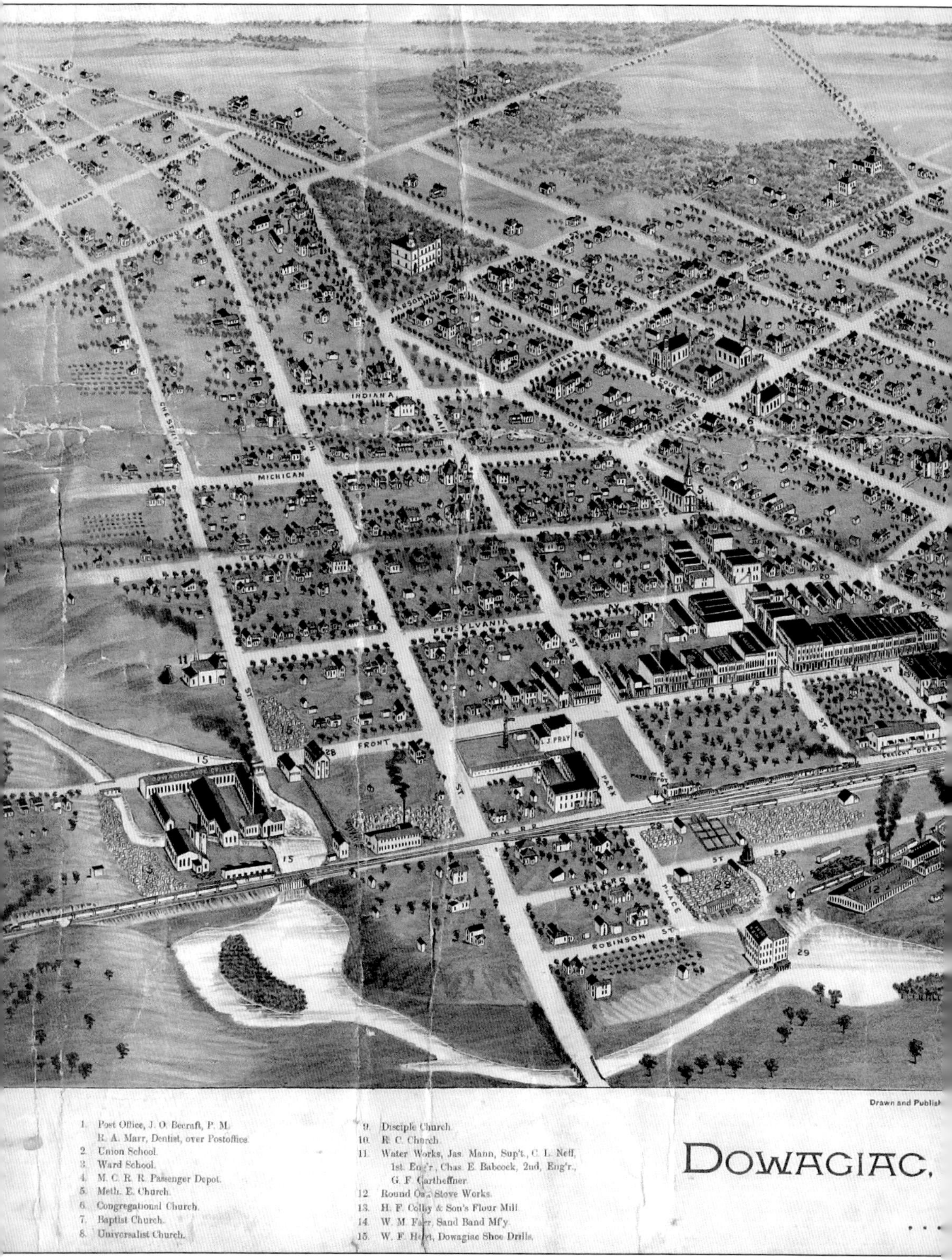

This bird's-eye view of Dowagiac dates to 1890.

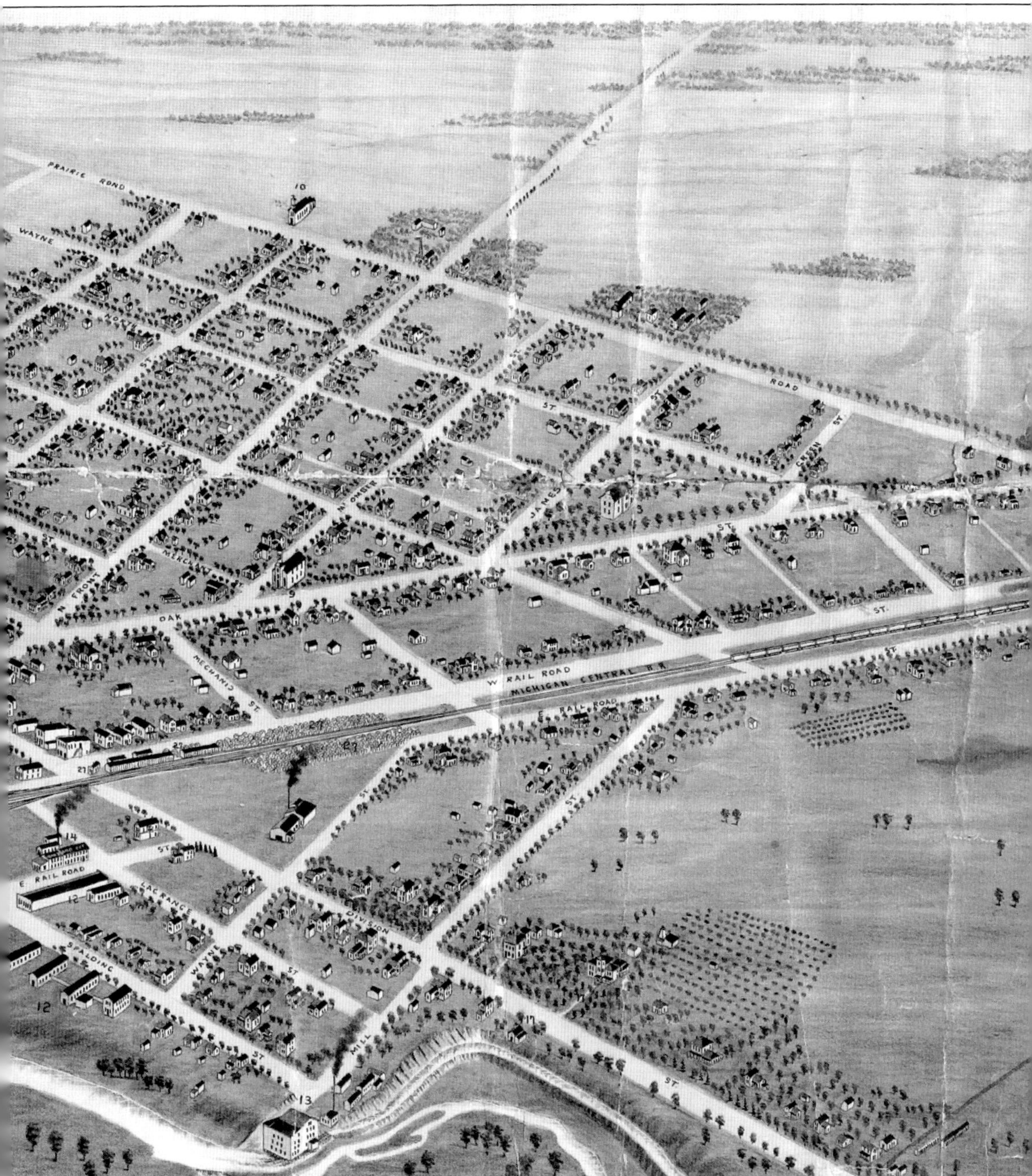

Ave., Milwaukee, Wis.

s Co., Mich.

. . . .

16. L. J. Pray, Wind Mills.
17. Ed. Pattison's Place.
18. Eugene Gilbert, Furniture, Picture Framing etc.
19. Butler Bros. Cigar Mnf'g.
20. J. M. Somers, Blacksmith Shop.
21. Coy. W. Hendryx, Attorney at Law.
22. C. L. Sherwood, Drugs and Stationery.
22. Chas. E. Swed, Attorney at Law, (over Drug Store.)
23. F. H. Essig, Dentist.
23. W. E. Parker, Physician and Surgeon.
24. A. M. Moon, Justice.
25. Joes. Keen, Board of Trade.
26. T. J. Edwards, Marble and Granite Works.
27. J. A. Lindsley & Co., Lumber Yard.
28. Chas. N. Parkinson, Repair Works.
29. Judd & Son, Plaining Mill and Lumber.

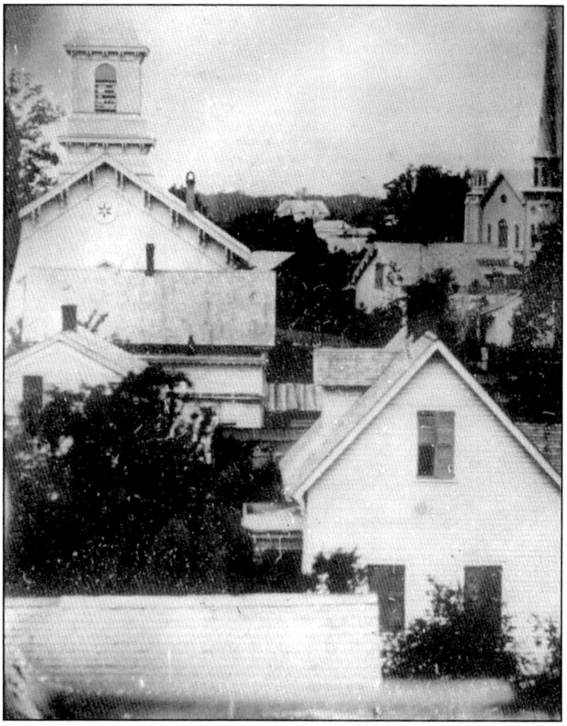

One of the earliest photographs of Dowagiac's downtown area, this *c.* 1865 image from a tintype shows several houses and churches. Like many cities, Dowagiac experienced a series of catastrophic fires in its early years, forcing change in building patterns and styles.

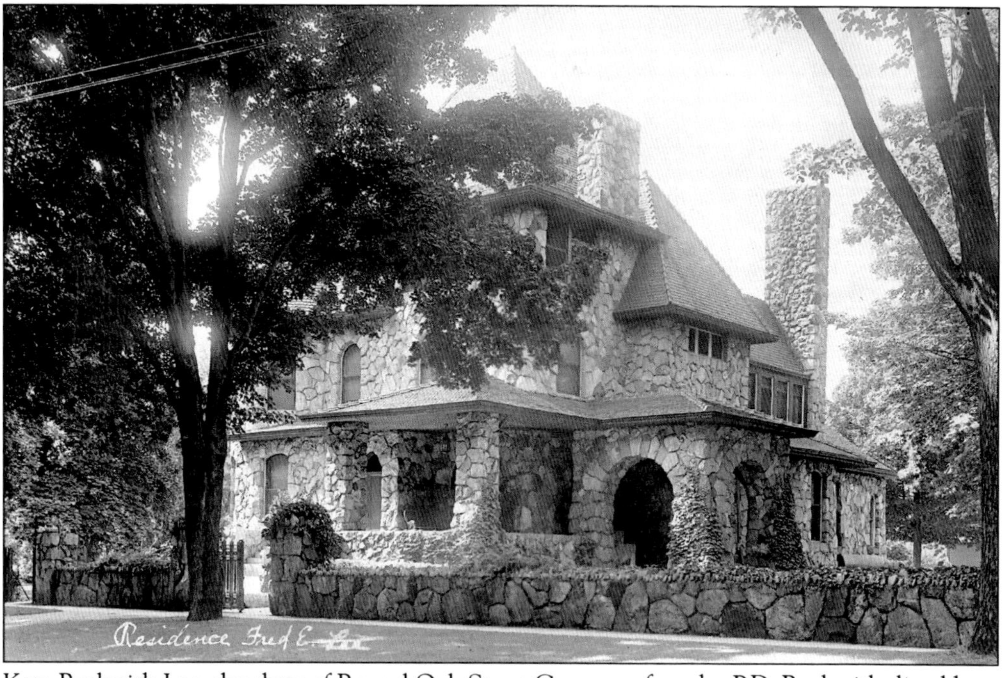

Kate Beckwith Lee, daughter of Round Oak Stove Company founder P.D. Beckwith, lived here with her husband, Fred Lee, and their daughter, Mary. The house, dubbed the Rockery, was completed *c.* 1895 and is in the Richardson Romanesque style, with characteristic round arches over doors and windows, and interior vaulting. It is made of local field stone. W.W. Brown of Chicago designed the home for entertaining.

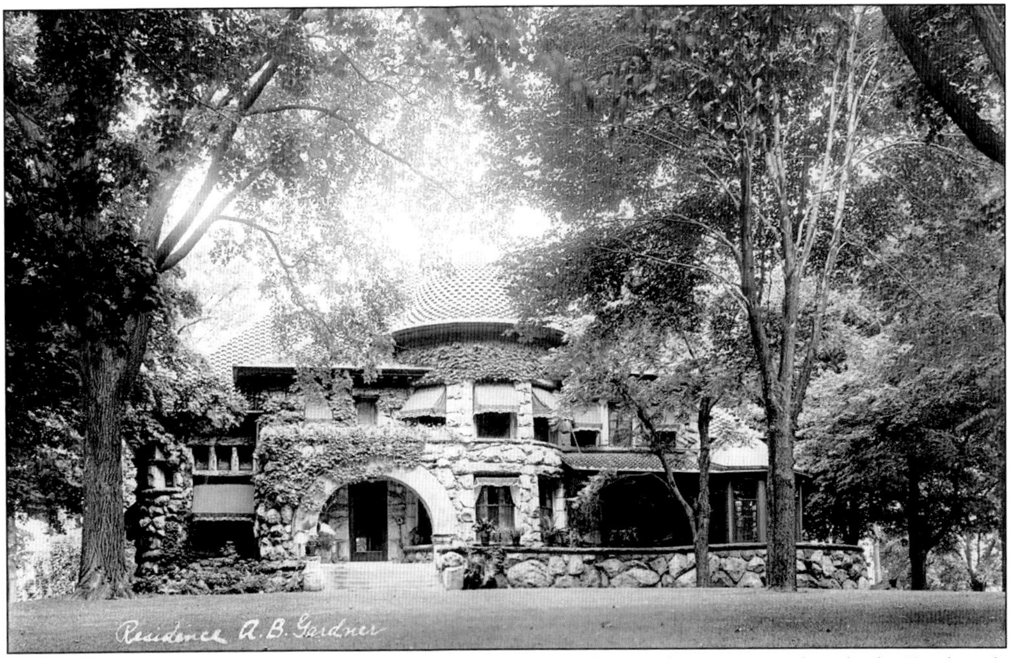

Another Richardson Romanesque style house, the Maples, is also associated with the Beckwith family. This house was built in 1896 by Archie Gardner, P.D. Beckwith's grandson by his daughter, Della. In addition to its majestic exterior, the house is known for its "Gold Room," with bird's-eye maple woodwork and staircase, exhibited at the Chicago World's Fair in 1893.

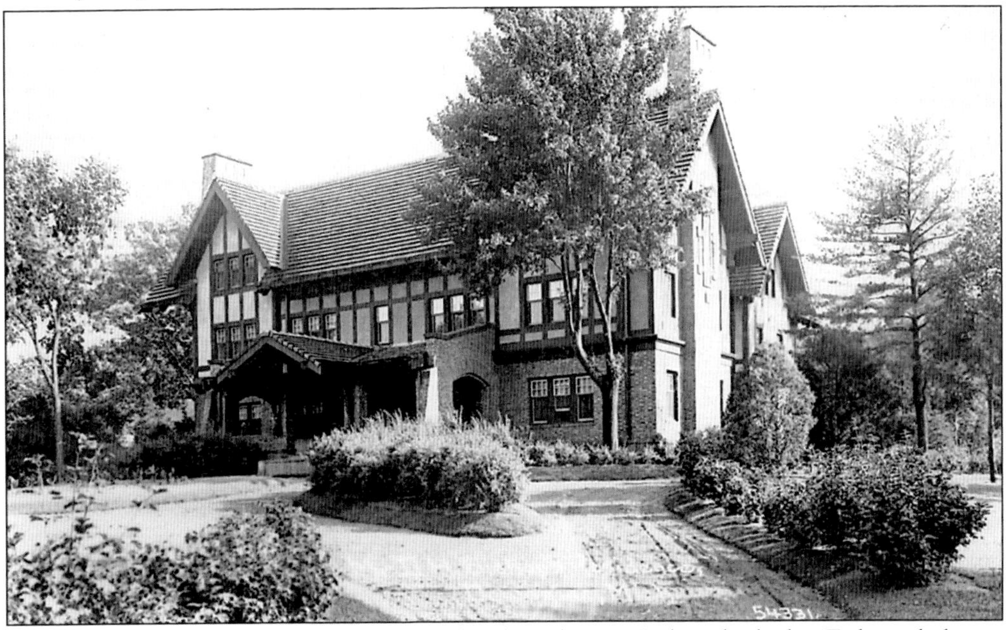

Mary Lee grew up in the Rockery. Her husband, Dickinson Bishop, built this Tudor-style house between 1910 and 1912. The decorative half-timber facade; tall, narrow windows; and massive chimneys were characteristic of this style. It had 43 rooms, including six bathrooms. Unfortunately, Mary Lee Bishop never lived in this house; she died in 1910 at the age of 22. The house was later used as a hospital and was razed in 1976.

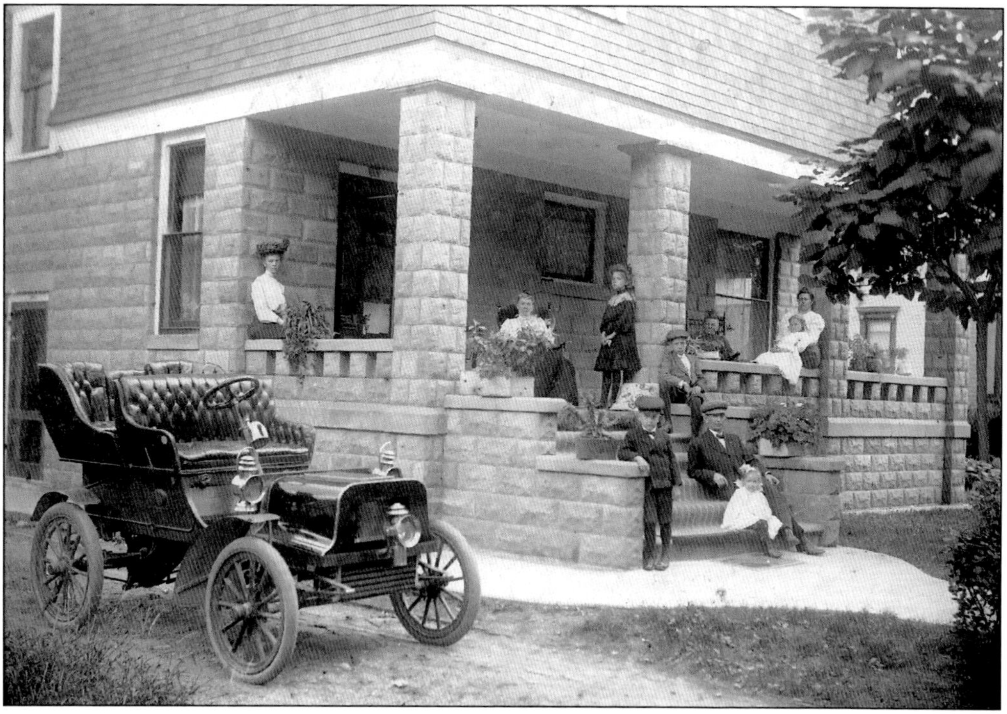

The Frank Richey family is assembled on the porch of their home on North Mill Street, c. 1906. The shingled upper level and wide porch are characteristic of the Shingle style of architecture, not quite as popular as the Queen Anne style of the same period. Mr. Richey, seated on the porch stairs, was a miller.

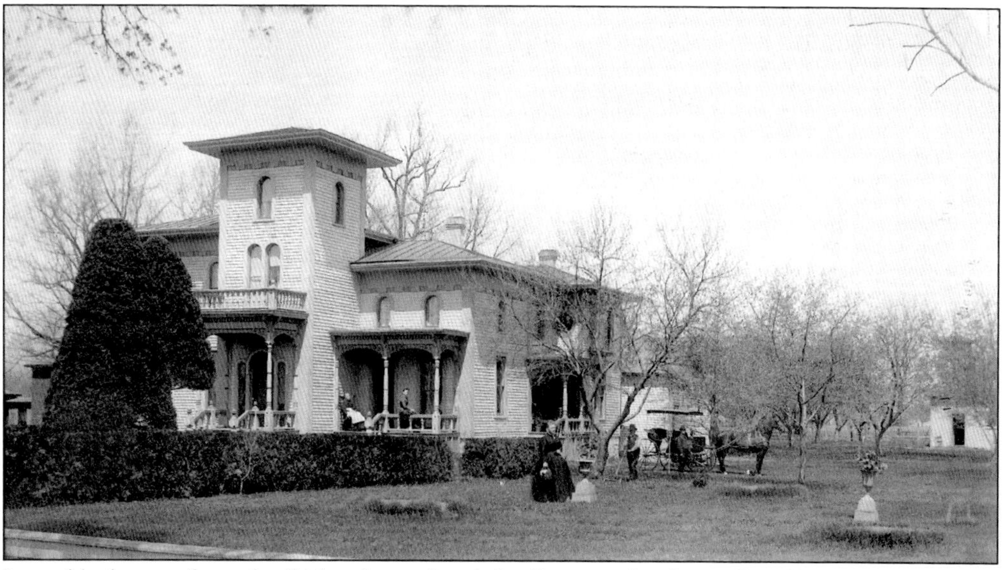

Just a block or so from the Richey home lived the Pattison family, on East Division Street. Mr. Pattison was a saloonkeeper and this photograph of his house, c. 1905, shows an Italianate style with tall, narrow, arched windows and a square tower. Mrs. Pattison is seated on the porch, left, with her daughter, Zella. Their neighbors, Mr. and Mrs. Guy Piper, and the Pattisons' hired man are in the yard.

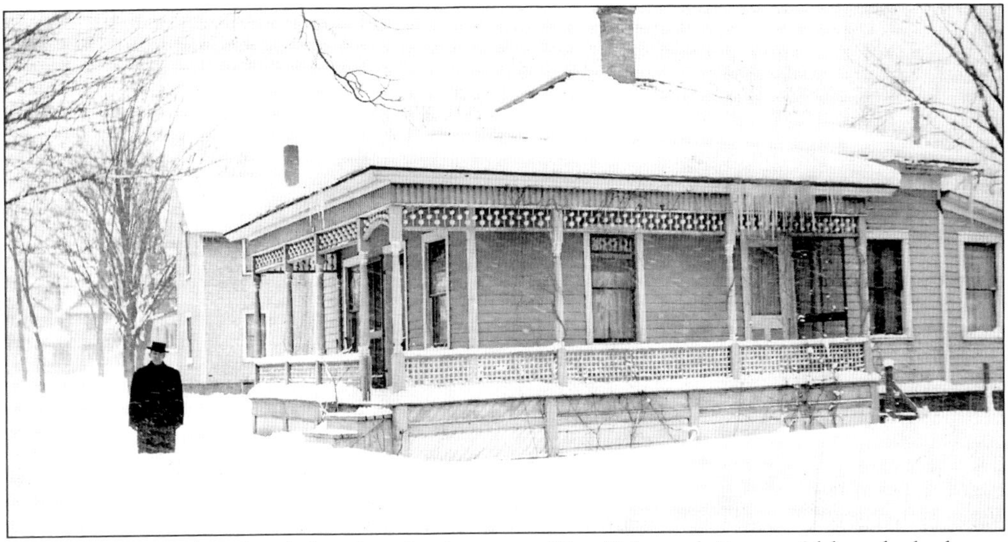

The Arthur Larzelere family lived in this house on West Telegraph Street. Although the house sports Queen Anne-style spindlework and detailing in this 1914 photograph, it was actually built in the 1830s. The man standing outside is possibly Arthur Larzelere, who worked as a traveling salesman, livery and feed stable owner, and eventually an automobile garage owner.

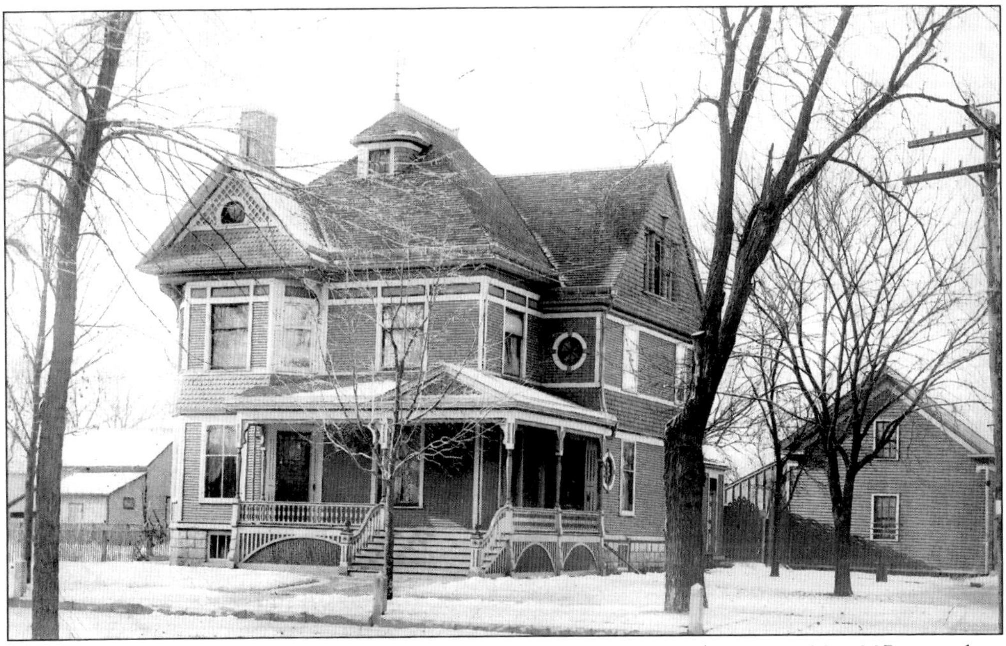

This photo of the Simeon Conklin house on Green Street, taken *c.* 1900–1907, reveals a common form of Queen Anne style architecture that was popular in the late 19th century. Conklin was born in New York in 1841 and came to Michigan with his family when he was a boy. He married Charlotte Swisher in 1861, was a successful farmer, and retired to Dowagiac and this house.

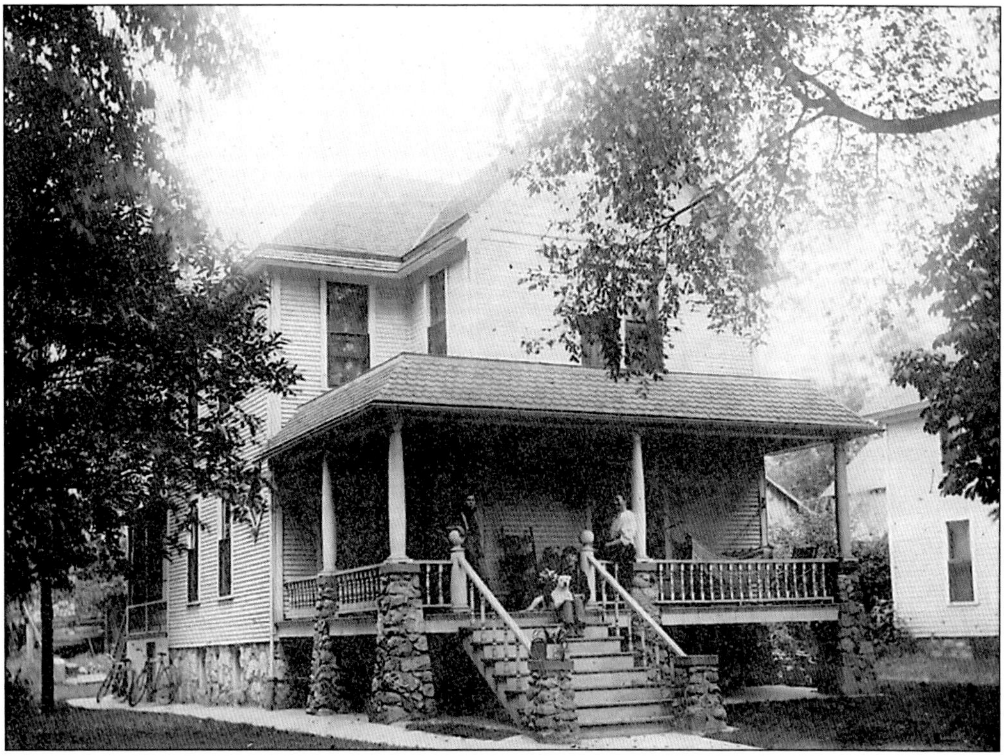

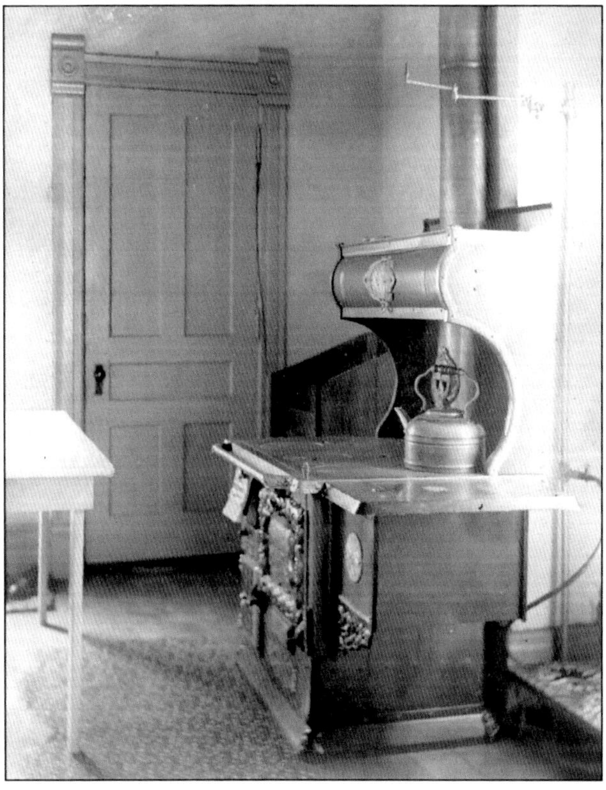

(above) The Skeeps family is pictured on the porch in this image of a house on Spruce Street. From left to right are Arthur, Henry, and Mrs. Skeeps. In 1900, Michael Skeeps was listed in the federal census as an iron moulder, probably for the Round Oak Stove Company. By 1910, however, he had died and his wife had remarried a local baker, Loren Eckert. This photograph dates to c. 1905 and shows a typical frame house with a gable front and wing.

(left) Photographs of interior spaces are valuable clues to the past. This photograph of the Warren Palmer home on Spruce Street shows a c. 1900 Round Oak cooking stove. Mr. Warren, like so many Dowagiac residents, was an employee of the Round Oak Stove Company in the early part of the 1900s.

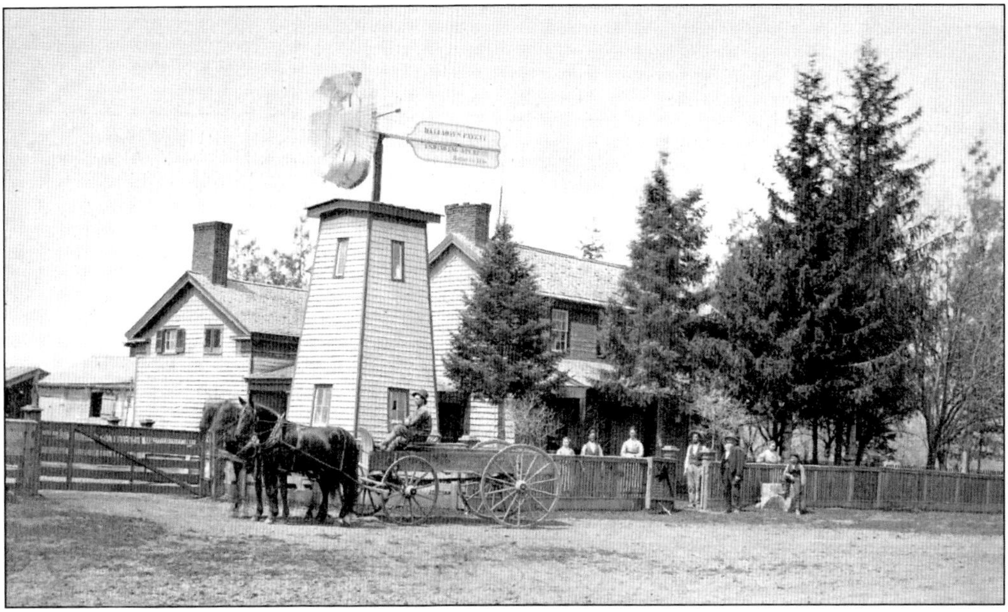

The Stephen Wright farm was located a few miles from Dowagiac at Oak Grove Road and Beeson Street. Stephen Wright was born in Ohio in 1816. The family came to Michigan when Stephen was 12 years old. This photograph of the farm dates from around 1900. After Stephen's death, his son Charles farmed here. The Greek Revival features of the structures were the dominant style in rural areas in the latter part of the 19th century.

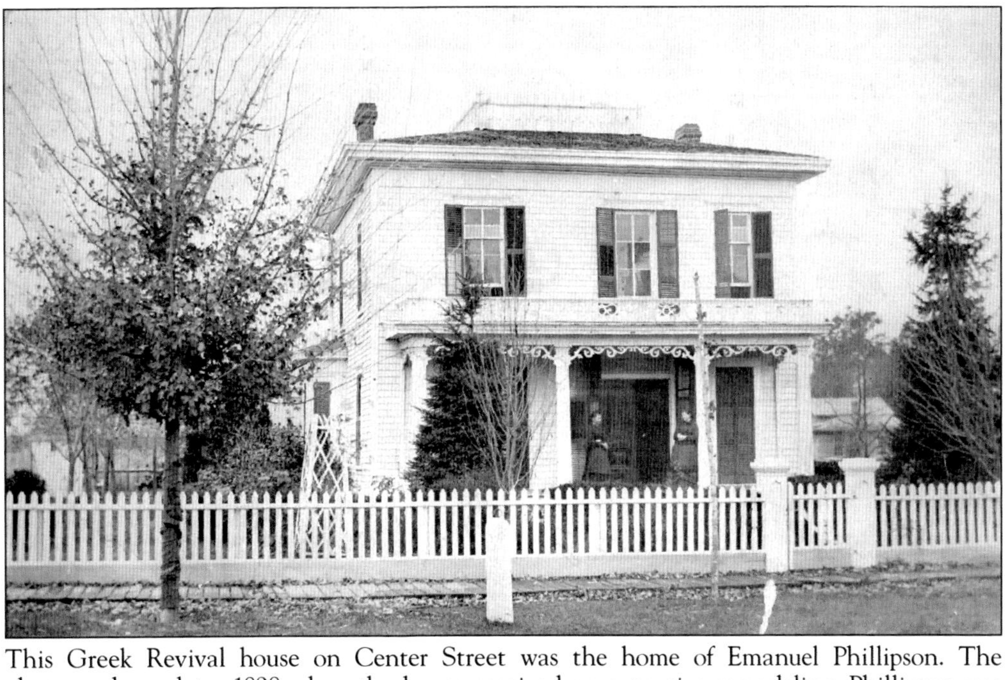

This Greek Revival house on Center Street was the home of Emanuel Phillipson. The photograph predates 1898 when the house received an extensive remodeling. Phillipson was born in Germany and came to Dowagiac in 1875, opening a clothing shop. The 1899 Dowagiac city directory stated, "Mr. Phillipson has a pleasant home in a fashionable quarter of the city, and enjoys his fireside and the companionship of his family to the fullest extent."

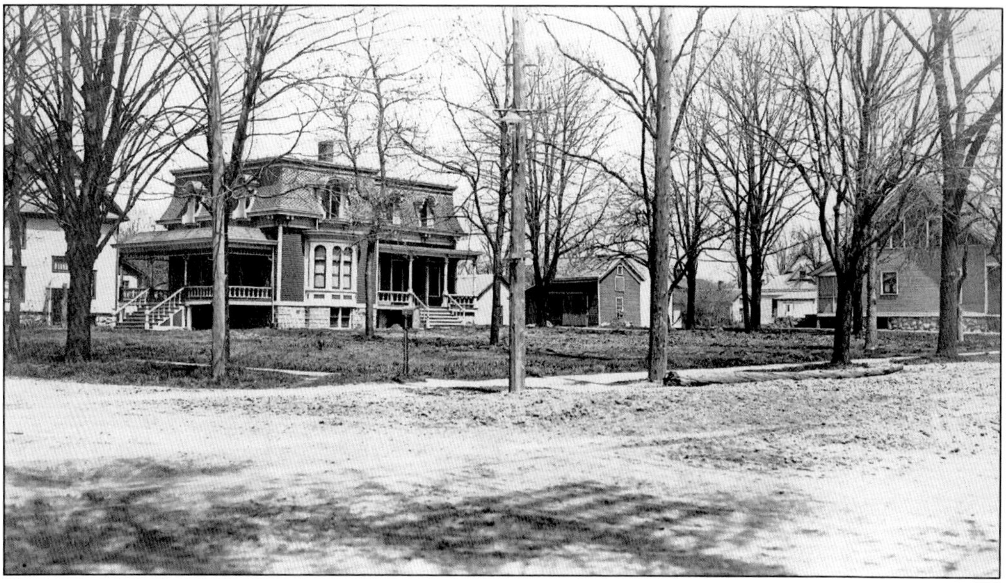

Dr. Casimer P. Prindle lived in this home at Orchard and Telegraph Streets with his wife, Adeline, in the 1860s and 1870s. The home is of the Second Empire style with a typical mansard roof and dormer windows. This was considered very modern for its time, imitating the latest French building styles. After the Panic of 1873, few houses were built in this style. The 1882 *History of Cass County* stated that Dr. Prindle did not like pretension or "use of high-flown language." He died in 1876.

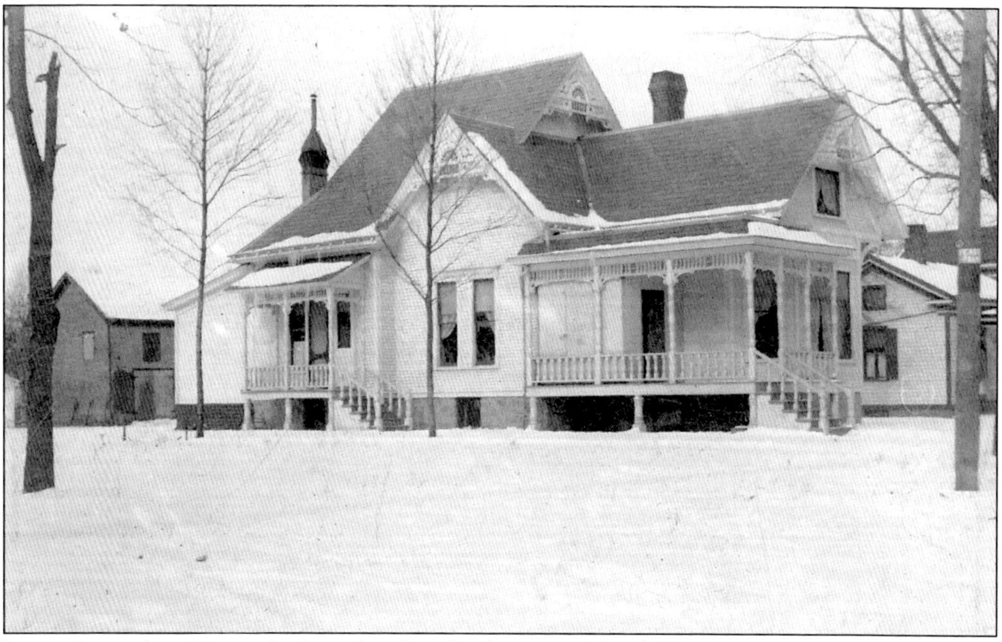

James Atwood and his wife, Ann, lived at this house on North Front Street. James was a farmer and dealer in livestock. This house shows that he was successful in his endeavors. It is a cross-gabled roof subtype of the very popular Queen Anne style. This photograph dates from c. 1910.

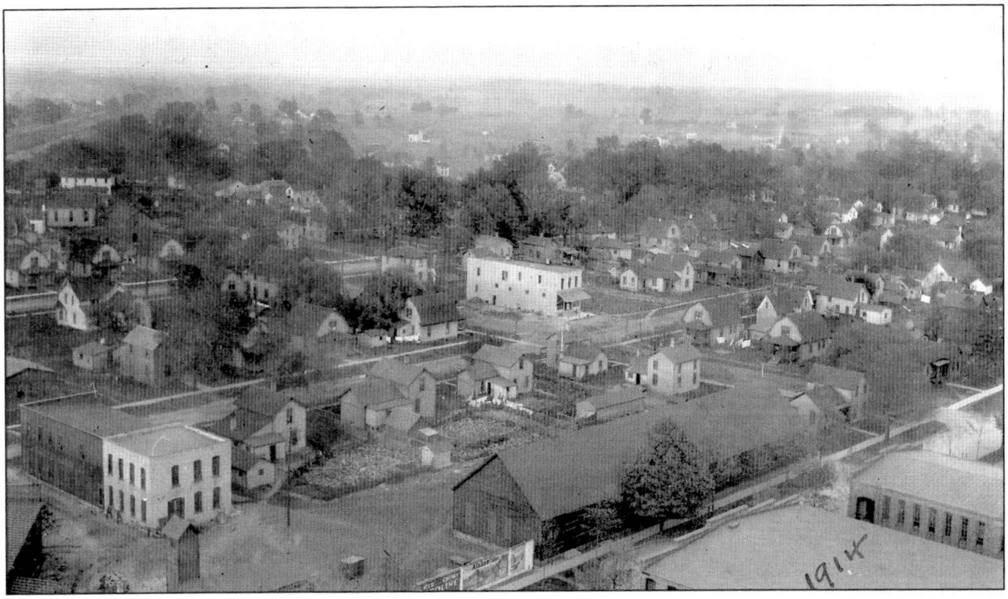

This is one in a series of 18 photographs showing a panoramic view of Dowagiac. The photographer, Raymond Garrison, climbed 153 feet atop a new chimney of the Round Oak Stove Company in 1914 to take the photographs. This view shows the area of Dowagiac east of the railroad tracks where many of the Round Oak Stove Company's workers lived. It is possible to see many of the Dutch Colonial-style houses that were built to house foreign workers who were brought in from Eastern Europe during a period of union demands for higher wages.

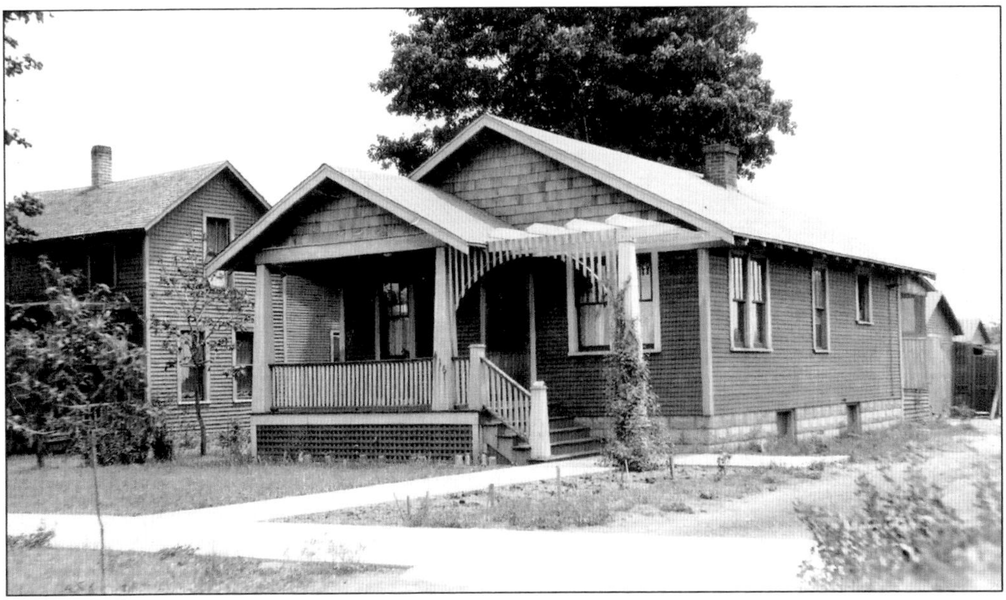

Ernest and Gladys Cochrane lived at this house on East Railroad Street. The house faces the railroad tracks and was an easy distance from the Round Oak Stove Company, where Mr. Cochrane worked in the press room. The house is of the Craftsman style, popular from 1905–1930. This photograph dates from 1910.

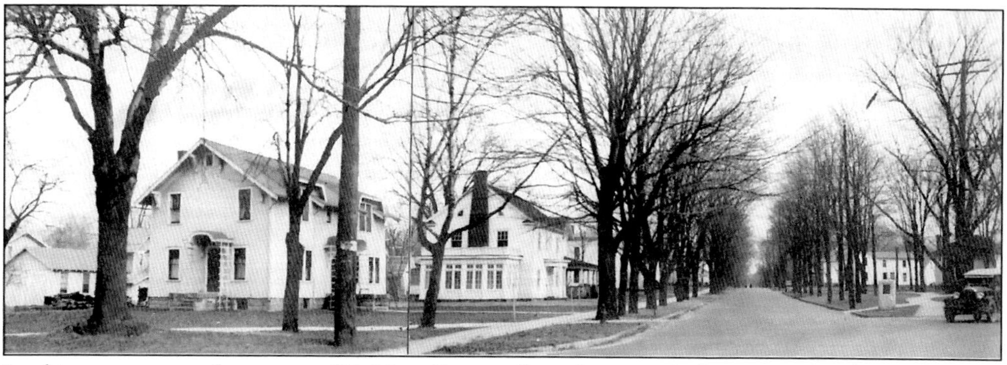

Looking east toward town on Division Street, this photograph from *c.* 1930 shows the E.E. Alliger house (foreground) and the Vernon Redner house. Mr. Alliger was the justice of the peace who sold real estate and insurance. Mr. Redner was a grocer. Across the street from the houses stands a low, stone monument to Civil War veterans from Dowagiac. The monument currently stands about a block from this position. These houses represent the Colonial Revival architectural style, which predominated American building after 1910.

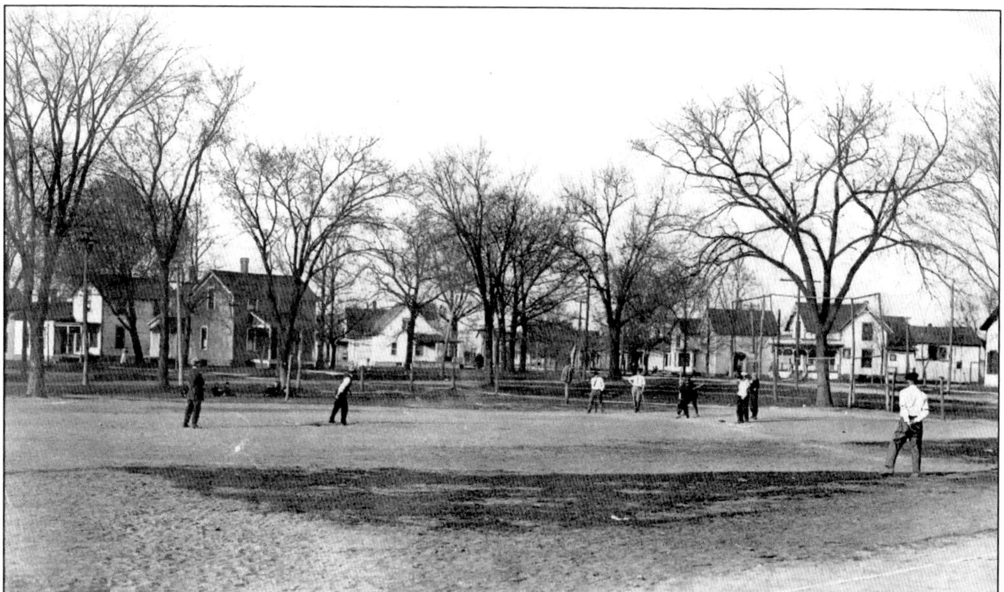

This photo of a casual game of baseball in the 1910s also shows the neighborhood surrounding Oak Street School. It reveals a variety of houses, typical of Midwestern cities like Dowagiac.

Eight

The ABCs of Dowagiac's Schools

Dowagiac had a progressive school system in its earliest days. In fact, it had a school in 1840, before the village even existed. The school, the first in Michigan west of Detroit, used citizen taxes for operations, making it one of the first public schools in the state. Pioneer families like the Hamiltons and McOmbers, used the school for a couple of years before it closed due to many parents' fears of the "immorality" their children were learning there. Students then attended some of the nearby township schools.

After the village was incorporated in 1858, several schoolhouses were built to accommodate the growing population. A school built in 1856 burned down three years later and was replaced in 1861 by the Dowagiac Union School building—the site served Dowagiac students until 2005. The Union School served both as a high school and primary school until 1903. In 1864, Dowagiac built the Ward School building on Oak Street, and the site has housed a school ever since.

In 1903, the city greatly expanded the Ward School and created the Oak Street School, which served as kindergarten, primary school, high school, and the Cass County Normal School. The Union School then became a primary school until it was razed in 1924 for construction of the new Dowagiac Central High School. The Central School was used as the high school until 1962, when the city built a new high school and Central was converted to a middle school.

McKinley School was also added in 1903 to serve students on the south side of town. Other city buildings were used as schools over the years, including the L.J. Pray Building, which served as the Front Street School for part of the late 1890s and early 1900s.

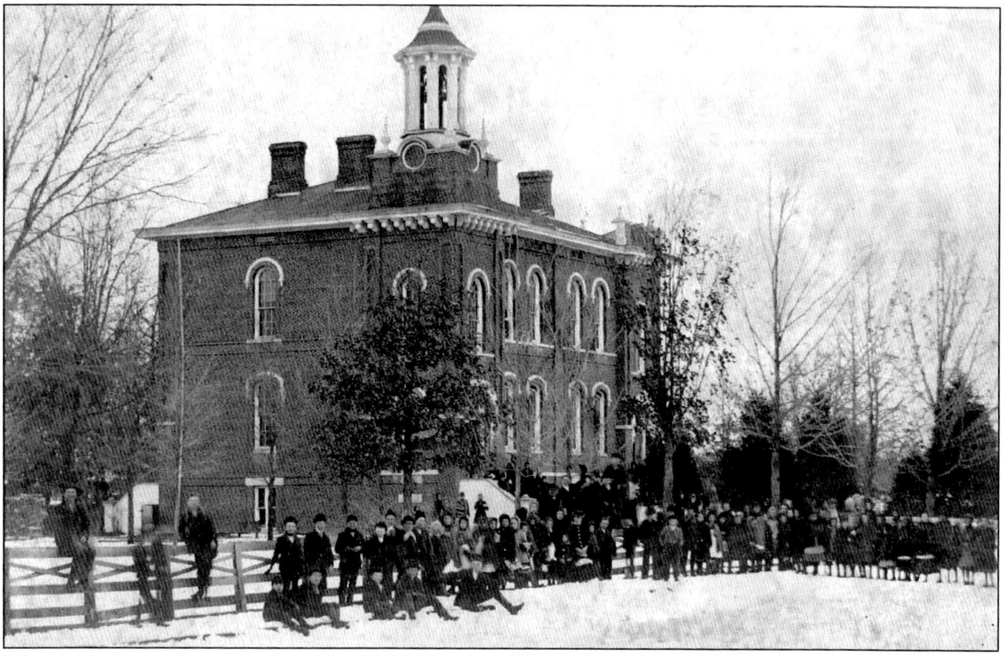

This is the best photograph of the old Dowagiac Union School in the Museum at Southwestern Michigan College's collection. The school was built in 1861 at the corner of Parsonage Street and Main Street (now Division Street). The photo dates to the 1880s and shows the entire building, grounds, and student body. Sources indicate that additional wings were added sometime in the 1880s—this photo was taken before the wings were added.

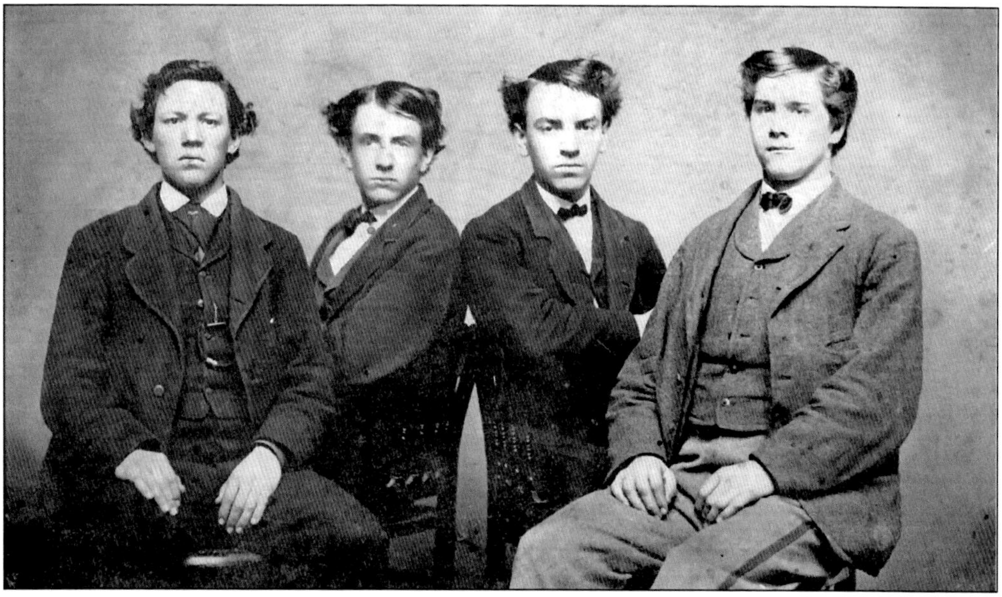

The Dowagiac High School Class of 1870 is pictured, from left to right: Charles Bailey, Charles Foster, Frank ReShore, and Allan Woodruff. They all went on to succeed in life. Bailey founded the *Tri-Weekly Monitor* of Dowagiac. Foster went to West Point and remained in the Army. ReShore started his own flower business in Dowagiac. Woodruff, who took the train to Dowagiac from Watervliet to attend Dowagiac's school, became a businessman in Watervliet.

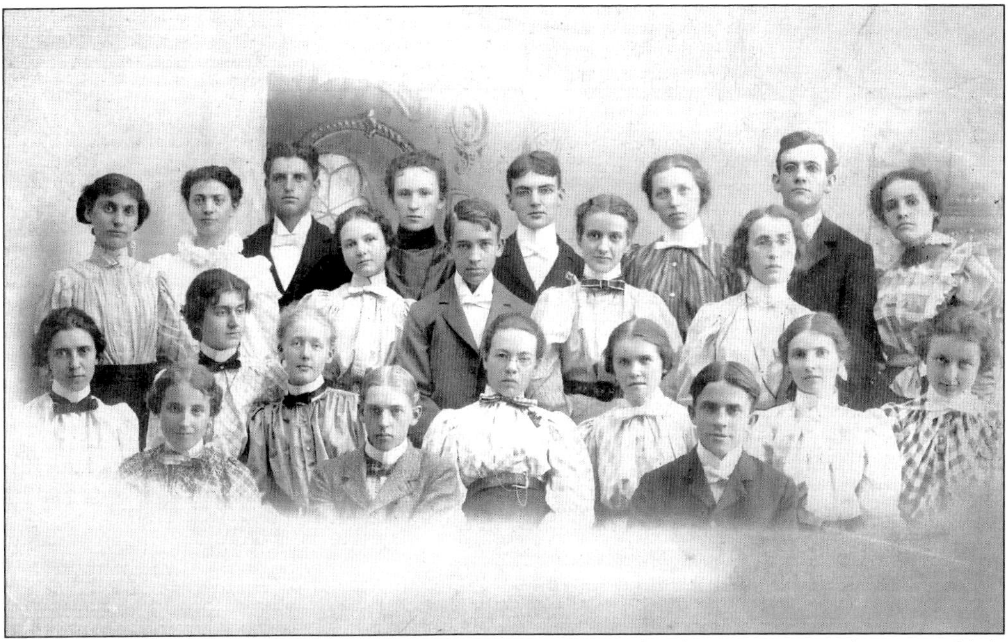

Dowagiac High School's Class of 1898, shown here, was the first Dowagiac class to publish a yearbook, titled *Once Told Tales.* According to the annual, students could graduate with specialties in one of six areas: Classical and Latin, Classical, Latin, Scientific, English, or English and German.

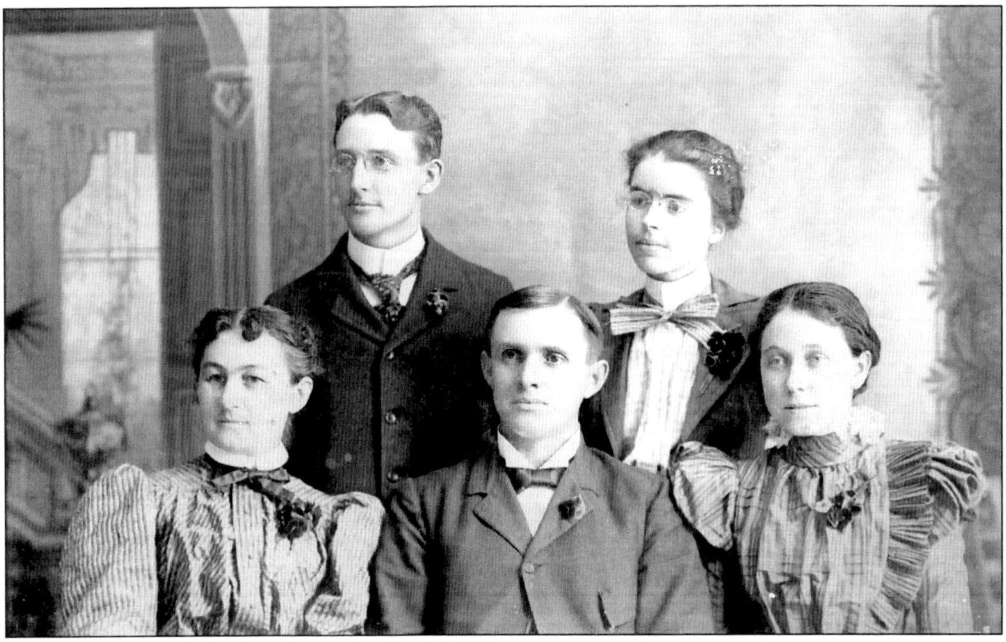

This is an 1898 photograph of the Dowagiac High School faculty. W.E. Conkling, school superintendent, is seated in the front row along with Evelyn Smith and Nettie Tyron (order unknown). George Green, the principal, and Lena Judd (soon to be Lena Judd Green) are standing. This photograph appeared in *Once Told Tales*, and according to a note accompanying the book, Lena Judd worked hard to help the students publish it.

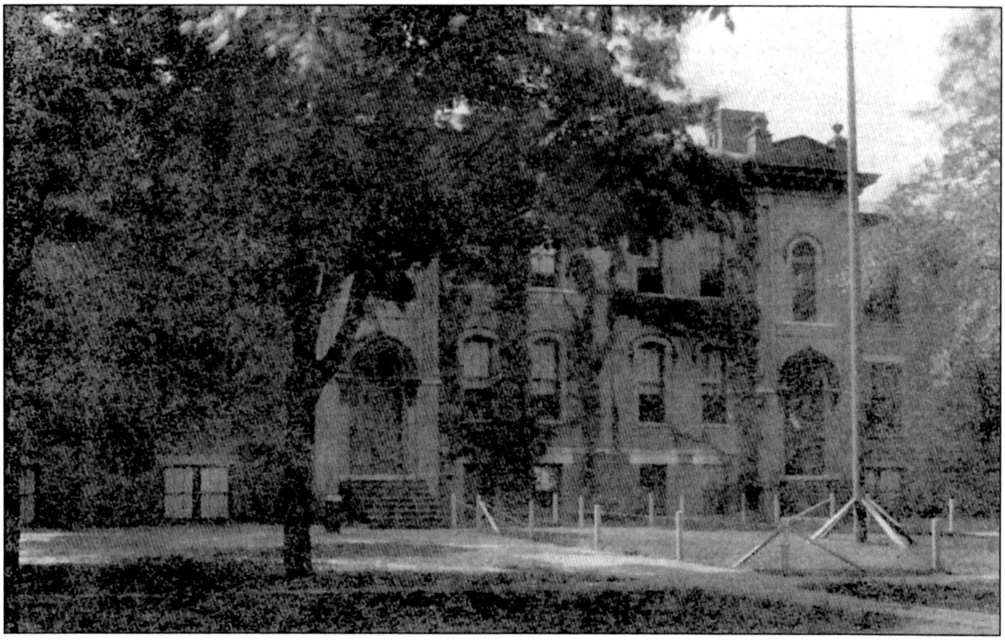

This photo shows the old Dowagiac Union School in 1901. The wings had been added by this time and the trees had grown considerably since the earlier photograph of the school. The site—Division Street and Parsonage Street—has served as a school grounds since 1856. Fire destroyed the original school house in 1859 and the city built the Dowagiac Union School in 1861 at a cost of $7,000. The building was razed in 1924 for construction of the new Central School.

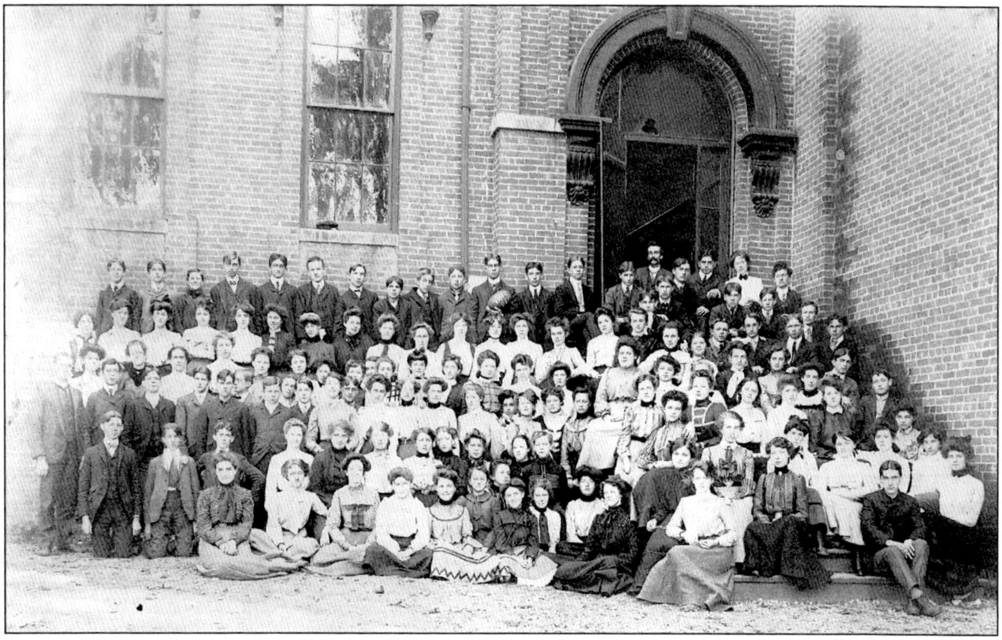

This is a 1902 image of one of the last high school classes to attend Dowagiac Union School. It appears to be the entire high school student body and one student in the back row is holding a football with "02" written on it. If the photograph was taken in the fall of 1902, this would be the last high school group at the school.

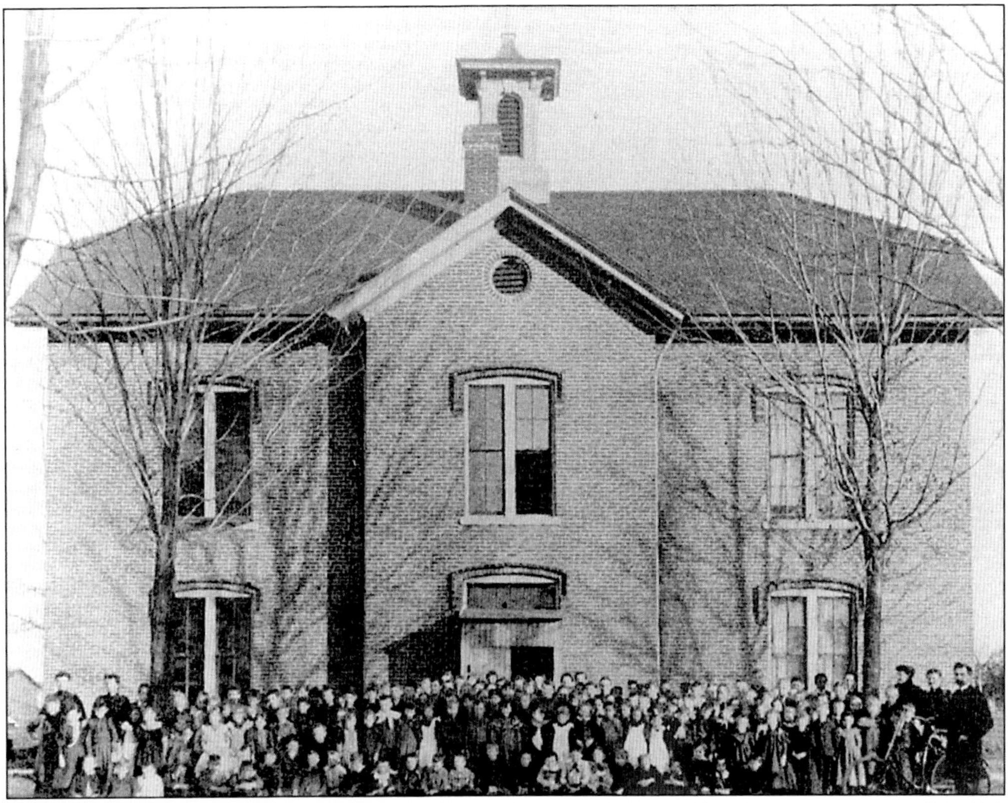

The Ward School, shown here in the 1890s, was built in 1864 on Oak Street at a cost of $5,000. It served as a primary education facility for residents of that section of town. The Ward School was expanded and reopened in 1903 serving as the high school, grade school, kindergarten, and Cass County Normal School.

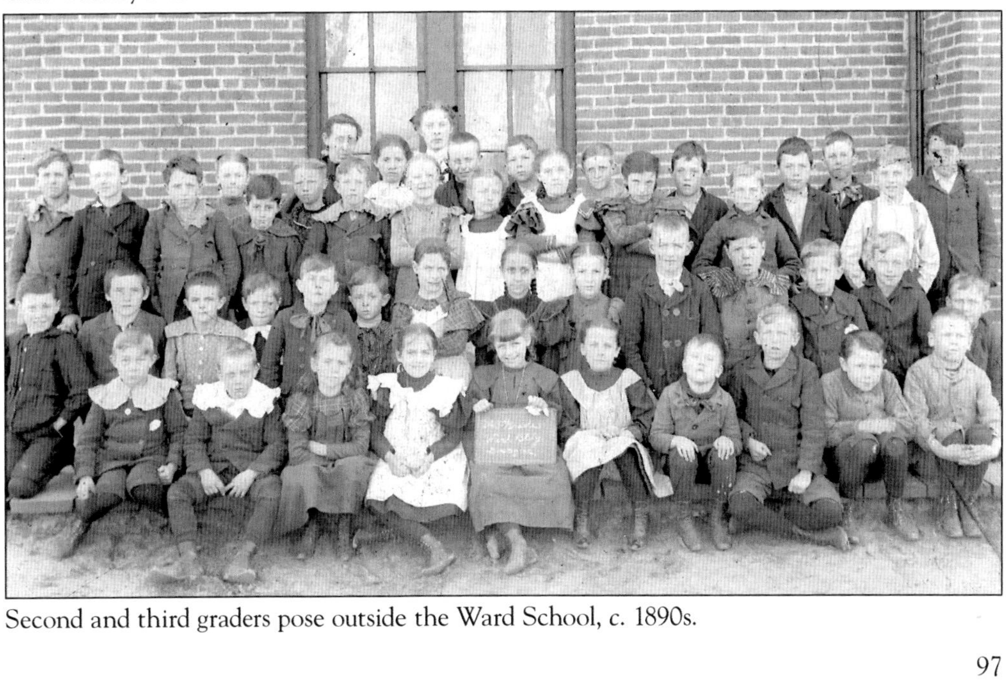

Second and third graders pose outside the Ward School, c. 1890s.

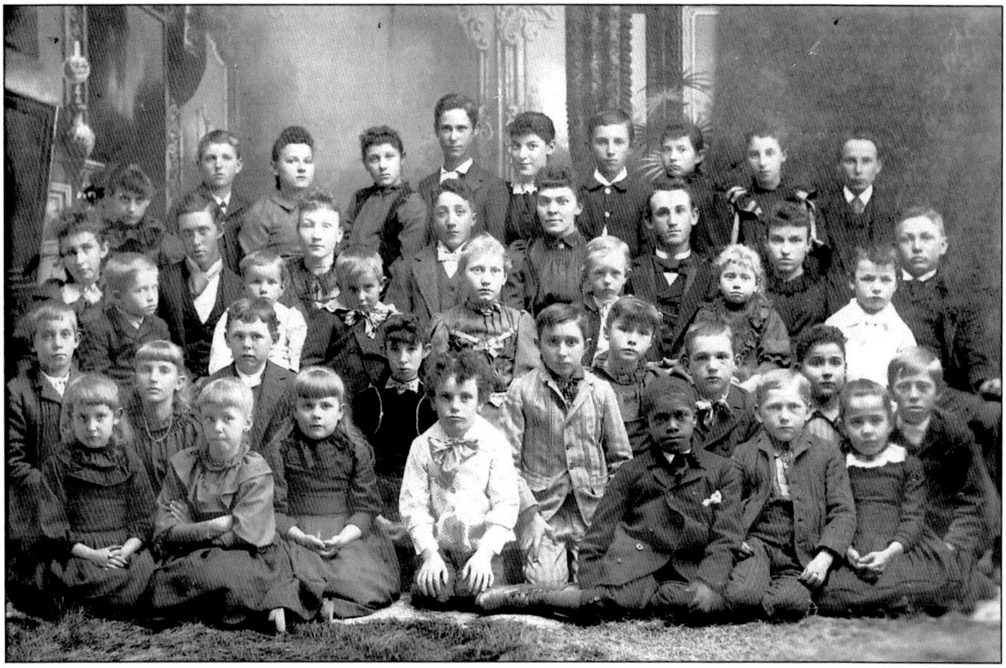

The Dowagiac area had many other schools—most in rural areas and some larger than others. Many had only one teacher and one room for all ages of children. This photograph shows the Peavine School students of 1893, taught by Ava Sink Judd. Peavine School was south of the city on Peavine Road in Pokagon Township.

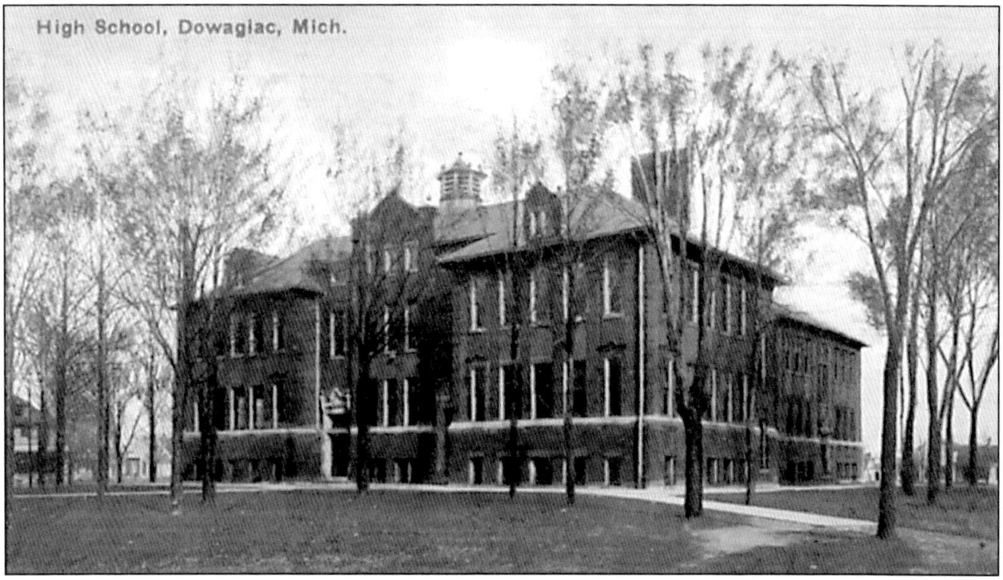

This commercial postcard shows the Dowagiac High School building on Oak Street—formerly the Ward School. As this photo shows, the addition made to the Ward School was substantial. The Ward School section of the building was in the rear and was still used as a kindergarten and first grade. This school served both as the high school and grade school—high school on the second floor and grade school on the first floor. The building was used as the high school until 1926.

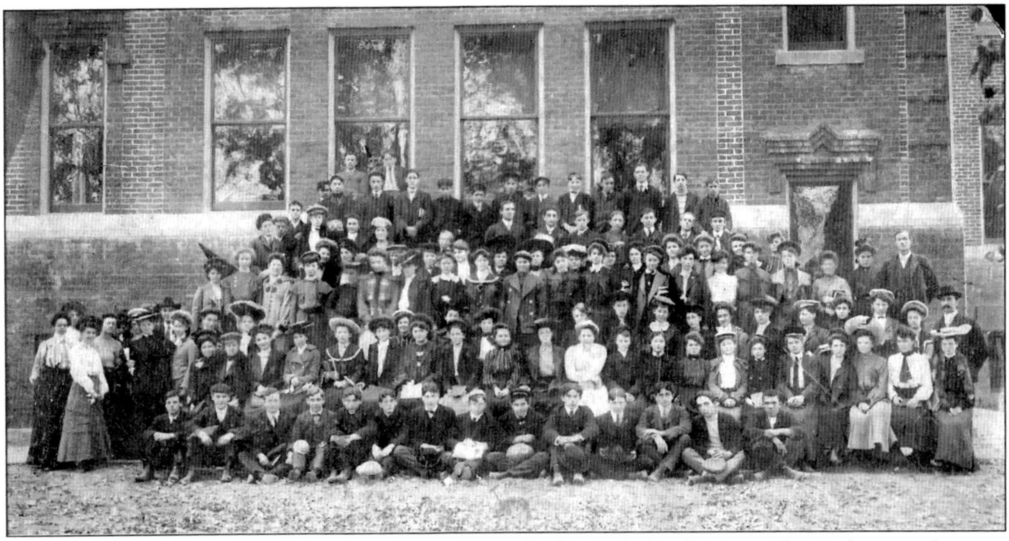

This photograph of the high school student body and faculty may have been taken to commemorate the opening of the new school building in 1903. Two boys, one in the front row center and one in top row left, hold footballs with "03" on them, dating the photograph to the first fall the school was used. Standing in the center of the photograph is longtime school superintendent and Dowagiac High School alumnus (Class of 1881), W.E. Conkling.

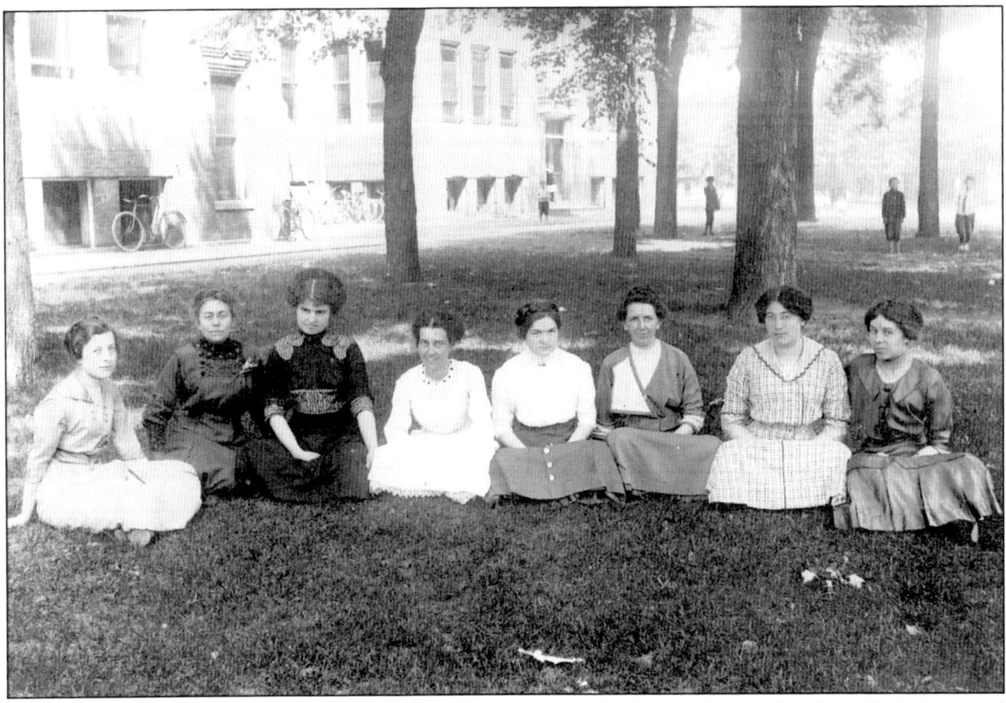

The Oak Street School (grade school) teachers pose on the lawn of the school in 1910. Pictured are, from left to right: Bessie Stahl, Tera Southworth, E'Lora Root, Eva Brown, Alleyne Gilbert, Nellie Dunning, Amy Acton, and Katheryn Born. Stahl and Gilbert graduated from Dowagiac High School in 1909 and probably attended the Cass County Normal School during the year after their high school graduation.

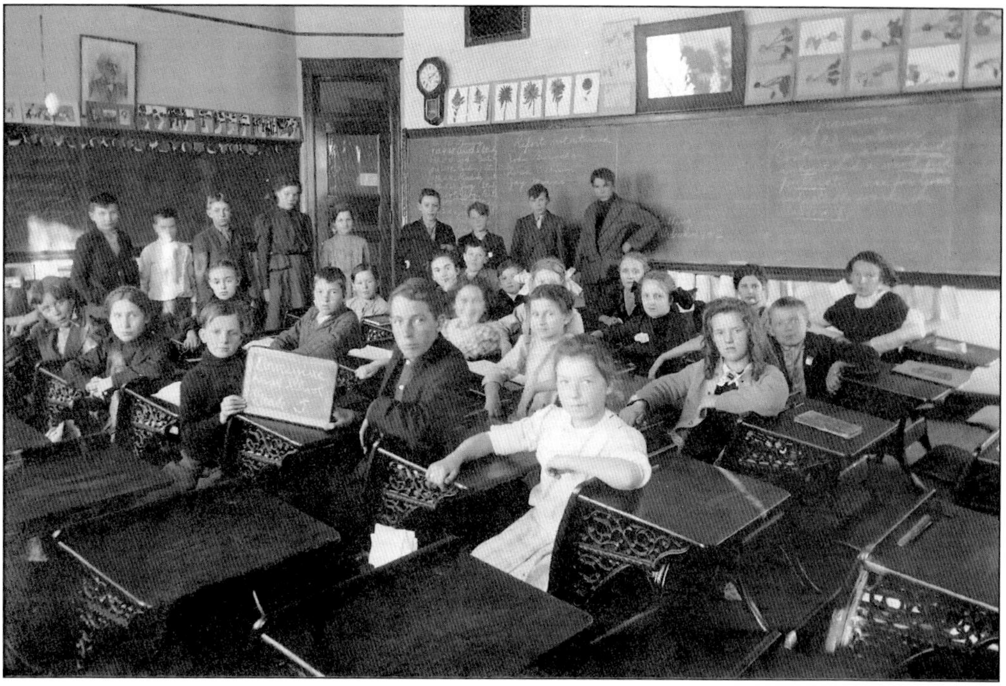

Other photographs documented some of the classrooms in the new school. This photo is the fifth grade class in the Oak Street School. Below is the high school chemistry lab in 1903. According to the 1904 yearbook, Mr. James Weyant was the teacher of this class.

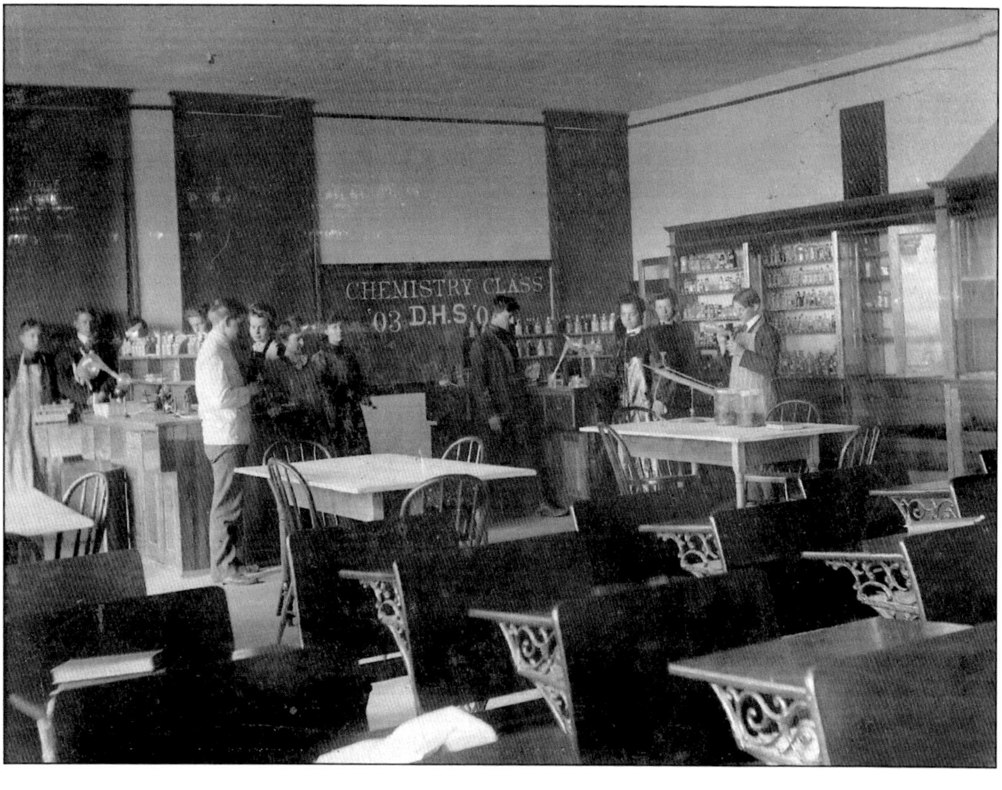

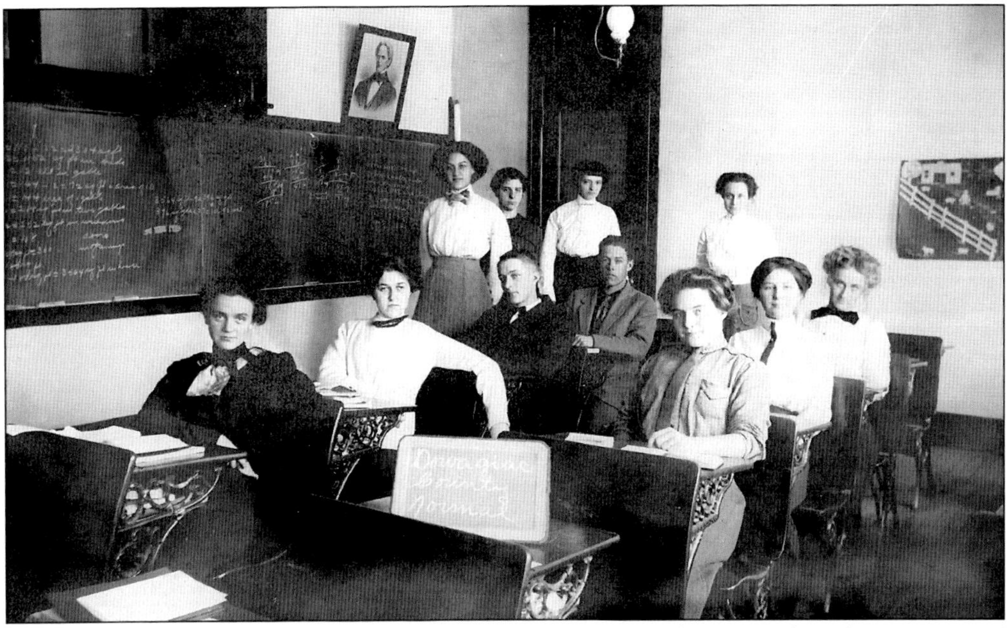

Future teachers pose inside a Dowagiac classroom in 1912. The state of Michigan operated a system of schools, called Normal schools, to train high school graduates to be teachers. Classrooms in the school on Oak Street were used for the Cass County Normal School, which remained active into the late 1950s. The students are identified from left to right: (right row) Frances Smith, Madge Straub (or Nellie Curtis), and Imo Kreighbaum; (left row) Rosamond Hurst, Maybelle Westfall, Lisle Stevens, and Ellwood Hathaway; and (standing) Anna Pearl Jones, Ethel Savage, Shirley Ross, and Loretta Fitzpatrick, the teacher.

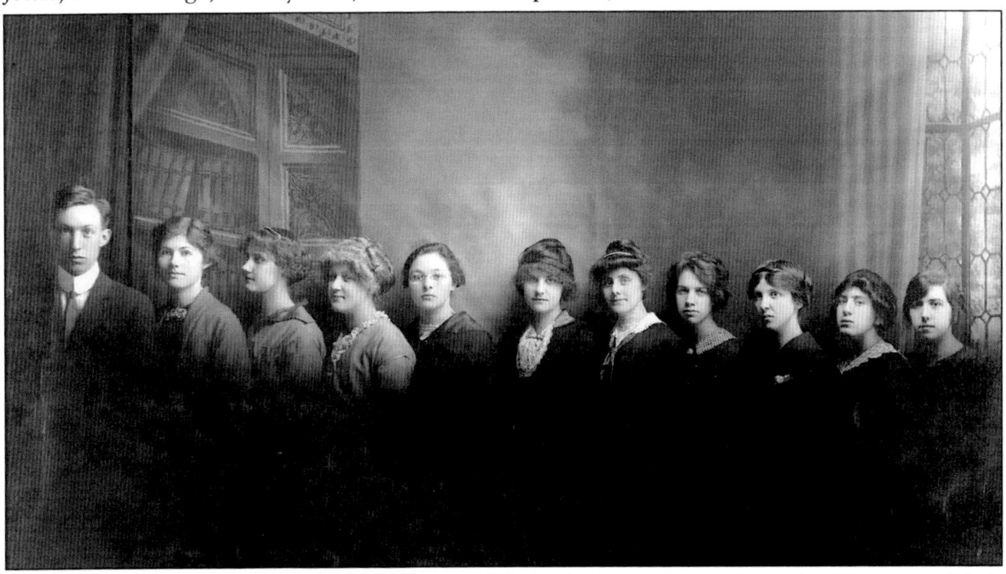

This photograph of the 1914 Cass County Normal class appeared in the Dowagiac High School yearbook, *The Advance*. From left to right are the following: Herman Bower, La Verne Argabright, Harriet Van Antwerp, Wilma Stevens, Geneva Ratliff, Cleo Cligh, Loretta Fitzpatrick (principal), Lois Tice, Lois Paxson, Jane Brown, and Helen McKenzie. Mabel and Hazel Shepherdson also graduated with the class but are not pictured.

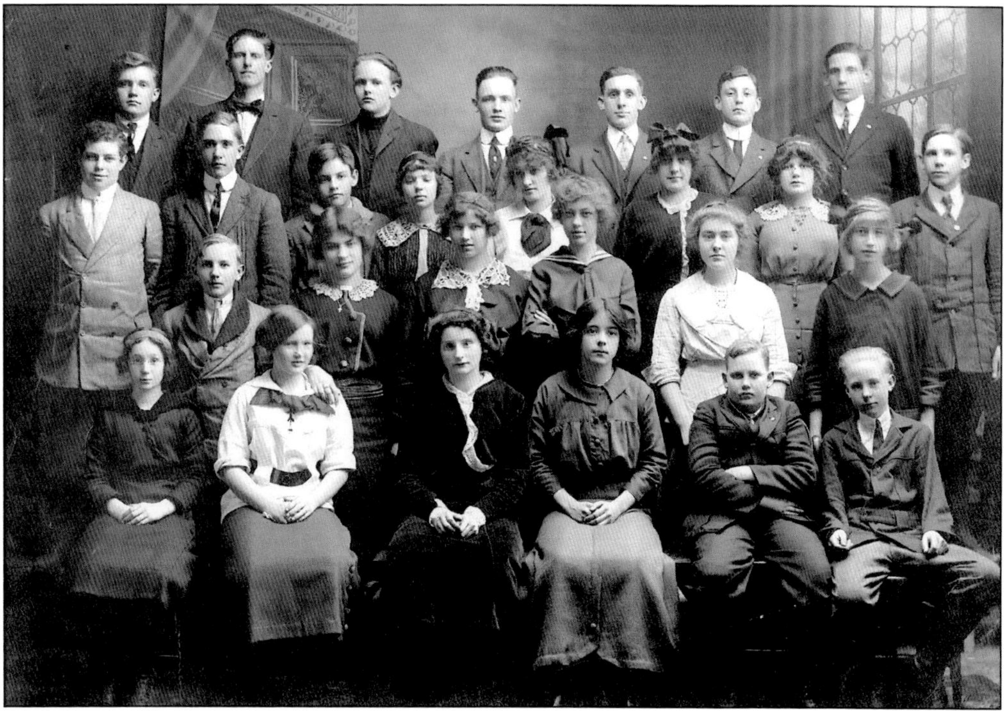

Dowagiac High School class sizes quickly grew after the new high school was opened in 1903. Fourteen students graduated in 1903, the last year in the old school. In 1909, 19 students graduated and in 1913 there were 21 graduates. This photograph is one of two needed to show the freshman class in 1914—there were 76 students in the class altogether. The growth in class size can be attributed to several factors, including the growing population of Dowagiac and the increased importance adults placed upon education for their children.

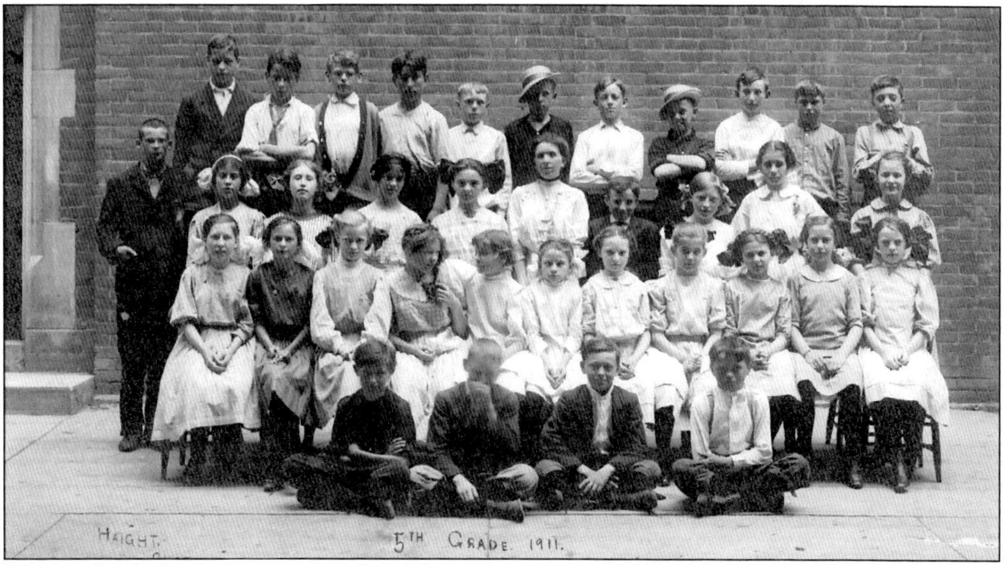

This is the fifth grade class outside of the Dowagiac High School building on Oak Street in 1911. Nellie Dunning, shown in an earlier photograph with her fellow teachers, is standing in the center of the photograph.

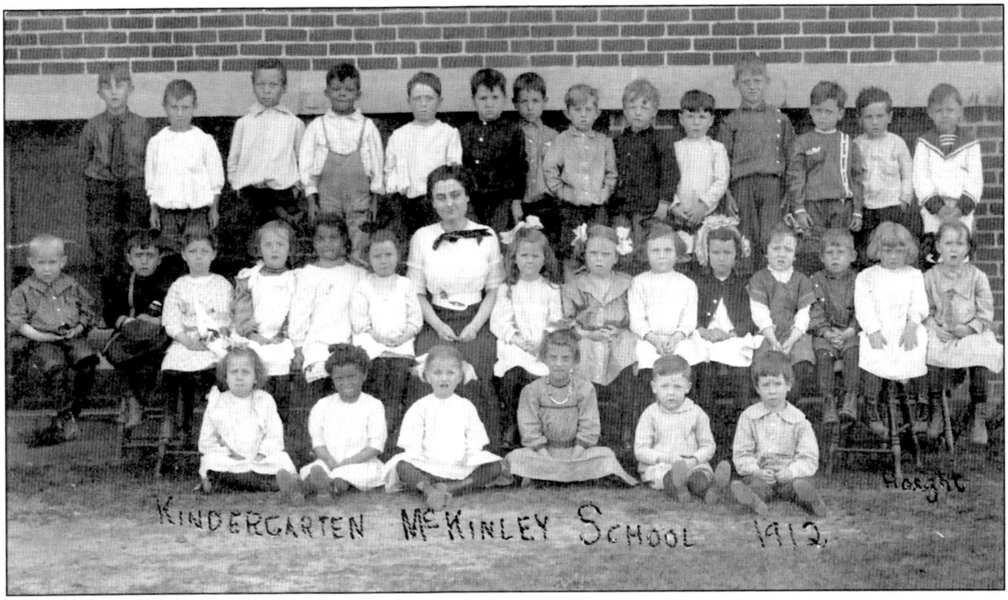

This image shows the 1912 McKinley School kindergarten class. The school was built on the south side of Dowagiac in 1903 on the training ground and encampment site of the 19th Michigan Infantry during the Civil War. Originally a four-room schoolhouse for six grades, McKinley underwent major renovations over the years and is still housing Dowagiac students.

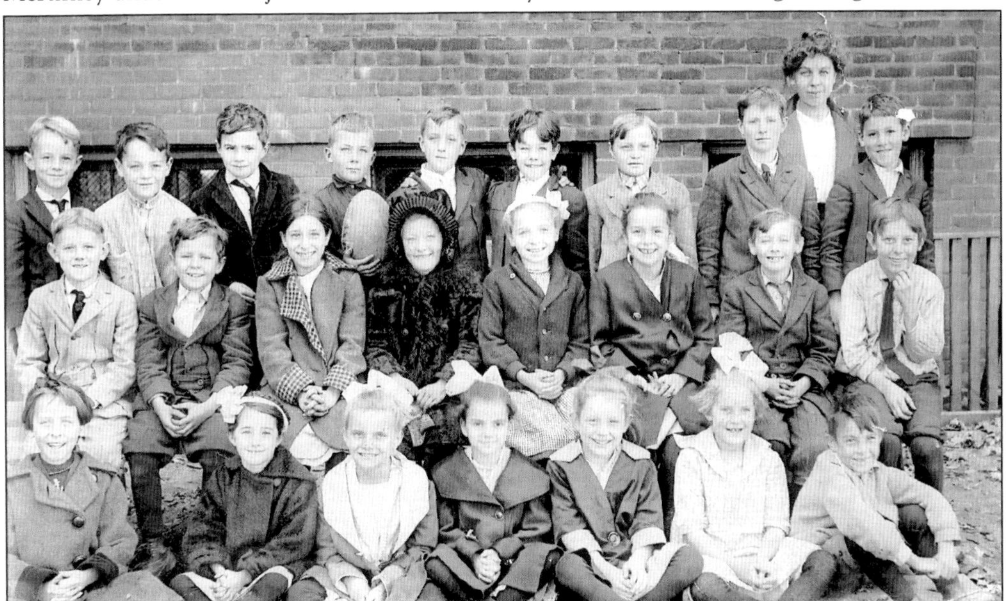

This is the Oak Street School third grade class of teacher Katheryn Born in 1914. The students are identified as, from left to right: (front row) Lena Phillips, Maybelle Sampson, Lila Gawthorop, Dorothy Avery, Evelyn Moulthrop, Helen Dunn, and Ernest Smith; (middle row) Ronald Paxson, Hugh Claspy, Mary Belsito, Gail Peterson, Marguerite Lonsberry, Beatrice Warner, Ralph Osborne, and Earl Rose; and (back row) Howard Paxson, Harold Reisch, Ray Wilson, Dick Reynolds, Kermit Dawes, Henry Springsteen, Rudolph Shenk, Malcolm Broadhurst, Katheryn Born, and Harold Aldridge.

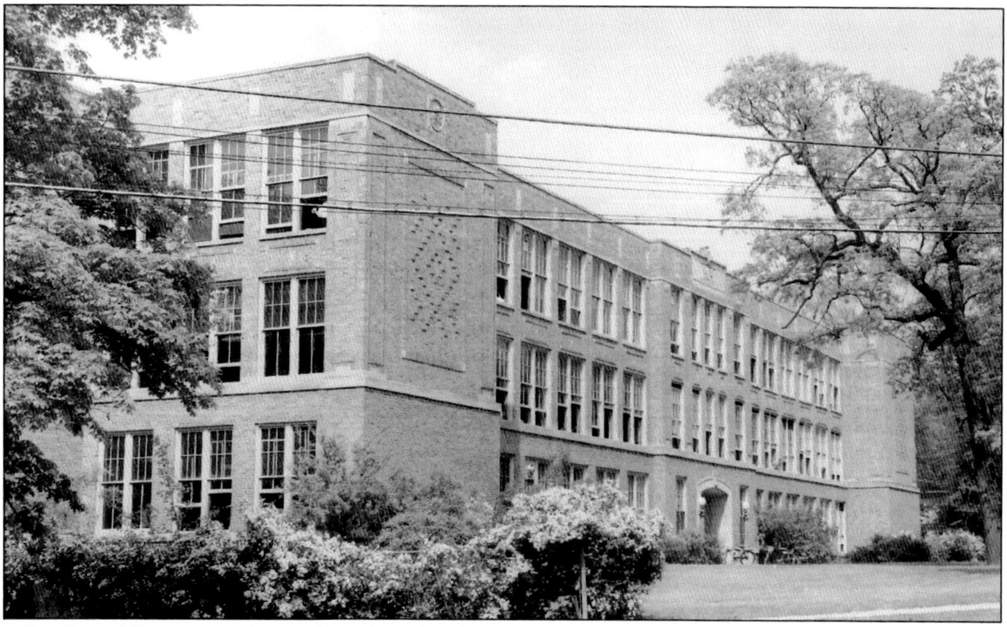

The "new" Dowagiac Central High School is pictured here; it opened in 1926. This building was erected on the site of the old Dowagiac Union School, erected in 1861 and torn down in 1924. This building served as the high school until 1962 and as a middle school until 2005.

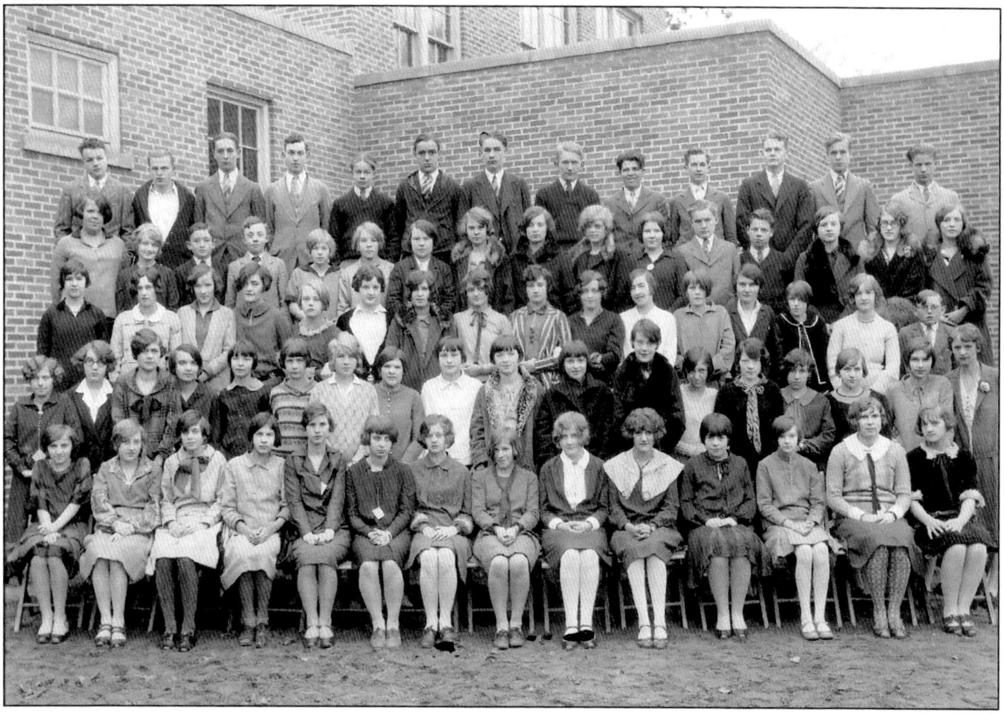

The 1928 Dowagiac High School glee club poses outside the new school. The 1928 yearbook, *The Wahoo*, mentioned that the club was taught by Mrs. Grace McLeod, at far right in the second row of this photograph. This is a large group—according to *The Wahoo*, enrollment was much larger than in previous years—and the boys and girls were taught separately.

Nine

A Sports Town

Whether a leisurely round of golf or an organized high school football game, sports have long played a role in Dowagiac society. Because there have been no professional teams (though Round Oak did have some professional players on its roster in the 1800s), high school athletics have spurred great interest among local citizens.

Of the major sports played today, baseball has the earliest documented history in Dowagiac. The first baseball club in Michigan was formed in Detroit in 1859; by 1861 Dowagiac had one of only nine teams in the state. In 1867, Dowagiac had two clubs, including the Fernaughts, and the city was one of two in the state to attempt to form a women's club—this was unsuccessful.

By the 1880s and 1890s, baseball was firmly established in Dowagiac; the City Leagues formed in the 20th century. As with many things in Dowagiac, the Round Oak Stove Company sponsored a baseball team, formed in 1887. It was very popular and the company continued to sponsor a team into the 1940s.

Dowagiac High School has had organized sports since the 1890s. R.V. Hinkle was the first documented athletic director at the school in 1907. The first football team was organized in 1896 under George Green. Over the past 110 years the team has achieved various degrees of success. Basketball was only intermittently played due to a lack of a high school gymnasium. The first documented team was the 1907 squad, which became the unofficial state champions—a feat not achieved since. The girls also had a basketball team, from 1907–1911 and during some years in the 1910s and 1920s. When the new school was built in 1926, it included a gymnasium, and basketball became a regular high school sport.

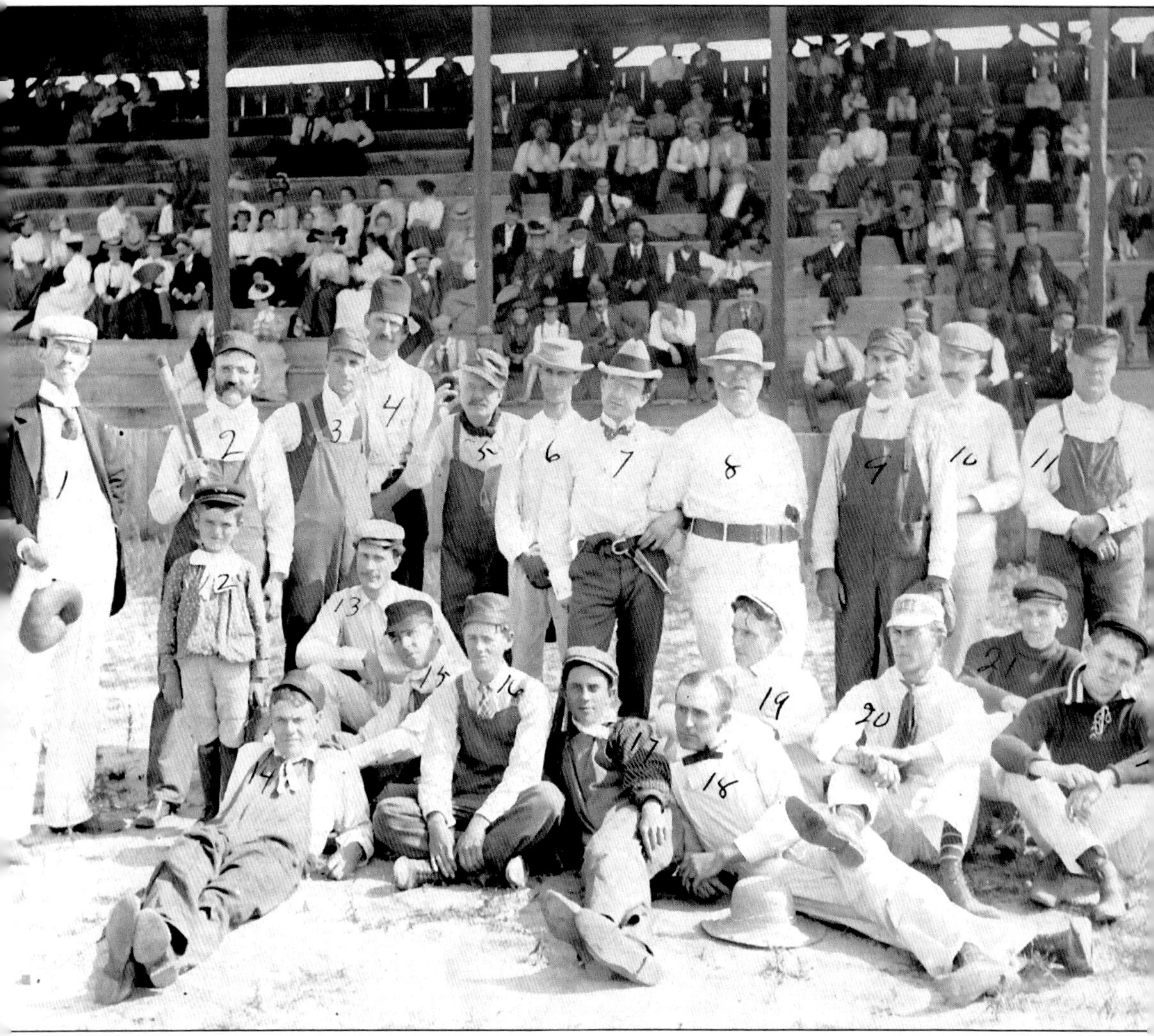

This photograph is titled "The Doctors vs. the Leans" and dates to the late 1890s. One team is composed of Dowagiac doctors and the other is a team of "upstarts." The men numbered "7" and "8" are the umpires and are both wearing sidearms.

The Round Oak Stove Company began sponsoring a baseball team in 1887. The owner, P.D. Beckwith, even set aside part of the company grounds for a baseball field. There was a Round Oak team for most of the next 60 years, with brief interruptions. This is a photo of the 1888 team and the players are, from left to right: (front row) P.H. Welch and Arthur Klock; (second row) Charles Hadding, George Hall, Henry Porter (manager), G.H. Flagg, and Elmer Neff; and (third row) W. Mumbry, A.J. Blair, E. Cullinine, and Henry Larzelere.

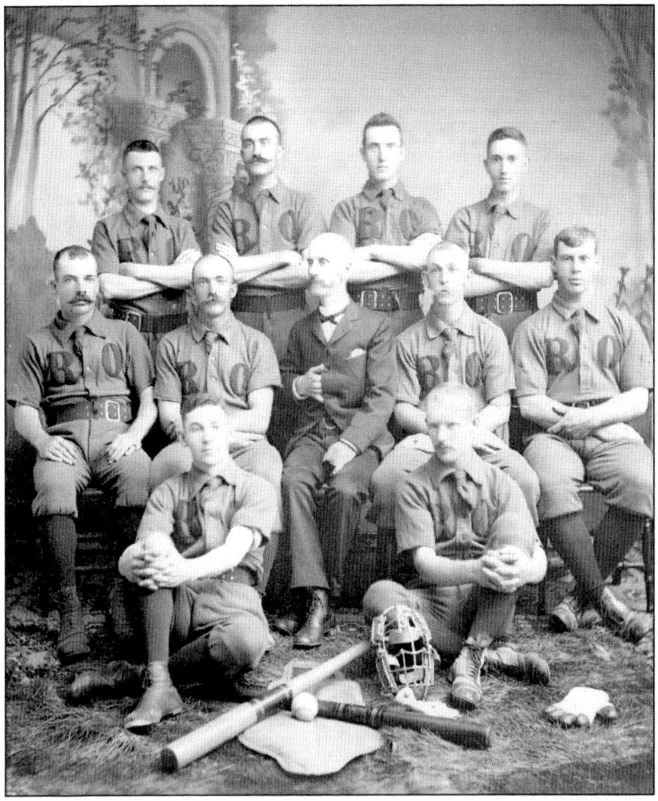

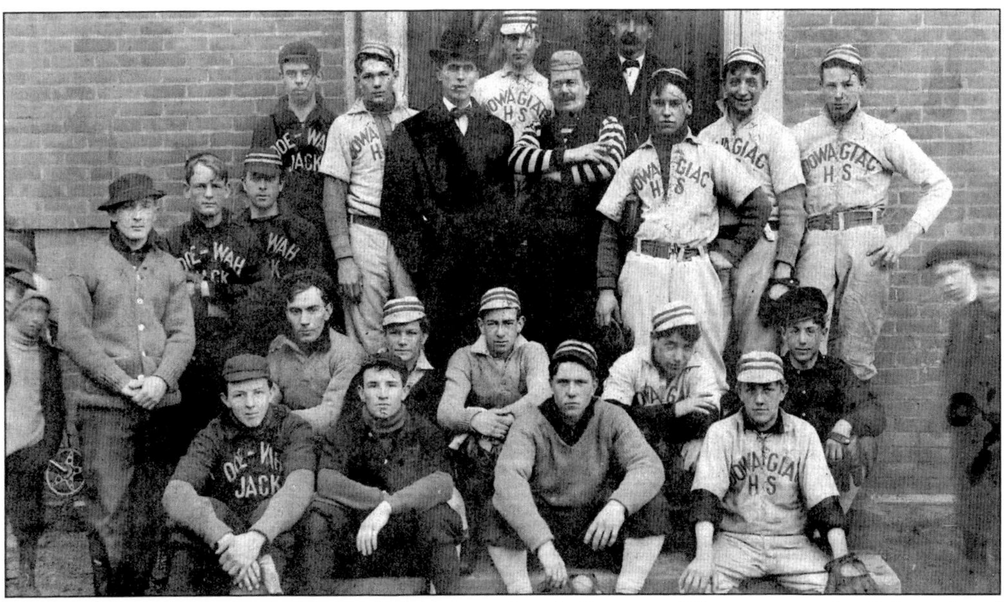

This photograph is dated 1904 and shows two baseball teams. The team in the light colored uniforms is from Dowagiac High School and the team in dark uniforms may be another high school team or the city team, the Doe-Wah-Jacks.

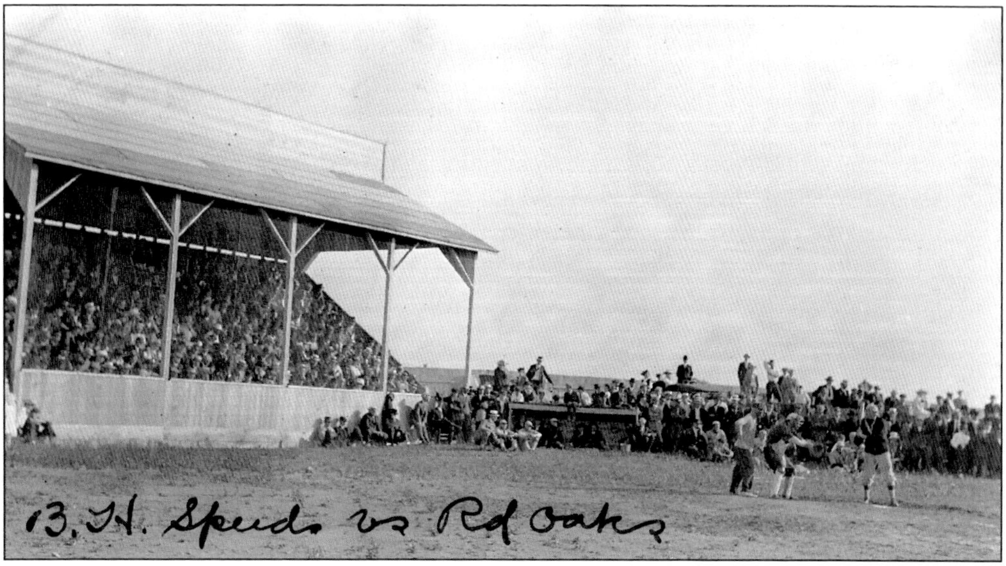

This photo shows the Round Oak baseball team in action against the Benton Harbor Speeds in 1915. Comparing this photo with the postcard below leads the authors to believe that this was taken at Dowagiac's baseball diamond.

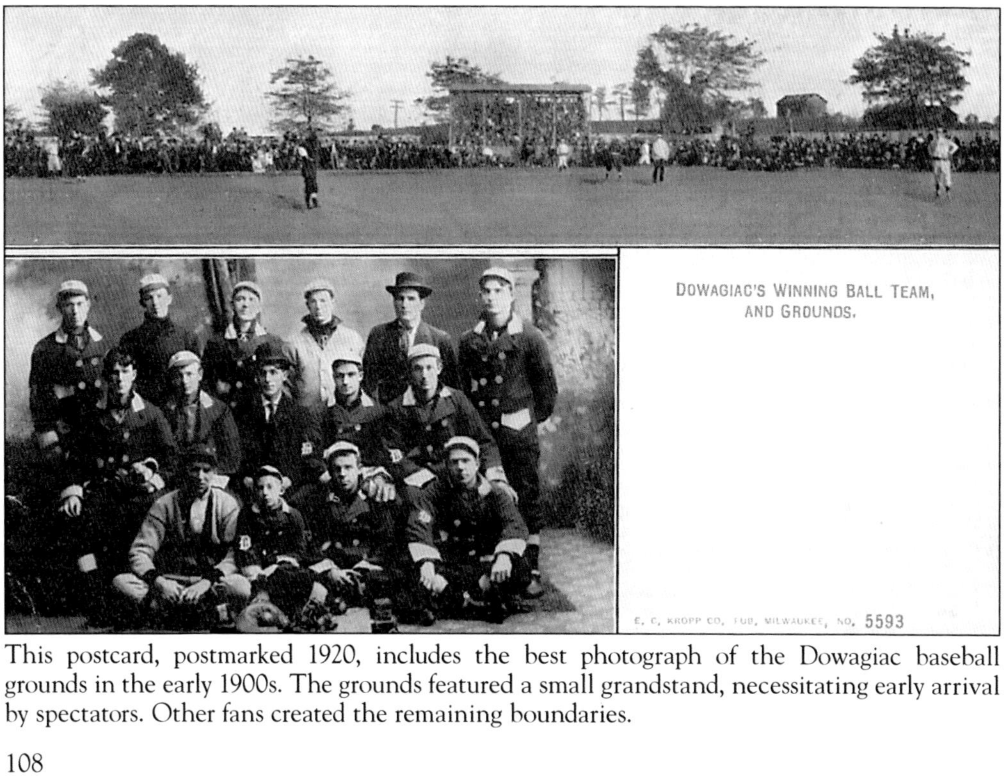

This postcard, postmarked 1920, includes the best photograph of the Dowagiac baseball grounds in the early 1900s. The grounds featured a small grandstand, necessitating early arrival by spectators. Other fans created the remaining boundaries.

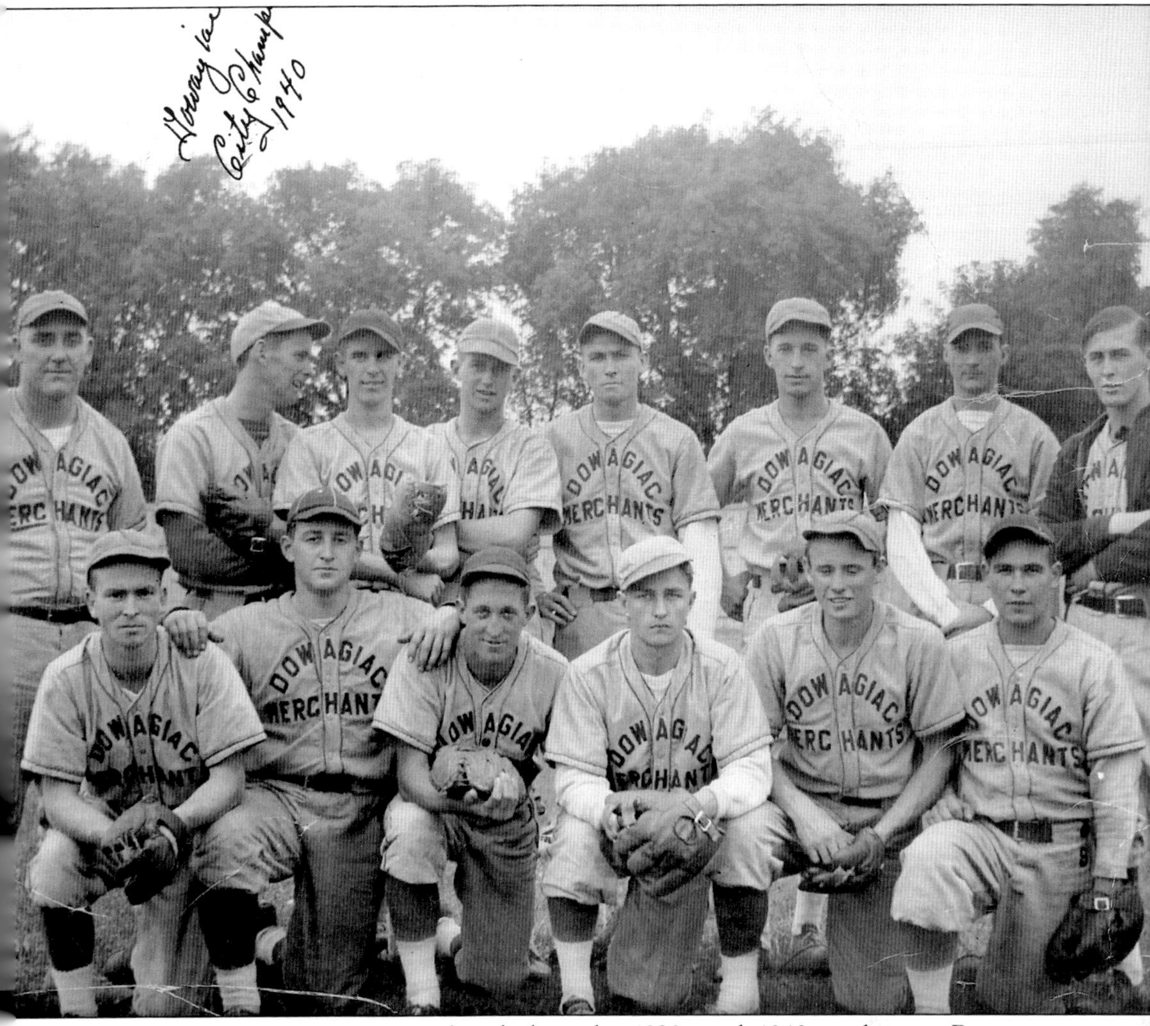

The Dowagiac City League was a big deal in the 1930s and 1940s and many Dowagiac businesses sponsored teams, including the Rudy Furnace Company, the Heddon Lure Company, and Round Oak. Formed in 1939, the Dowagiac Merchants team was sponsored by some of the downtown businesses and was composed of recent Dowagiac High School graduates. They made a good showing in 1939 before losing to Round Oak in the championship. In 1940, the Merchants won the championship before disbanding for five years during World War II. The team got back together in 1946 and won the championship one last time. Pictured are, from left to right, as follows: (front row) Erwin "Bud" Pond, Dave Moore, Bob Jessup, Don Griffis, Dan Brosnan, and Dick Bowers; and (back row) Mike Mott, Byron Rice, William "Cremo" Heimstra, Gerald "Bud" Rose, Joe Bartak, Jim Jessup, Gene Cowham, and Herb Schramm.

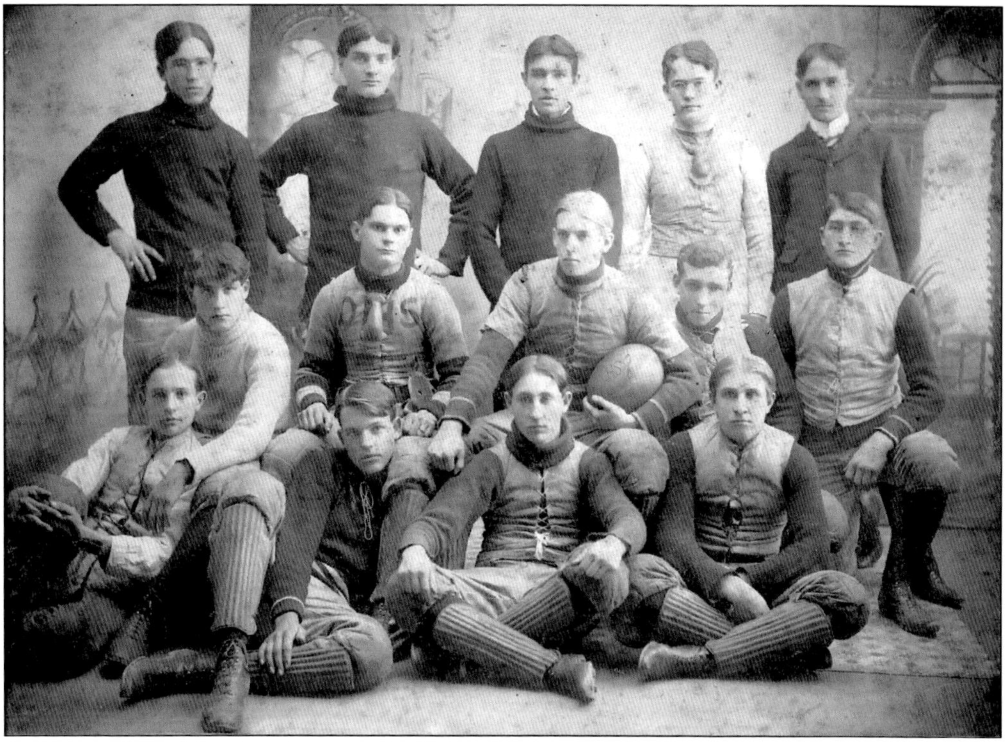

Dowagiac High School had its first football team in 1896 under George Green as coach. This is the 1898 team, and according to player Virgil Blanchard, the team had "no coach, usually someone from downtown who had played, Abe Oppenheim was one." Blanchard, pictured at the far right in the middle row, lived near Berrien Center and rode his bicycle to Dowagiac High School.

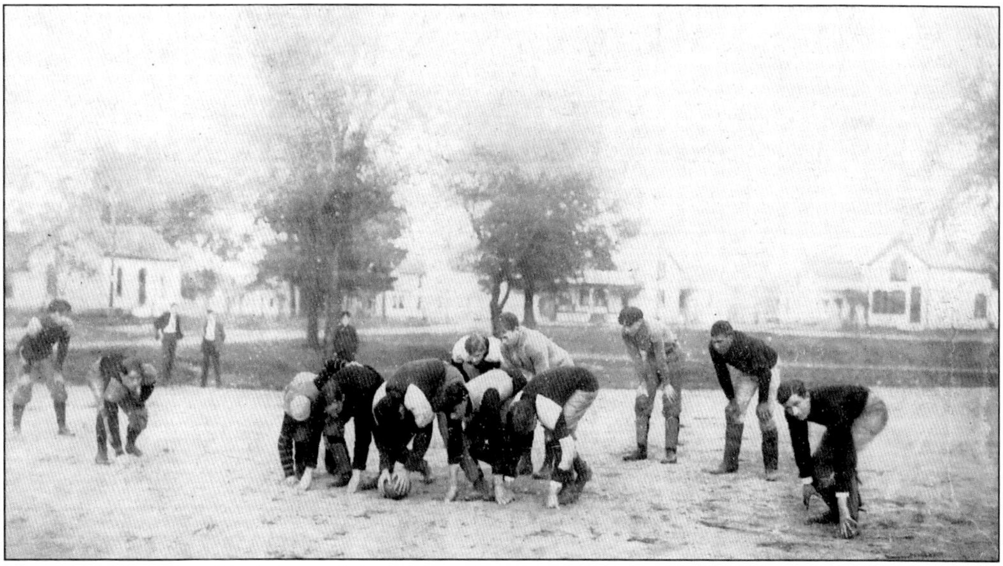

The 1903 Dowagiac High School football team practiced on a new field at the new high school grounds on Oak Street. Arch King, whose presence shows that the Dowagiac school and sports systems were integrated long before it was a national practice, is pictured second from right.

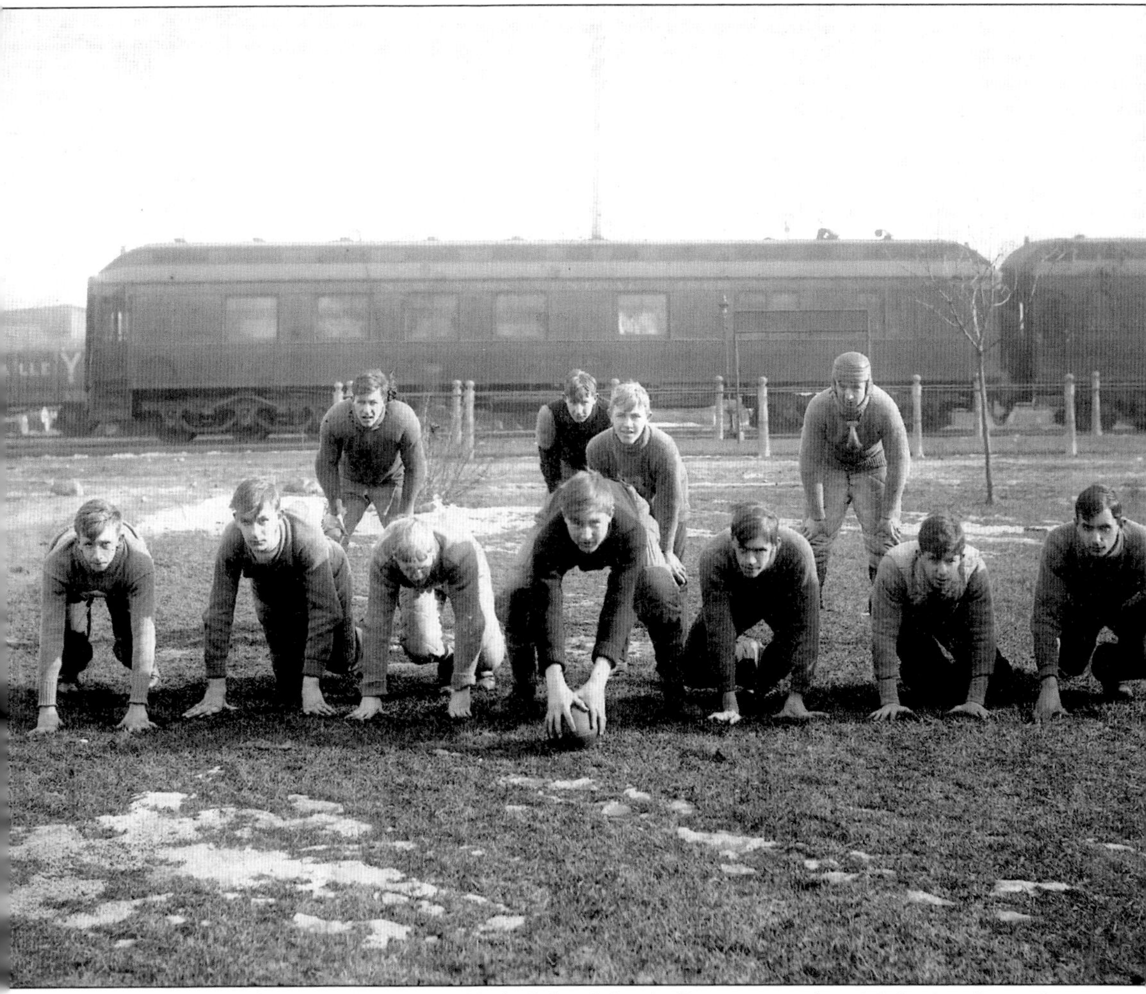

This photo shows the 1907 Dowagiac High School football team posed in Michigan Central Railroad Park. The linemen are identified from left to right: March Wells (right end), Carl Luke (right tackle), Lyle Stebbins (right guard), Ralph Stafford (center), Harry Parsons (left guard), Harvey Campbell (left tackle), and Harry White (left end). Behind the line are Gus Lindsley (right halfback), Harry Jones (fullback), Herman Rutter (quarterback), and Ford Lake (left halfback).

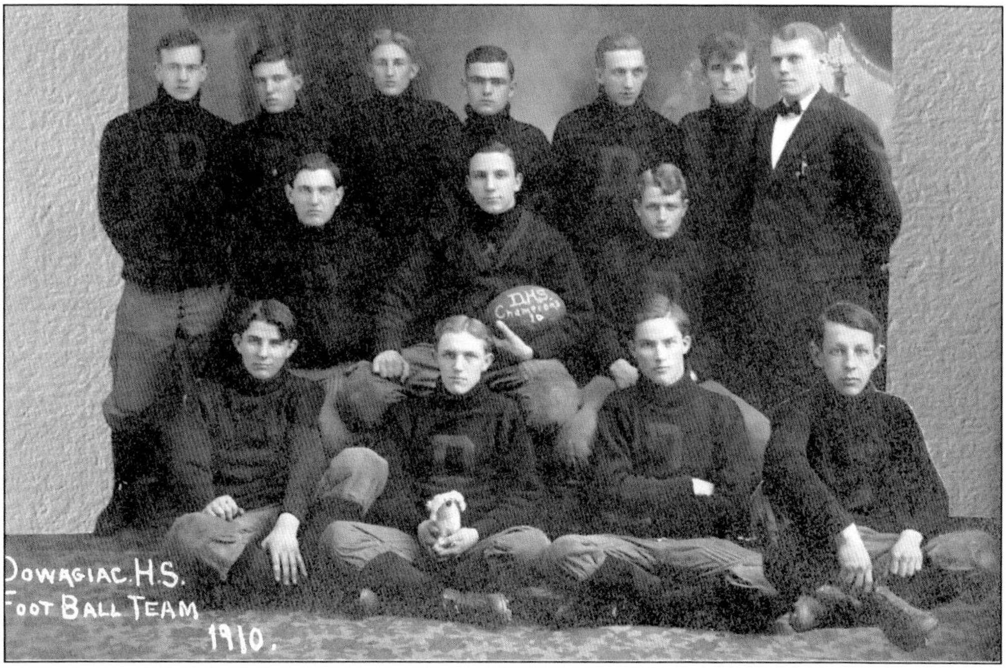

Though it is labeled as the 1910 team, this is the Dowagiac High School team that played in the 1909 football season. This team beat archrival Niles twice: 63–0 and 33–0. The yearbook notes that they held what may have been the first pep rally in Dowagiac history. "On the night before the first game, an 'agitation' meeting was held on campus. A large bonfire of boxes gave an excellent light, in which the D.H.S. yells were practiced and speeches were made by members of the school board, faculty, and team. This was a new stunt and succeeded in arousing considerable interest."

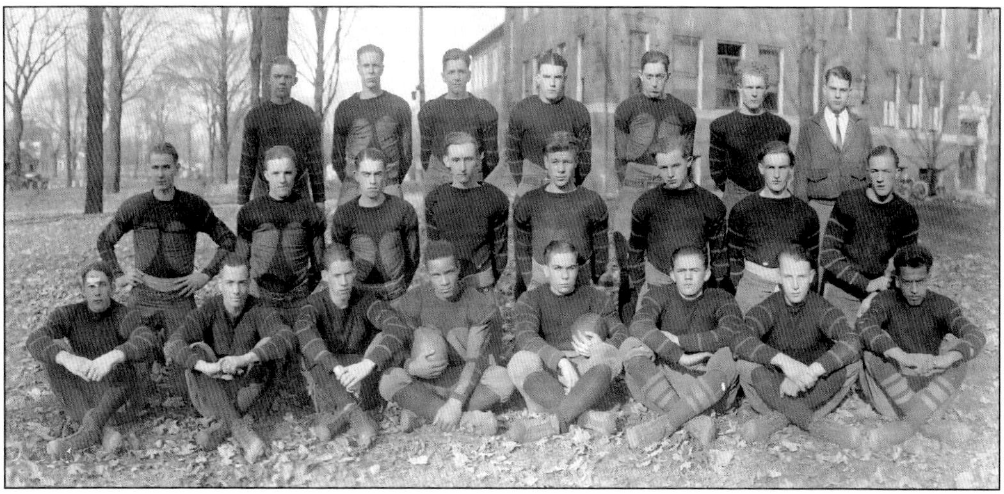

The 1924 Dowagiac High School football team went 6–3–1. They are posed here on the lawn of the high school on Oak Street, from left to right: (front row) Howard Billington, Earl Steimle, Oral Alriedge, Glenn White, Louis Lonsbury, Elmer Metras, Maurice Moulthrop, and Harold Wyne; (second row) Don Lamoreaux, Jake Mather, Gifford Fox, George Mersereau, Steven Martin, William Murrell, Ralph Burling, and Billie Barszcz; and (back row) John Metras, Paul Lieber, Wayne Maher, Dean Parrish, Max Allen, George V. Wilson, and Maurice Rector (captain).

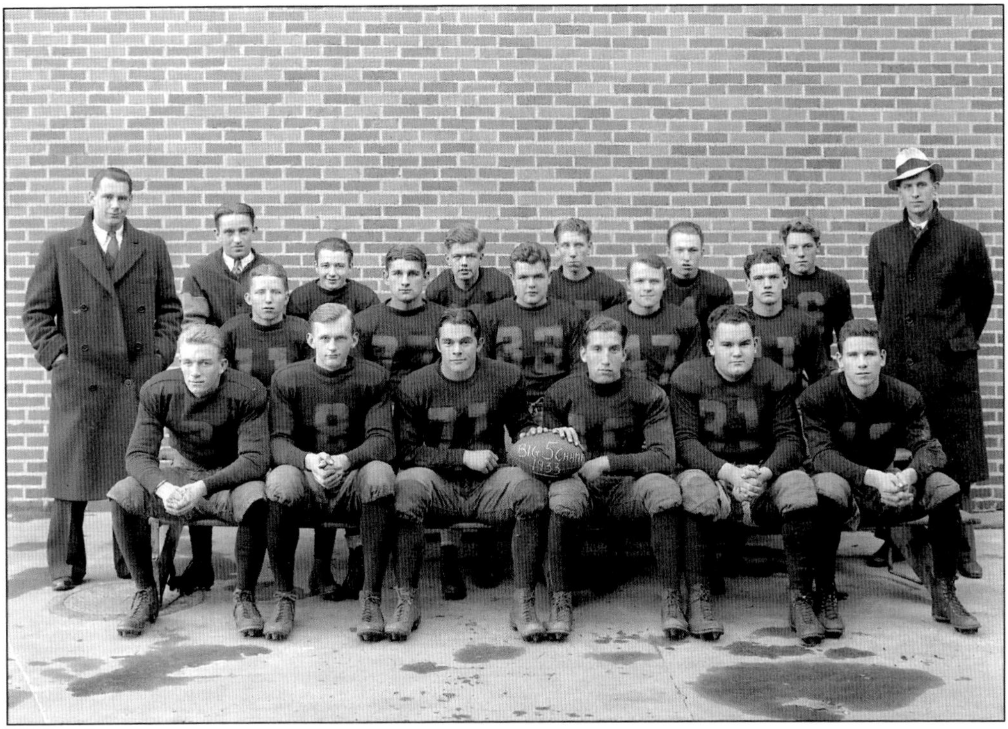

The 1933 Dowagiac High School football team was the first to repeat as Big-5 Conference champions. The team outscored its opponents that year 129–53 in marching to a 6–1–1 record. Pictured front row center with the football are captains Lee Zelner and Martin Kneller. Arthur Frontczak, seated second from the left in the second row, was voted to the All-State team that year. Standing at left is Assistant Coach Orra Morningstar, and standing at right is Head Coach James Lewis.

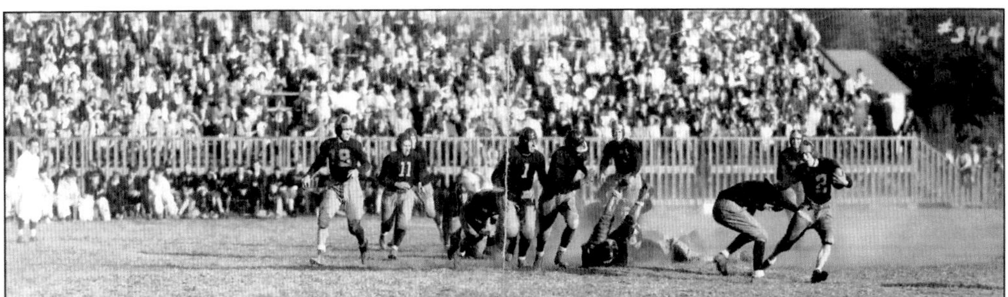

This action photo shows Dowagiac halfback Gordon Smith carrying the football during the school's homecoming game against St. Joseph on October 10, 1934. The game ended in a 6–6 tie despite runs of 40 and 43 yards by Smith. This is the first year that spectators enjoyed the large grandstands in the background, which were erected that season.

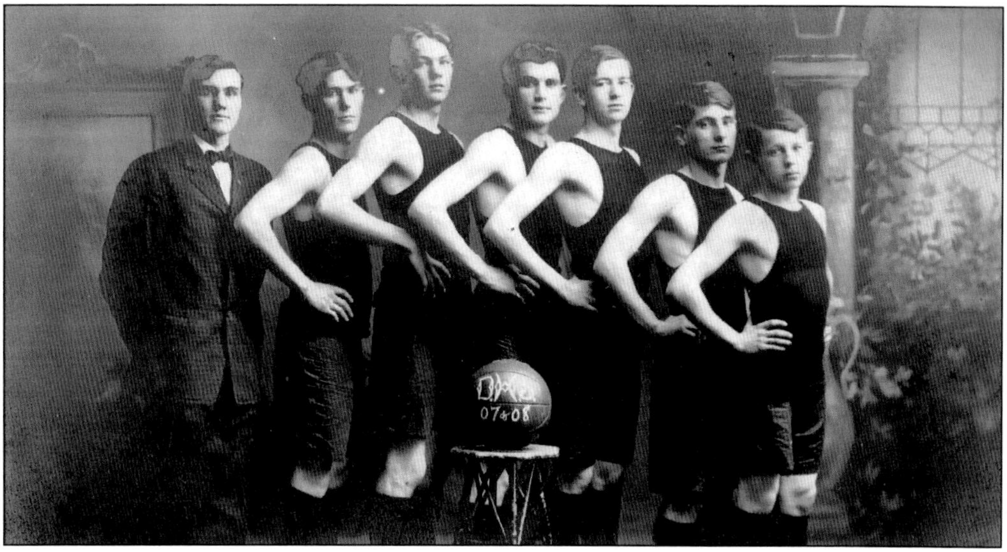

The 1907–1908 standout basketball team did not even have its own gymnasium. Instead they played at the old Round Oak Hall. The team, coached by J.C. Clarke, played so well against local teams, that they challenged the larger Kalamazoo High School to a game. According to the 1908 DHS yearbook, Kalamazoo condescended, and played a "practice" game against the smaller Dowagiac . . . and was beaten 35–21, giving Dowagiac the unofficial championship of southern Michigan. The locals then challenged Grand Rapids, who visited Dowagiac and were beaten 28–23 . . . after Grand Rapids led 19–8 at halftime! This gave Dowagiac the title of "The Championship Basketball Team of Michigan."

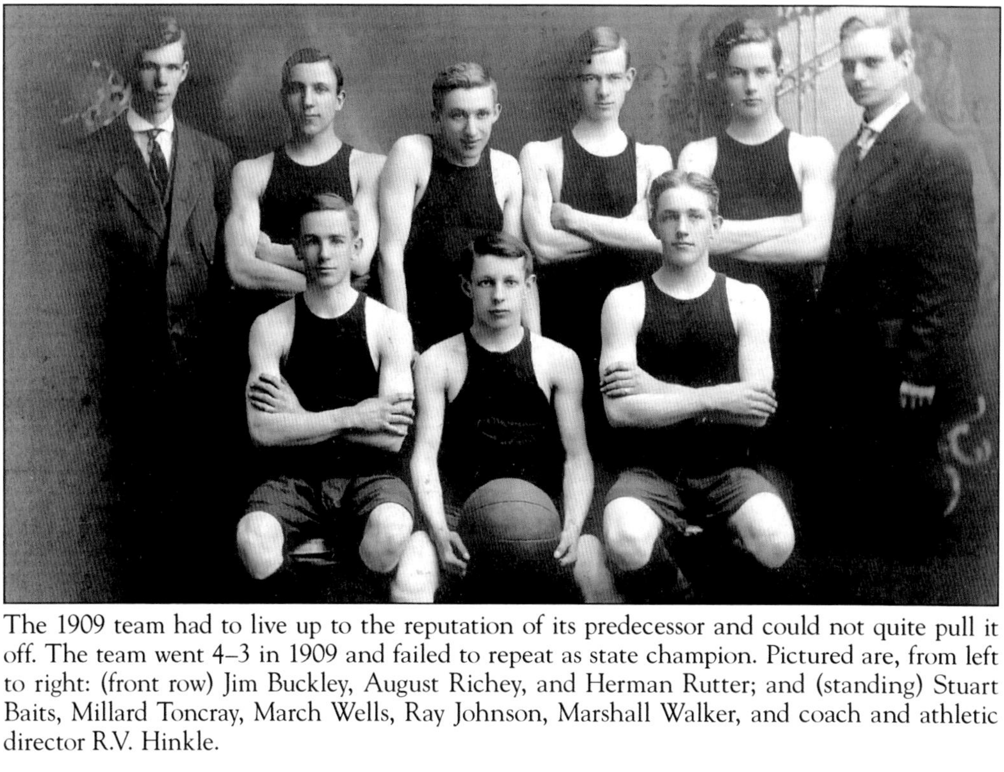

The 1909 team had to live up to the reputation of its predecessor and could not quite pull it off. The team went 4–3 in 1909 and failed to repeat as state champion. Pictured are, from left to right: (front row) Jim Buckley, August Richey, and Herman Rutter; and (standing) Stuart Baits, Millard Toncray, March Wells, Ray Johnson, Marshall Walker, and coach and athletic director R.V. Hinkle.

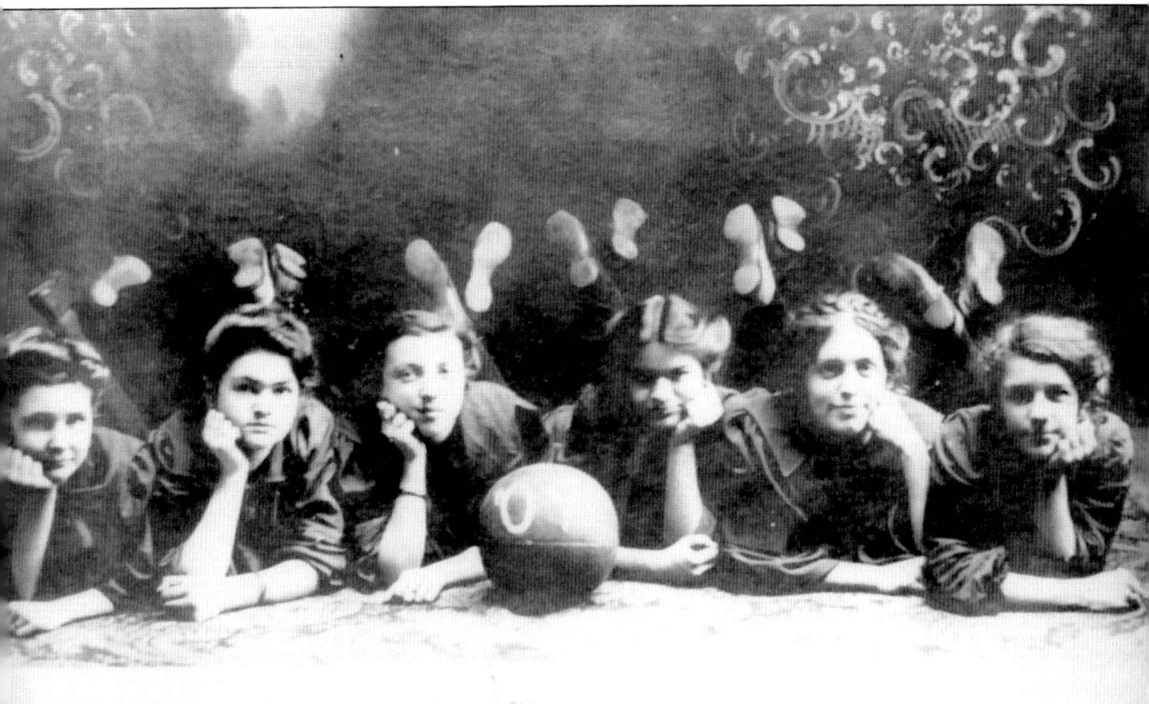

This is a photograph of the Dowagiac High School sophomore girls basketball team in 1907 (Class of 1909). Along with this photograph in the 1907 Dowagiac High School yearbook is a poem to the sophomore girls team, which began:

A Football team we have that's good,
A baseball team that's fine!
But the team we like the best of all
Is the basketball team of nineteen nine.

The players are, from left to right: Marie Park, Alleyne Gilbert, Faye Shurte, Mary Bishop, Mary Leeder, and Clara Gebhard. Their record in 1907 is unknown, but in 1909 they went 4–6.

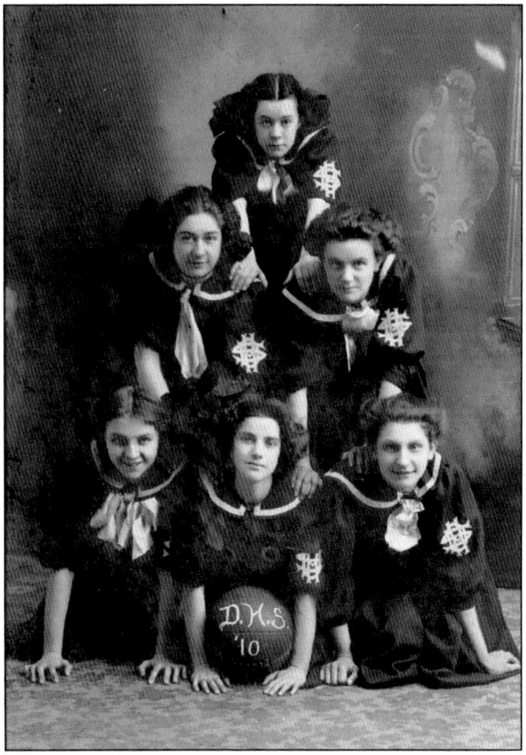

In 1910, the girls of Dowagiac High School formed the Girls' Athletic Association—complete with a constitution and officers. Lyla Wald served as basketball manager and the team went 3–3 for the season. From left to right are the following: (bottom) Marcia Conkling, Lyla Wald, and Gertrude Gebhard; (middle) Violet Kelso and Rosamond Hurst; and (top) Grace Campbell.

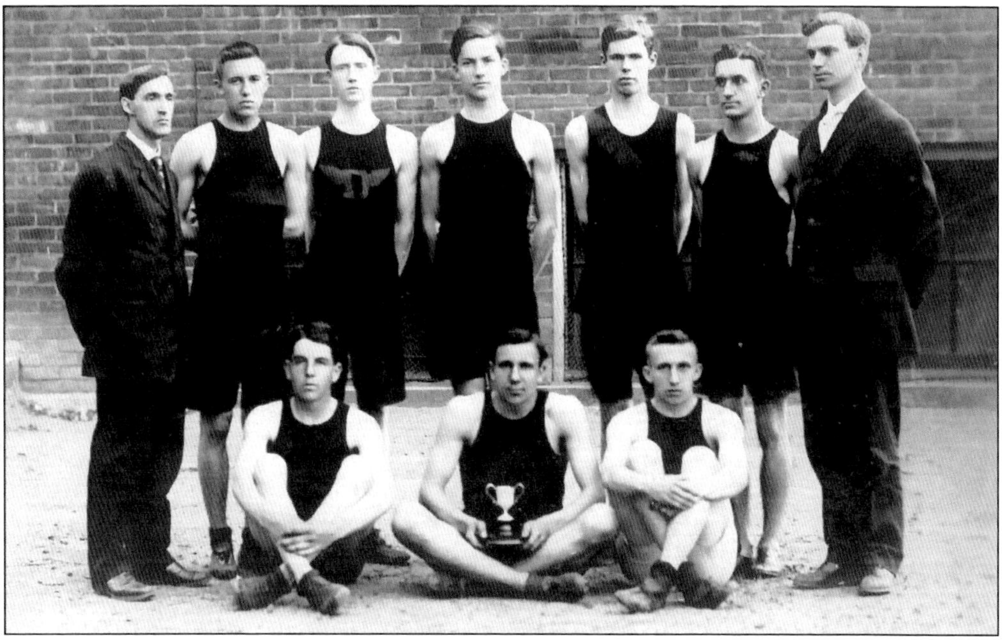

The 1909 DHS track and field team holds a loving cup it earned that year. According to the 1909 Dowagiac High School yearbook, "Two years ago this work [track and field] was unknown to us, but in these two years we have developed so astonishingly that we have twice won the Championship of Southwestern Michigan and have in our possession the handsome silver loving cup, which with one more victory becomes our permanent possession."

Ten

Fairs, Festivals, and Fun

Music, theatre, books, special celebrations, and hobbies are among the many pastimes enjoyed by residents of early Dowagiac. Especially in the days before radio and television, people made their own fun. Many special clubs were formed over the years. In the 1899 Dowagiac city directory several pages are devoted to clubs and organizations, including five bands, such as the Ideal Mandolin Banjo and Guitar Club and the Dowagiac Round Oak Band. Secret and Benevolent Organizations were very popular at this time. Thirty-one are listed in the directory; among them: Independent Order of Odd Fellows, Catholic Knights and Ladies of America, Tribe of Ben Hur, Ancient Order of United Workers, Royal Arcanum, and the Kingsbury Chapter of the Royal Arch Masons, meeting the first Wednesday after the full moon.

Other clubs targeted hobbies and interests, like the City Whist Club, and the enigmatic Married People Pleasure Club. Churches offered many opportunities for activity as did schools and employers. The Round Oak Company sponsored its own baseball team and a plot of land near the company was used as a baseball park.

The lakes surrounding Dowagiac have attracted many to their shores for recreation. Indian Lake, just three miles from Dowagiac, had several resorts, beaches, and pleasure craft to entertain lake-goers. Once the interurban train route was established in 1911, it became even easier for Dowagiac residents to visit Indian Lake. Summer residences sprang up around the lake, and it continues to be an attraction today.

The earliest library in Dowagiac was built on Front Street by P.D. Beckwith in 1885. The Ladies Library Association was a very active organization; Beckwith himself served as its president at one time. A Carnegie library replaced the original building in 1903 and continues to serve the community.

There have been several theatres in Dowagiac that through time have offered plays, vaudeville, concerts, and motion pictures. In addition to traveling troupes, local productions were highly popular. The theatre in the Beckwith Memorial Building opened on Front Street in 1893 as a memorial to P.D. Beckwith, who died in 1889. The theatre building, located at the corner of Beeson and Front Streets, was of the Romanesque style and constructed of Lake Superior red sandstone. P.D. Beckwith's love of the arts was signified on the exterior of the building in 19 busts of famous artists and writers, including Beethoven, Chopin, Voltaire, Thomas Paine, and Victor Hugo, with a bust of Beckwith in the center. During the dedication of the of the building, Robert G. Ingersoll, a noted orator and agnostic, stated that the building was a fitting memorial to a man who, ". . . fought the battle of his life alone and whose heart grew nobler and gentler with success; to one who tried to make a heaven here, who believed in the blessed gospel of cheerfulness, of happy lives, of laughter and love." Over the years the building housed the post office, Round Oak Stove Company offices, a restaurant, the Lee State Bank, a pool hall, and the City Council meeting room.

Fairs, circuses, and celebrations were also favorite pastimes and the Dowagiac Union Fair drew many residents as participants.

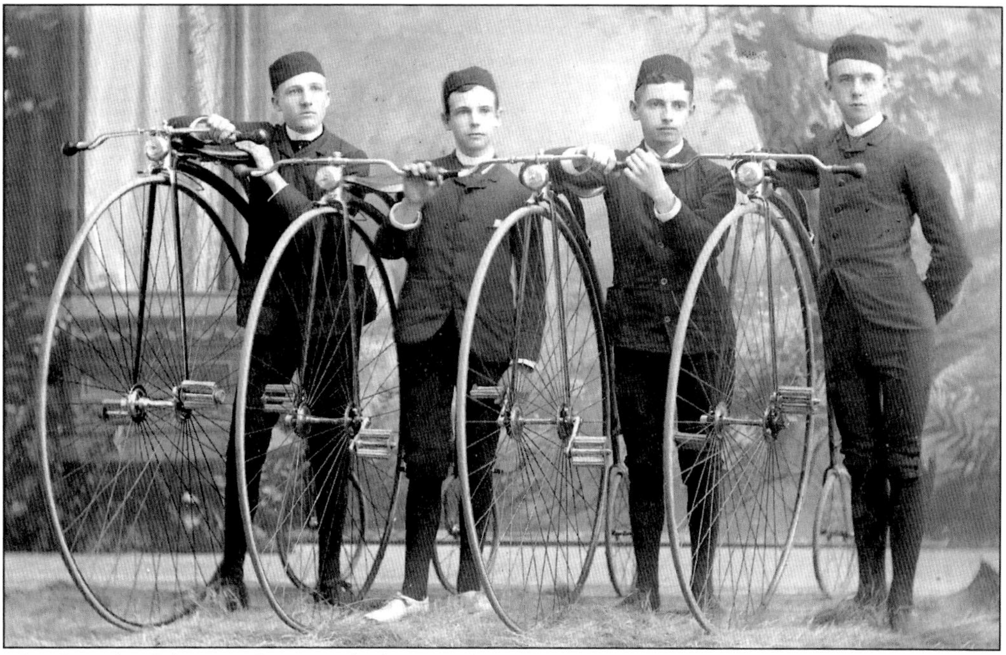

This bicycle club was photographed around 1885. Pictured from left are Frank Perry, Harry Bigelow, Lewis Bigelow, and Harry Dewey.

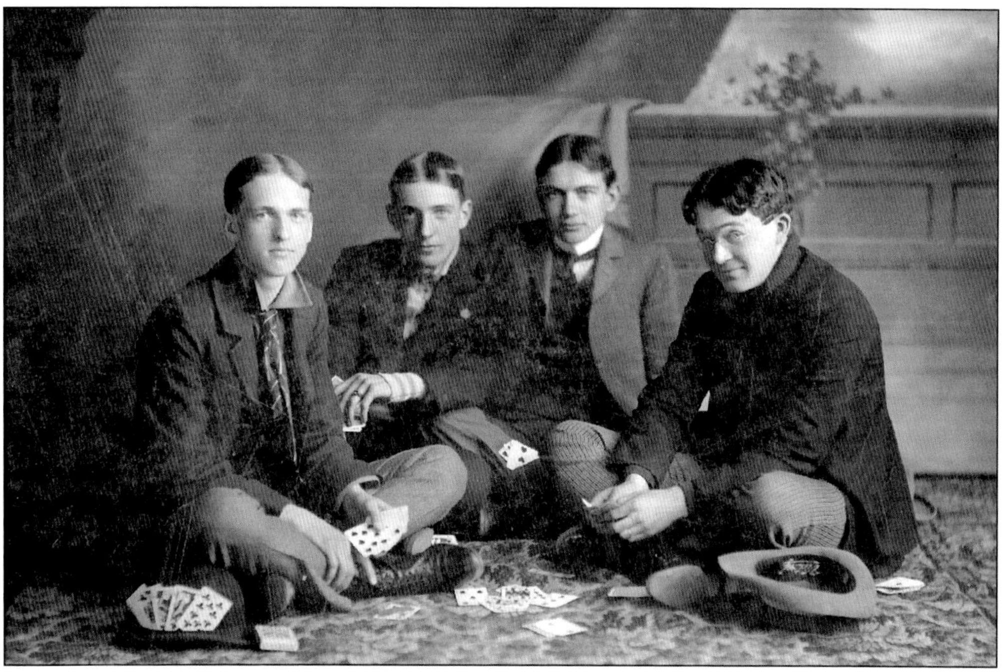

Another form of entertainment was card playing. This c. 1899 studio photograph illustrates these young men's penchant for cards. Irving Phillipson is third from the left. Phillipson was an 1899 graduate of Dowagiac Union School and attended West Point.

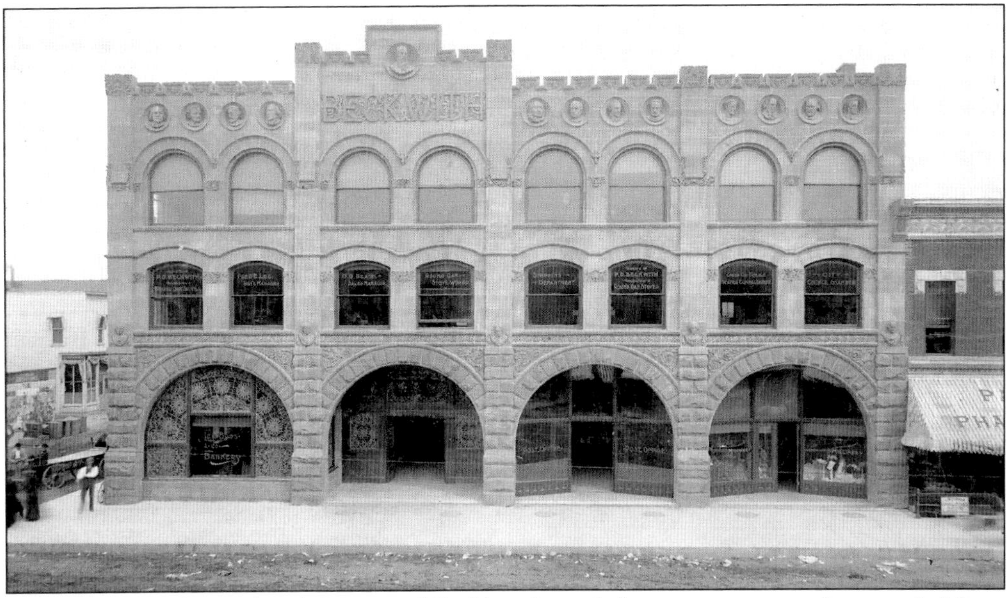

The theatre in the Beckwith Memorial Building hosted theatre companies that traveled from Chicago to Detroit. It started showing movies in 1910 and vaudeville acts also appeared. The building was razed in 1967.

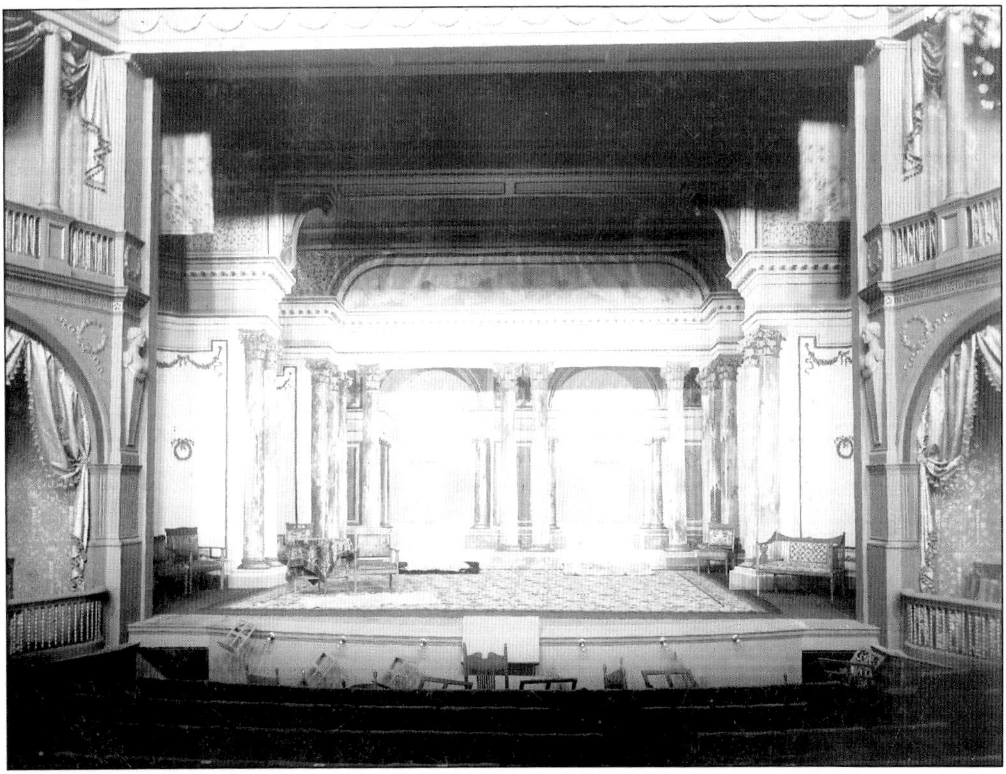

The interior of the theatre in the Beckwith Memorial Building shows Greek Revival features including Greek keys on the stage curtain, friezes, arches, busts, and Ionic columns. The theatre seated 700.

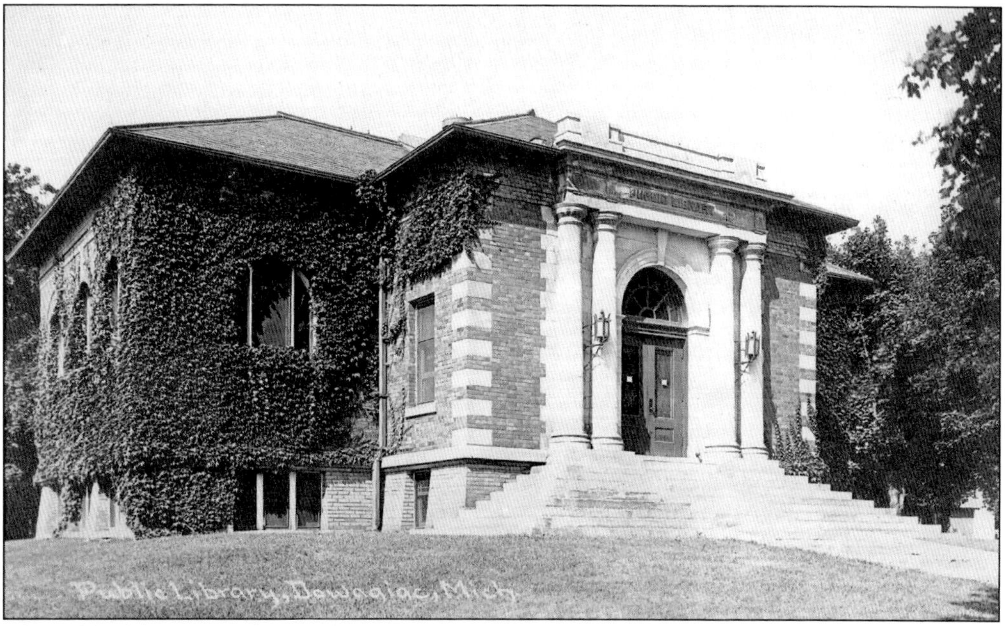

The public library was designed by Berkley Brandt, a 30-year-old architect from Chicago. The construction was funded with $12,500 from Andrew Carnegie, and the estate of P.D. Beckwith provided two city lots on Commercial Street for the site. The library opened in 1903, replacing an earlier library built by Beckwith on the corner of Front and Division Streets.

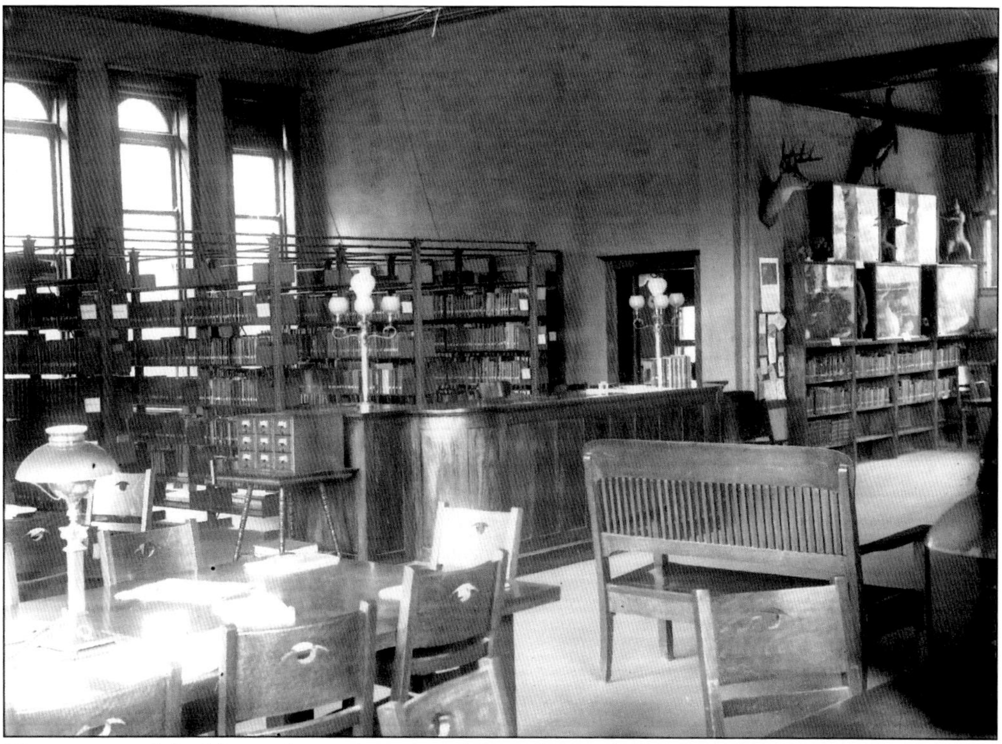

The interior of the library shows the original furnishing of Mission-style chairs and tables. The library remains in use, though it has received major remodeling.

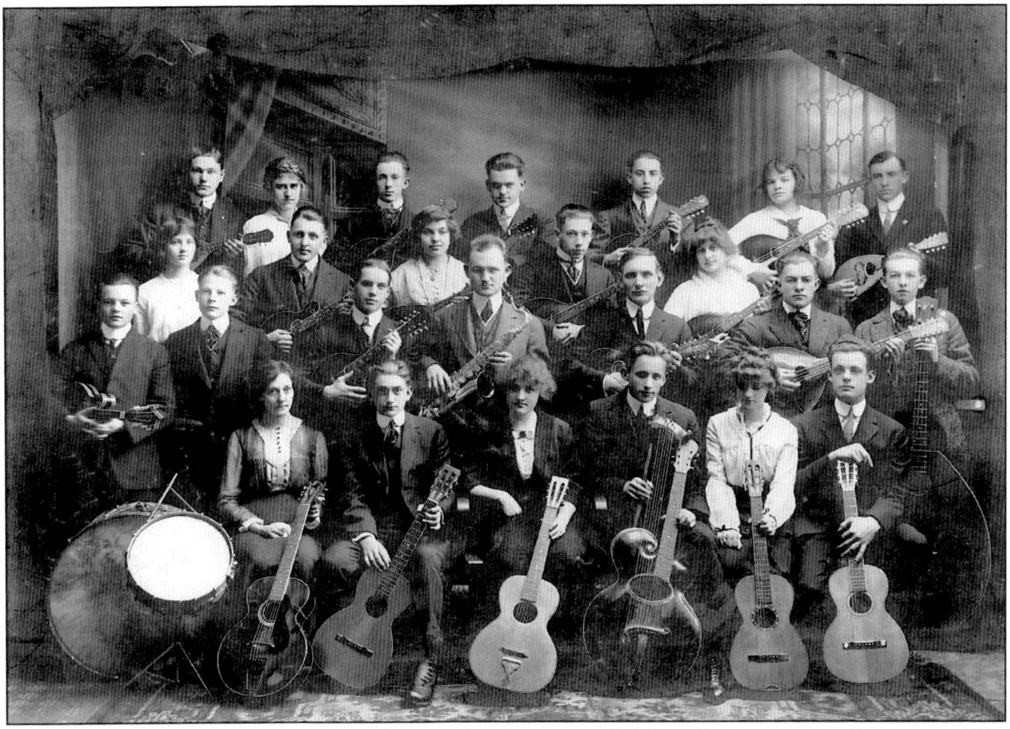

Music provided many Dowagiac residents with pleasure and allowed talents to be showcased. The Dowagiac High School Mandolin Club of 1914 was directed by Superintendent P.F. McCormick.

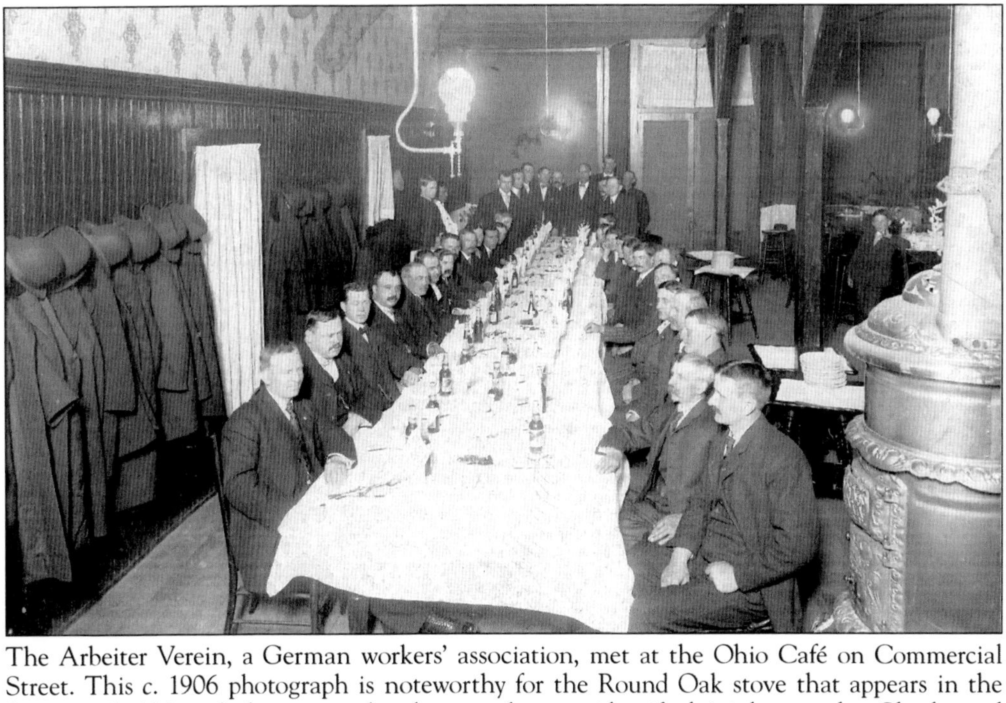

The Arbeiter Verein, a German workers' association, met at the Ohio Café on Commercial Street. This *c.* 1906 photograph is noteworthy for the Round Oak stove that appears in the foreground. Although the men in the photograph are unidentified, it is known that Charles and Adam Stahl and Michael Skeeps are pictured.

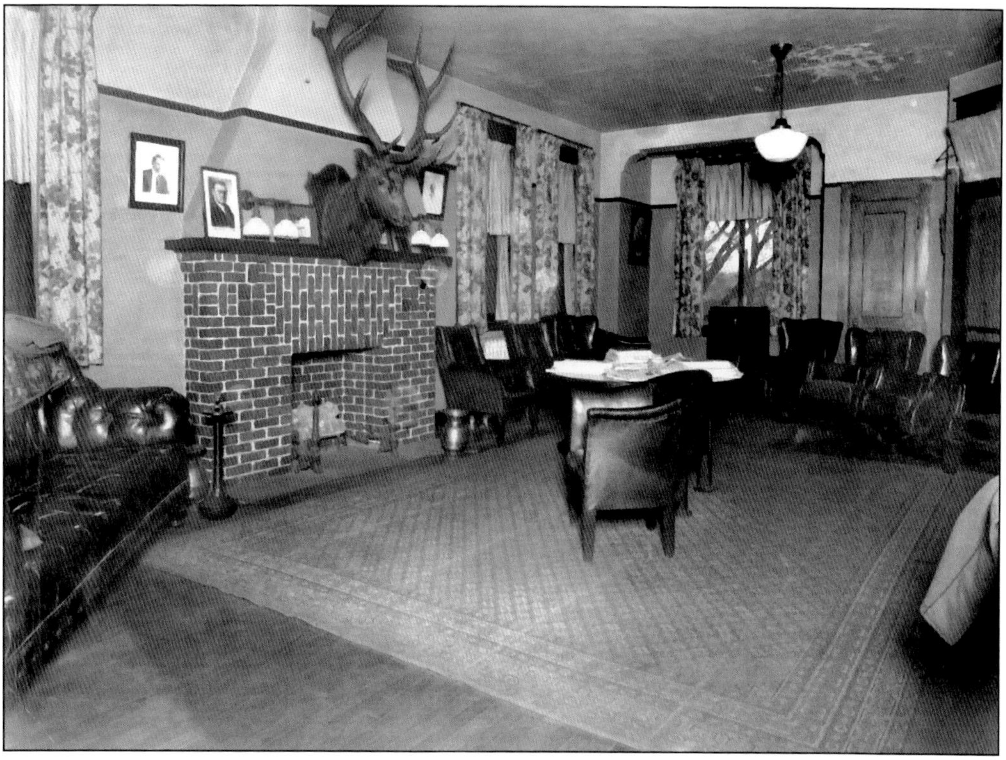

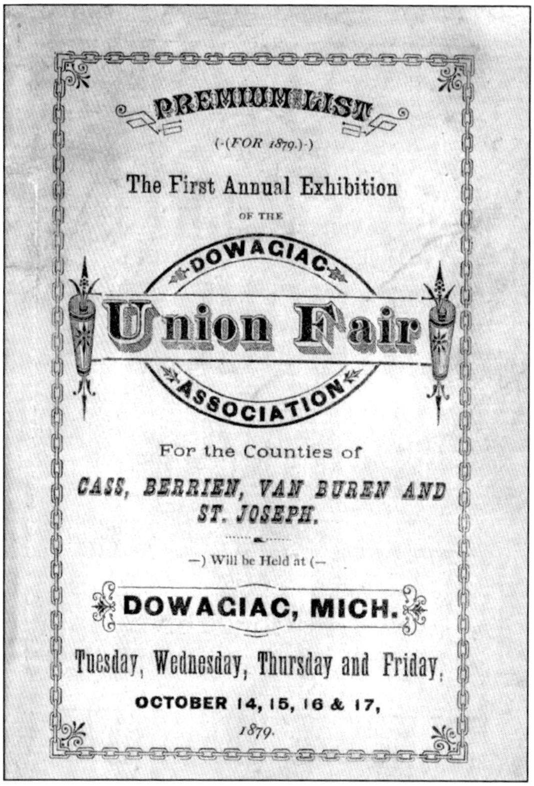
PREMIUM LIST

(-(FOR 1879.)-)

The First Annual Exhibition

OF THE

DOWAGIAC

Union Fair

ASSOCIATION

For the Counties of

CASS, BERRIEN, VAN BUREN AND ST. JOSEPH.

—) Will be Held at (—

DOWAGIAC, MICH.

Tuesday, Wednesday, Thursday and Friday,

OCTOBER 14, 15, 16 & 17,

1879.

(above) The Benevolent and Protective Order of Elks' headquarters building was built in 1913 on Front Street. Fraternal organizations of this kind were very popular around the turn of the century and offered their members status in the community, but also fun. This building had a ladies' parlor, a gentlemen's parlor, a reading room, a private office for the secretary, a billiard room, card room, dining room, buffet room, and kitchen.

(left) Fairs were huge attractions for residents of Dowagiac. This is a premium list for the first Dowagiac Union Fair, held in 1879 at the fairgrounds east of the city.

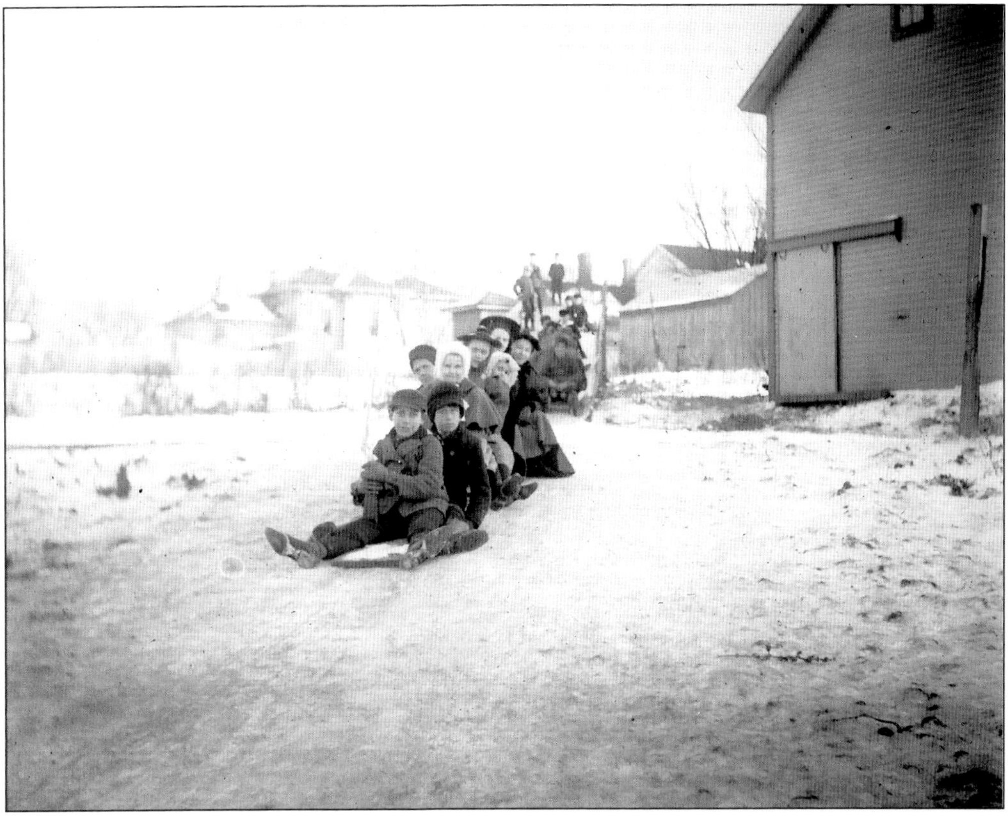

Sledding was a popular pastime in the same way it is today. Abundant snow, a sled, and a hill were all that were necessary to create some fun.

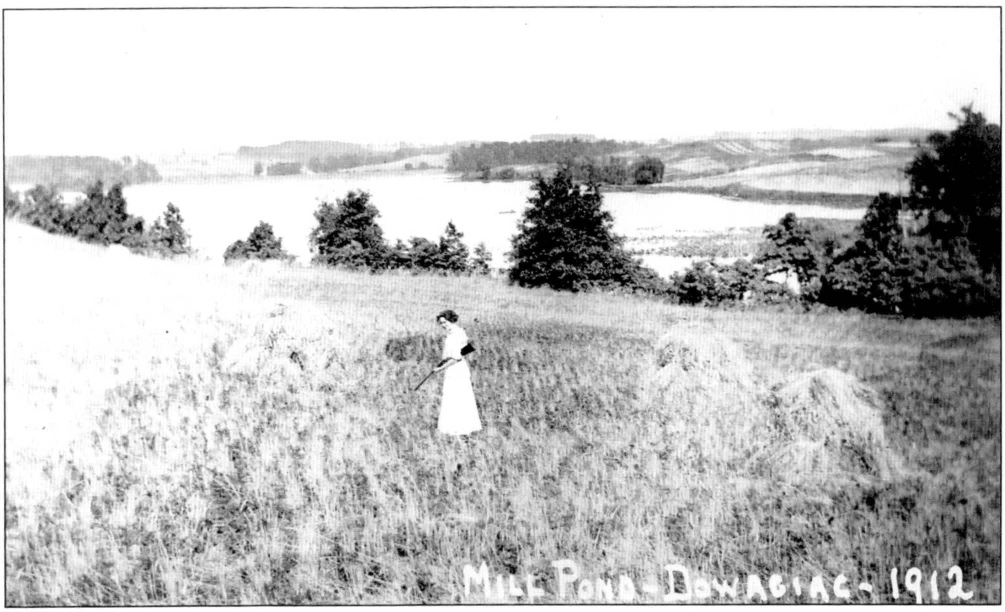

Given its rural setting, it would not be unusual to see Dowagiac residents out hunting in nearby fields. This 1912 postcard image shows an unidentified woman at the Mill Pond.

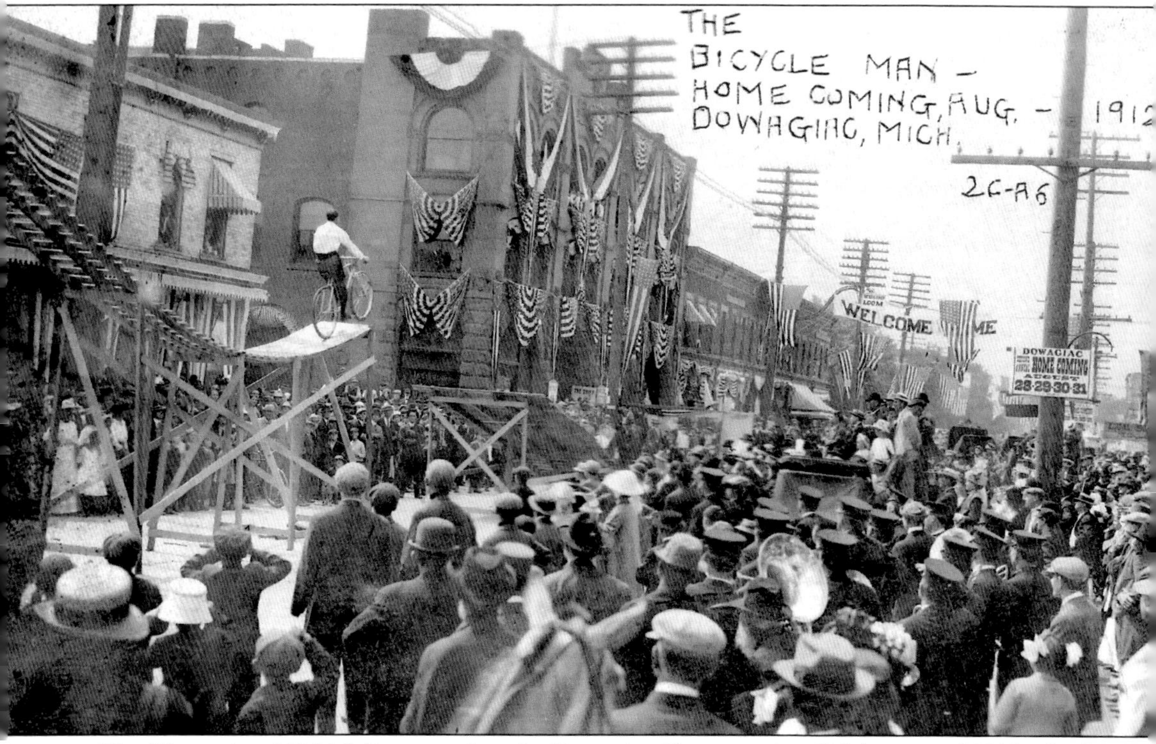

The "Sensational DeVolo" appeared at the Dowagiac Homecoming Celebration of 1912, which took place August 28–31. This photograph shows DeVolo thrilling the crowd with his "ride for life" on a wooden bicycle ramp along Front Street. Music during the entire celebration was provided by the Round Oak Band.

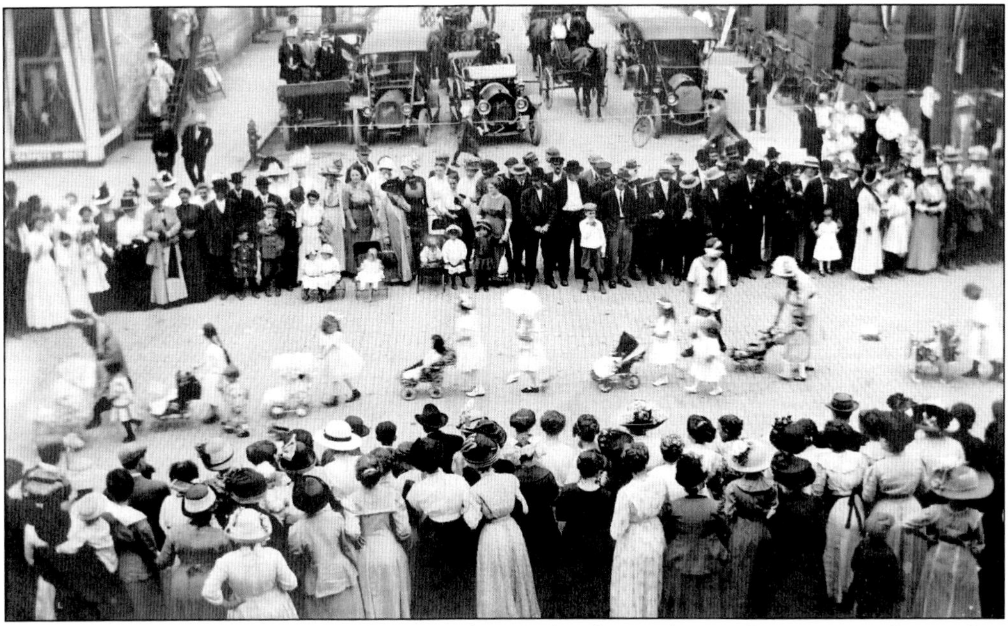

The Dowagiac Homecoming Celebration of 1912 also featured several attractions designed to welcome former Dowagiac residents home for a visit. Among the festivities was a "Unique Doll Parade" in which children pushed their diminutive charges down Front Street.

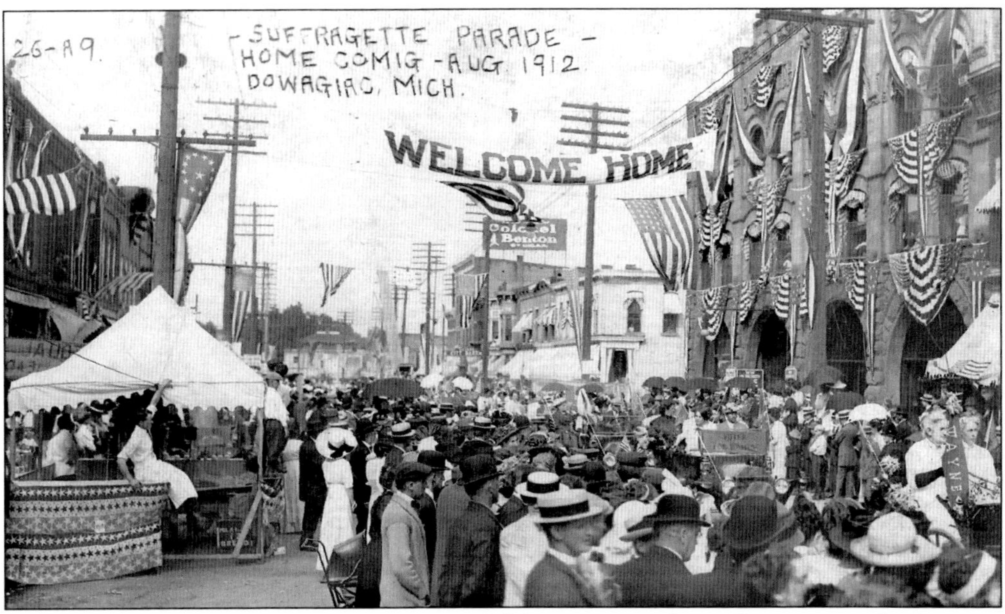

Another aspect of the 1912 Homecoming Celebration was the suffragette parade. Patriotic bunting and a "welcome home" banner adorn Front Street. Women with flags and signs reading "Votes for Women" carry the suffrage message to onlookers.

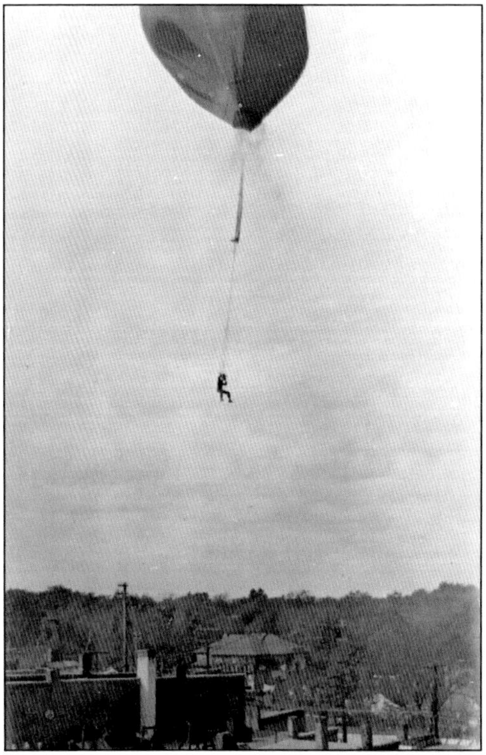

The new Carnegie library can be seen in this photograph, as a parachutist, part of an aerial circus, descends over town. The event was to celebrate the dedication of a new fountain in a town park, later named for Willis M. Farr. Mr. Farr was a city booster and owner of a sand band manufacturing company. A sand band was placed on wagons to keep excess mud off the wheels. This photograph dates to c. 1914.

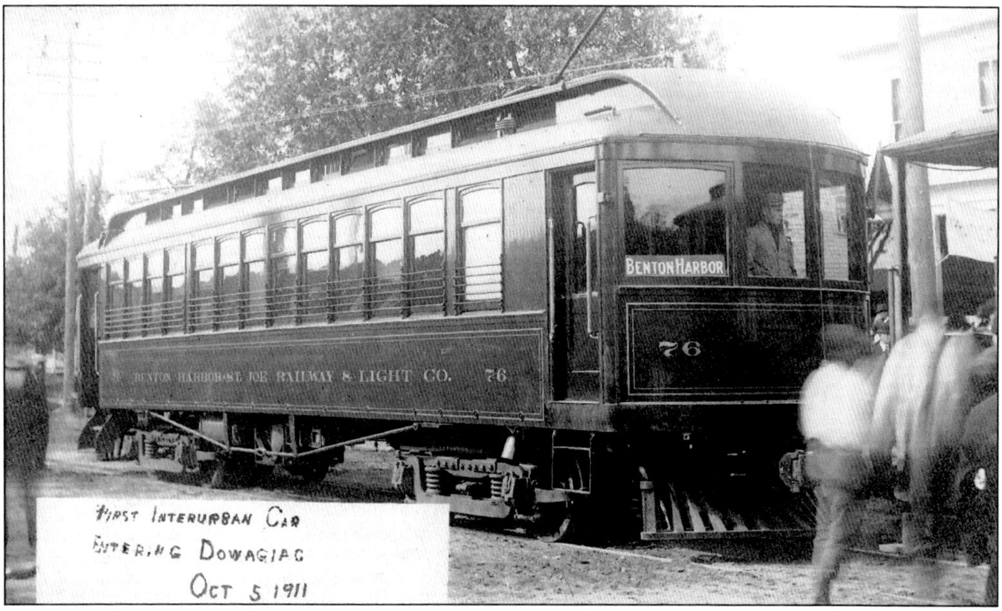

The arrival of the interurban train system to Dowagiac in 1911 meant affordable and convenient travel from Dowagiac to Indian Lake for recreation, or Benton Harbor for shopping. This photograph was taken when the first train arrived in Dowagiac on October 5, 1911, during the Homecoming Celebration's "Interurban Day." Steam whistles from the Dowagiac Manufacturing Company, Round Oak Stove Company, and the City Water Works blew upon the train's arrival and the Round Oak Band broke into a rousing march.

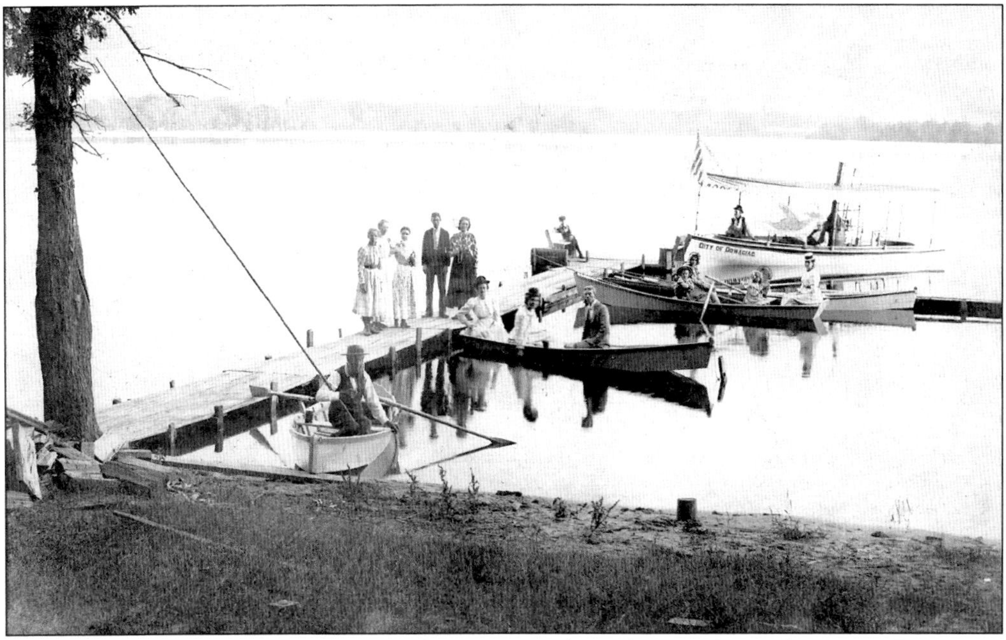

Indian Lake is located just 10 miles east of Dowagiac and was the site of several resorts in Dowagiac's early years. This 1892 photograph shows the Ely and Tice families, among others, setting out for some boating fun. *The City of Dowagiac* pleasure boat can be seen in the background.

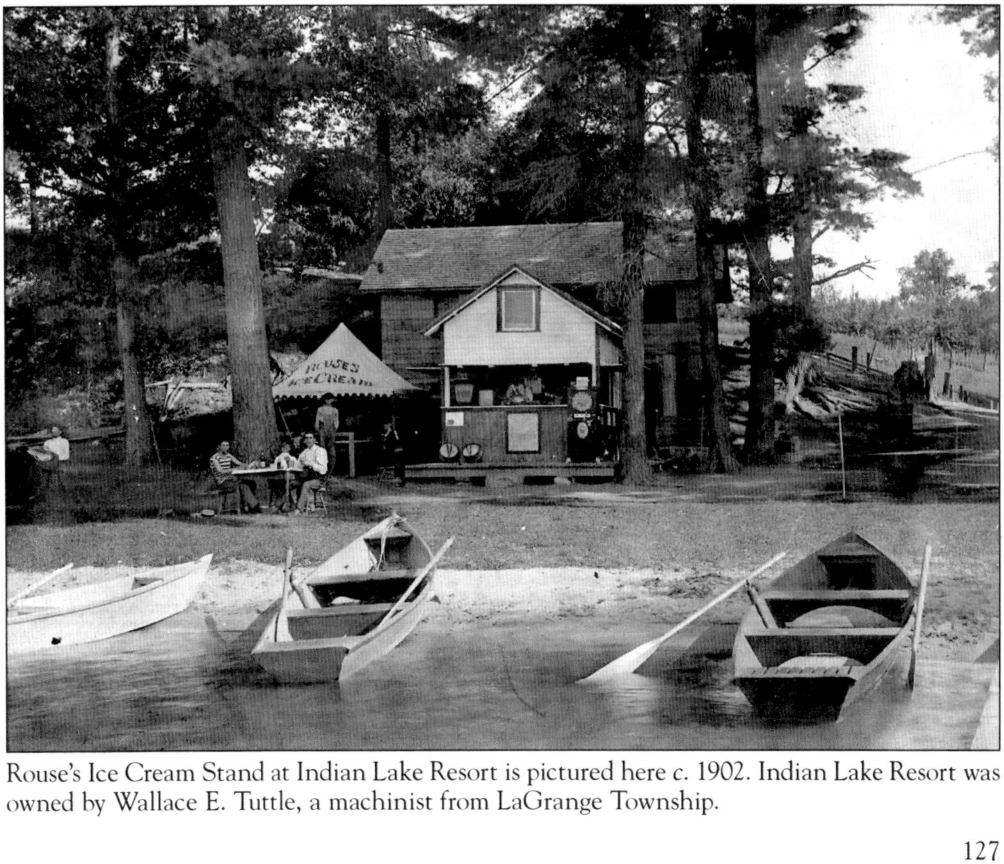

Rouse's Ice Cream Stand at Indian Lake Resort is pictured here *c.* 1902. Indian Lake Resort was owned by Wallace E. Tuttle, a machinist from LaGrange Township.

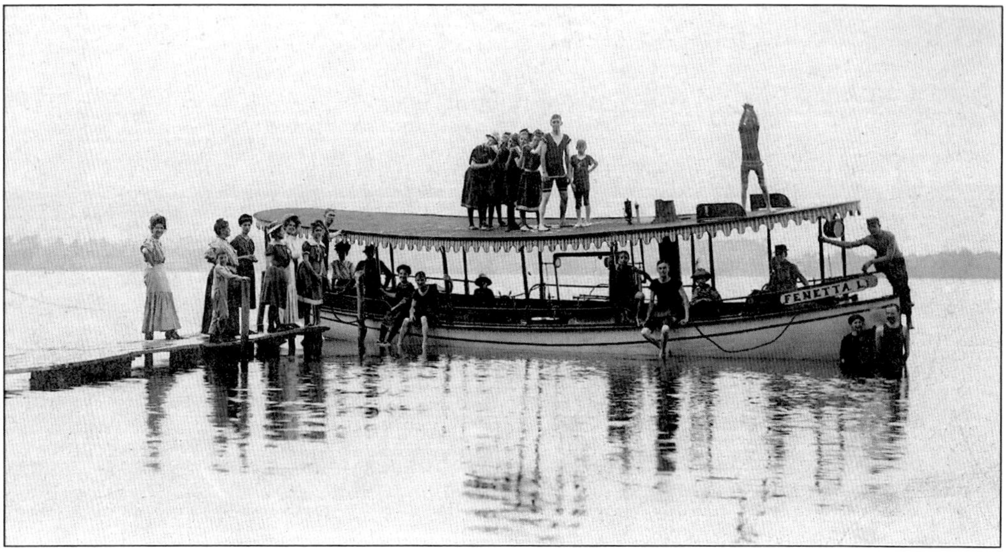

The *Fenetta L.* was a steam-powered sightseeing boat that plied the waters of Indian Lake. Named for the wife of resort owner Wallace Tuttle, the *Fenetta L.* began running around 1906 and was a popular attraction for several decades. This photograph is from c. 1910.

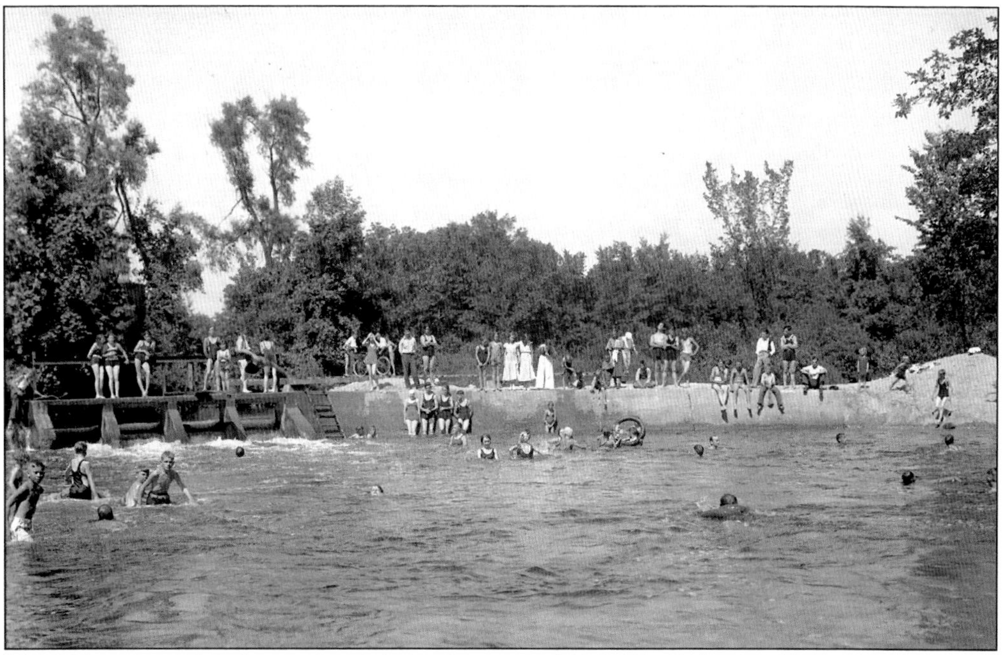

The old swimming hole was located on the east side of town behind the Round Oak Stove Company. This photograph is dated c. 1920. The swimmers are unidentified except for John Bobik, at the far left foreground.